Empowering the Performer

By Daniel Labonne

Unanswered questions about a unique experiment

With the Performing Arts & Cultural Development

TAMARE
HOUSE

Empowering the Performer

The right of Daniel Labonne to be identified as Author of this work has been asserted in accordance with sections 77 and 78 of the Copyright, Designs and Patents Act, 1988.

First published in Great Britain with TamaRe House, April 2012
25 Brixton Station Road, London, SW9 8PB, United Kingdom
+44 (0)844 357 2592, info@tamarehouse.com, www.tamarehouse.co.uk

Copyright © Daniel Labonne, 2012

A CIP catalogue record for this book is available from the British Library.

This employs acid free paper and meets all ANSI standards for archival quality paper.

ISBN: 978-1-908552-14-3

INTRODUCING

FACE

(Foundation for Arts, Creativity & Exchange)

To the youth of Africa

Life is not a 'brief candle.' It is a splendid torch that I want to make burn as brightly as possible before handing on to future generations.

George Bernard Shaw
Playwright (Ireland)

TABLE OF CONTENTS

Prologue

By Dr. Issa Asgarally

At a time when the third globalisation is unfurling, channelled by an unprecedented media revolution, as we grow aware of the necessity to "empower" certain key players of the social life, it seems to me that the project of Daniel Labonne comes at the right moment.

Daniel Labonne has had a long and rich career first as an actor, then as director before becoming a playwright and, finally, an administrator of performing arts. On the basis of his strong and tremendous field experience coupled with years of study and reflection at the University of London, he set up ACTPA, an African centre for the training of performing artists, stressing the multi-fold representativeness of performing arts that brings together "a performer, a performance and an audience"

His *Diamond Theory* is fascinating and full of promise, because it places performing arts in the centre of four development plans: personal, social, national and economic. First of all, it is evident that a performer's personal development is enriched by the learning of fundamentals such as dance, drama, stage management, techniques of production, acting and singing. As regards to the social development, Daniel Labonne reminds with good reason that performing arts are an integral part of African societies as they inspire and support every aspect of social life. Besides, performing arts can form the core of a cultural industry in Africa, considering the fact that if culture is priceless, it does have a cost. Through training, performing artists are given a chance to become entrepreneurs, teachers, hence, active players in the economic

Daniel Labonne

development; and performing arts, a vehicle to foster the development of a cultural industry and support its expansion in the national industry. Finally, in the Diamond theory, it is a different type of gem, a non-mineral...

Also innovative is the neologism 'Drumma' created by Daniel Labonne, combining *Drum*, omnipresent in Africa, and *Drama*, western by origin but global in outreach, allowing the specific and the universal to come to terms. As he justly points out: Drumma, in order to feel and hear the pulse of a continent reduced to silence. And here I quote Aimé Césaire: "Ma conception de l'universel est celle d'un universel riche de tout le particulier, riche de tous les particuliers..." [My concept of the universal embraces a term enriched with all its particularities and pluralities].

Being committed to cross-cultural exchange, I think that Daniel Labonne's project fits harmoniously therein. I shall echo the forceful assertion he made: "Underdevelopment is not only about underperforming economies, tyrannical leaders and ethnic warfare. It may be about the inability to listen to each other." To listen and speak to each other, is precisely one of the stakes in intercultural exchange. The absence of others deprives me of existence, wrote Hannah Arendt.

In show business, he says, Africa has a lot to give and to receive from Europe, from America, from Asia. However, before speaking to the world, it is essential for Africa to speak to herself first, making sure that the process of exchange starts at home, among African countries. And already there, the work to be undertaken is huge! Because it implies the need to prevail over the lack of organisation, resistance to change and corruption - the losing trifecta of a rich continent - and, after the martyrdom of slave trade and colonialism, to put an end to the supplement of self-damnation known as negrology. But once the work being launched, the cultural meeting - which formerly failed - between Africa and Europe could eventually begin. Besides, given the African origin of a large number of the population in America, the relations between both continents would only be stronger and mutually beneficial. And obviously, it would be of sheer advantage to the millenary civilisations of China and India to establish cultural ties with the cradle of civilisation. In brief, if Africa makes strategic choices in line with requirements and gets really integrated in the current globalisation process and if, in turn, the other continents change their stereotyped representations of Africa, the intercultural exchange between these four continents will be in a position to soar up. Indeed, as I mentioned in previous writings, the intercultural does not see the various cultures as competitors for the title of "the greatest" or "the most developed", but rather, forming a whole, as majestic and symphonic movements, the history of humanity with its variations and differences. In this particular perspective, Daniel Labonne's project is crucial.

Daniel Labonne

ABBREVIATIONS

FACE	Foundation for Arts, Creativity & Exchange (Proposed Funding Body)
ACE	African Centre of Exchange (Proposed permanent regional school of Performing Arts)
ACTPA	African Centre for the Training of Performing Artists (The Experiment)
ATEX	African Theatre Exchange (The project managers of ACTPA)
UAPA	Union of African Performing Artists (The association of Artists from 15 countries)
ISC	International Scientific Council set up to advise the coordinator in London in 1987.
CASTLE ARTS	Venue for ACTPA made available by the Government of Zimbabwe in 1990
AFSYMWORK	African Symposium Workshop organised in Mauritius in 1988 as a mini ACTPA in operation
ATEX Round Table	International Meeting in February 1998 in Paris with major partners from Europe, Africa and America
FOOTPRINTS	Title of the first production Made in Castle Arts - a dance-drama with an inter-African cast
LUCY & ME	Title of course 2 at Castle Arts, devised by ATEX on the theme of Anthropology and Performing

	Arts. Title of the play at the end of the same course.
OAU	Organisation of African Unity. Now African Union grouping most countries of the African continent.
UNESCO	United Nations Education Science and Culture Organisation
ACI/ICA	African Cultural Institute formerly based in Dakar, Senegal and now out of operation.

EXCHANGE	*A term used in this research as a new concept applied to the creative process in training performers of Africa. A pragmatic approach to end the isolation of African performing arts and the limited market of their products by expanding the distribution prospects; potentially, an original form of live performance Made-in-Africa, depending upon further research.*
DIAMOND THEORY	*Theory developed by Daniel Labonne applied to the cultural development of Africa. The theory is based upon practical work, including the work done with ACTPA and ATEX in 1990s. The theory encapsulates one clear result from an original experiment inserted in the World Decade for Cultural Development.*
DRUMMA	*Term coined by Daniel Labonne in his academic study to describe dramatic arts preceding Ancient Greek Drama, namely live arts across*

Africa. Name to be eventually given to new a theatre building in the African city of tomorrow.

DEVELOPMENT THROUGH CREATIVITY
Title of the MPhil Thesis of Daniel Labonne at University of London.

Daniel Labonne

LET THE AFRICAN PHOENIX RISE

Too many people have been involved

Too much effort and too many resources invested

Too much hope has been raised

Too many nations would eventually benefit

Too many artists have placed their faith in it

Too many sacrifices have been accepted

Too many lies have been told

Too many talents yet long to blossom

This report is but a testimony of time

Supported with authentic photographs taken

Along years of sheer hard work

But duty ends when a task is fully done

We remain confident that, in the end, truth will overcome

That deep seated belief and decades of labour will bear fruits

To benefit the young and free the thespian's song

There was a need to draw a line over the past and pave the way for the future

If it still matters to say thank you, more importantly

It is about shaking off the ashes so the phoenix may rise

Daniel Labonne

Daniel Labonne

INTRODUCTION

Daring to Dream *1

The reader may have to figure out whether this book is a report, a memoir or a recommended action plan. My only apology lies in the very unique nature of the subject matter, as the raw facts in Chapter One will establish. Behind the factual history, the reader will find three undeniable dimensions that partly explain the uniqueness of the matter. First, the continental representation as a core dimension of the project; then the spotlight placed over the ill-defined performing arts of Africa; finally, the unusual responsibility placed over the shoulders of one man to deliver a rather daunting undertaking. The experiment broke new ground as it evolved, away from the mandate that usually flows from identifiable authority. Somehow, the project managed to rely upon voluntary initiatives and personal investment, quite close to the mixture of responsibility and freedom that vitally nourish theatre both the arts and enterprise.

The two most reliable parameters to gauge the experiment are there to guide the reader: twenty seven years after the inception of the project, the same person could hardly be blamed for sheer personal ambition or momentary madness. But the best scientific claim lies in the crucial need factor. Is a school of performing arts capable of handling the incalculable wealth of forms and content from across sub-Saharan Africa required?

As long as a need is not addressed and that an alternative has not been found to bridge a gap that hampers progress, any effort ought to be objectively worthwhile. Such is the basic premise of this book. During the evaluation of the experiment, the actual monitoring of a cultural project with a continental dimension presented academic relevance. But, in this book, I shall go further. Not only am I returning to Africa what belongs to Africa, but I propose to do it in direct language in order to reach the high school student or the civil servant. Performing arts in Africa are not exclusive to a trade or locked up in a village or a building: they remain a vibrant expression of life at the present tense.

Because, the whole experiment is pragmatic and applied to a prevailing situation in developing Africa, an action plan is contained in the book. I could not state the facts and list down the problems without pointing a finger towards a workable solution.

In 1993, I produced a first draft of this book with an abundance of photographs I had taken alongside the research and study towards establishing a new school of performing arts open to Africans from various regions of the continent. The last words of this pictorial report were 'Time will tell.'

Time has spoken, and twenty years later, I would contend that the theatre and the performing arts are picking up a fresh relevance in the modern world as a counter-balance useful to the modern man. Performing arts have kept this old faculty of restoring the fundamental nature of being humans, endowed with the consciousness of living one day at a time and having to negotiate between our duties, our mortality, our common heritage and our immediate environment. More than ever before, in the digital age, it matters that we remind ourselves that we are made up of living cells and that we are first a body.

In Sub-Saharan Africa, the relevance of live arts has never really been left out of communal living or individual consciousness. So far, life has tended to be punctuated by story, ritual, dance, song and performance that keep the individual bonded to the other, to nature, to the ancestors and to the cosmos. Is modernity worth discarding such practices? Or is it that there is an urgency for Africa and Africans to preserve live forms of human expression and sharing, to be considered as endangered

Daniel Labonne

heritage? Isn't it more urgent to focus upon the need to pull the young African away from the temptation of violence or emigration? Whatever may be the answer to these questions, our main concern is the study of the role of the performing arts within a context that has been colonised by the economist: the wonderland of development. Our research has tended to indicate that, applied to black Africa, theatre and the performing arts ought NOT to become a tool in the hands of the super-powerful economic guru. On the contrary, the performing arts in Africa have retained enough life-blood to allow for a fresh transfusion that may boost the economic outcome of a patchy and rather painful development so far. Provided the cultural dimension is handled differently and creatively. Provided an alternative agent is identified and adequately trained.

The term 'cultural development' applies precisely to this inside-out vision that may have a better chance of transforming and enriching the lives of millions. However, to contain the forces that tend to limit the complexities of life to statistical data and economic performance, both the function and forms of the performing arts would need a fundamental re-appraisal. A starting point would be the training of the performing artist of Africa. Next, the education of the young African may be enriched as academic knowledge makes room for this stream of human artistic practices from the early beginnings. That is why, in the second training programme organised at Castle Arts, in 1991, I chose the title LUCY & ME: to restore continuity and relevance to a plundered vision of history and culture. Rightly or wrongly, we undertook serious research in an attempt to bridge anthropology and performing arts. Farfetched? Perhaps, but the adult performers involved did not think so. We did go to the Museum of Addis Ababa to visit Lucy, the diminutive African lady, magically fascinating as one imagines flesh over millennia-old bones...

That there had been a strange link between modern pop music with the incidence of the title of a song (Lucy) written by the European group (The Beatles) had not been a damper on our efforts to hammer out a strategy to train adequately the performer in Africa, by Africans and for Africa. On the contrary: African studies cannot be exclusive by rejection. In anthropological terms, to be African is also to remain doggedly inclusive by assuming the motherly responsibility of having nurtured humanity with all its subsequent plurality. It matters that Africa is not perceived as a depressing closed ghetto in the books of a blinkered historian, but a vast field of colourful forms of unpredictable expressions of life, bursting with vigour and meaning. The arts of Africa are there for the sharing - the basic meaning given to 'exchange.' There is evidence of African roots in the development of world popular music in the last 100 years. As modernity attracts a constant flow to urban life, the performing artist of Africa is in danger of being cut off from oral tradition at home and reduced to underpinning other cultures. This experiment suggests he or she ought to be taught how significant progress could be achieved through 'a process of exchange' with fellow Africans. This process involves tapping into the rich and varied forms of performing arts of a vast continent. In a dangerous world pulled to the brink of standardisation and self-destruction, there is also an additional responsibility for the performer to act as the guardian and mediator of oral tradition.

Restoring the link and continuity in the brief history of homo-sapiens has become an urgent task. Development had been for most Africans a dramatic struggle for survival with one step forward and one step back. With LUCY & ME, in 1991, the performers recruited from many parts of the African continent (and from South America) accepted the challenge and responded creatively with an original script and a staged performance at the end of an 11-week training course in Southern Africa. Twenty years later, in 2011, Lilian Thuram publishes in France the essential book 'Mes Etoiles Noires' (*My Black Stars*) with the subtitle 'De Lucy a Barack Obama' (*From Lucy to Barack Obama*). The need to restore continuity and repair the memory is an ongoing task, no matter who takes the initiative and what particular shape that initiative may take.

Daniel Labonne

Time has spoken.

What may have been perceived as farfetched and ambitious in 1991, as we struggled to establish a purposeful school of performing arts relevant to Africa, is being indirectly approved with Thruram's remarkable book. For it all began with an upright, thinking Lucy. In the latest episode of the human saga, the son of an African has validated his thinking and his talent by qualifying for the most important job of our times: President of the United States of America. Has a link been restored in real time between Lucy and Obama? Lilian Thuram sets the record right on his own terms, with the list of pioneers who have, along the way, restored dignity and credibility to a battered group of human beings, still classified as 'black.' Were Princess Anna Zingha of Angola, Toussaint Louverture of Haiti or Martin Luther-King of America really exceptional? Were they merely trying to be 'black?' No. They were just as human and they did their best just as others had in history. The problem lies with 'the others.' Jean-Paul Sartre stigmatised 'the others' as the earthly representation of hell (L'enfer, c'est les autres.) Breaking down the wall of racial prejudice and restoring the missing pages of human history matter. But let us quote Lilian Thuram. *'If we really want to change our society, fight against racism, it cannot be through positive discrimination, nor through community empowerment ('communautarisme'). Only by changing our shared imaginings, shall we be able to get closer to each other and to break free from cultural barriers; only then would we be in a position to go beyond the major obstacle hidden behind such words as "visible minority", "diversity" - the "you" as opposed to the "us" determined by the colour of the skin.'* *2 What time is telling me through the voice of the ex-footballer Lilian Thuram is this: 'changing our shared imaginings' may take many forms; but it is essential to find innovative methods of educating the young and restoring the facts so human beings do not lose faith in themselves and in our ability to learn from both our mistakes and our heroes. Note the word 'shared' which implies exploration and exposure through 'exchange,' the method used in our experiment.

The African who has never left Africa and lives fully integrated in his or her community is neither a 'visible minority,' nor is the colour of the skin an obsessive reality. Except for the worse and most extreme example of visible majority and legalised discrimination during the Apartheid system in South Africa, dismantled by another hero in Thuram's book: Rolihlahla Nelson Mandela. Dozens of other independent African countries are no ideal place to live in; nor is their development proving a modern pyramid of achievements. On the contrary, under-achievement and constant set-backs plague the recent history of many African countries. War, famine and poor leadership have tended to become endemic. From out of Africa, blame is systematically apportioned as to suggest that because 'they' are not like 'us:' that 'they' may always try but 'they' will never succeed... Understand, 'we' are superior or 'they' are inferior and doomed... Thuram is again right by insisting that *'The black man is not better than the white man; the white man is not better than the black man; there is no such thing as the black man's mission; nor is there the white man's burden; no black ethics, no white intelligence. There is no black history, no white history. We must reclaim the entire history of the world to better understand each other and to teach our children.'* New terms of 'exchange' are essential for a new mindset. And the poorer we are, the harder we must try.

Time is telling all of us that skin colour (black, white or yellow) is becoming increasingly an irrelevant consideration. The old planet earth is getting tired of our stubbornness and our cruelty. The experiment with the ACTPA Project was not 'a black experience' intended to establish any superiority; nor was it about venting off anger against any form of oppression in a Southern Africa torn by racial conflict. It was only a peaceful attempt to talk and listen to each other in a creative environment, using training as 'the horizontal method:' then, to make sense out of that state of peaceful togetherness and formulate the utopia - through drama and performing arts - whereby fellow Africans are able to think for themselves and create freely without the constant external arbitration, away from fabricated need to follow a role-model.

Daniel Labonne

The records will show that our experiment was both successful and promising. This book is mainly about setting the records right for the young. It is also a matter of informing the largest number about what it really takes to conceive and manage a development project in Africa. Education is after all what really matters to achieve lasting progress. I also felt a duty to return to Africans what belongs to Africa, so lessons may be learned and other performers may take over from our past efforts. More importantly, the training project dedicated to performing artists was about breaking free from whatever others may say and think about Africans. It was about daring a different way to imagine cultural development on our own terms, in a future Africa. It was about comparing notes between neighbours, irrespective of the achievements of others; it was about a mindset that neutralises both slavery and colonisation; it was about grooming the undervalued talents scattered all over the African continent and fusing creatively a fragmented vision into a harmonious whole. In short, it was about restoring the damaged link between LUCY and ME.

That was no political project but an artistic enterprise with minimal and short-term dependence upon friends of goodwill. There was no hidden motive to emulate or diminish the success achieved elsewhere, or to toe any line set out by experiences culturally rooted in other lands. Cultural development must necessarily mean minding one's own business, and that is basically what we tried to do. What's wrong with that? For reasons that ought to be explained, it was unfinished business. Perhaps the reader might understand better after considering the content of this book and guard against the same pitfalls in future experiments. With this book, another pragmatic measure is being taken with FACE. The foundation will receive the findings of a promising experiment with the aim of seeking for permanent structures and lasting benefits. But where we must insist as we address this comprehensive report to the young of Africa is this: never stop yourself from daring to dream!

Professor Albert Mawere Opoku of Ghana once taught me an African proverb that insists upon the virtues of self-help and discourages the temptation to respond to blame with blame. *'The man who does not lick his lips cannot blame the harmattan for drying them.'*[3]

I met Professor Opoku, the Founder of the National Dance Ensemble of Ghana, at the University of Legon, during the field work that provided the foundation to this vast experiment in the performing arts. What the professor means is this: when things go bad, do not blame nature or others; just do what you can. Most of the time the effort will pay off, at least it will pacify nature and ensure you do have a future.

Well, Professor, we have licked our lips and we have nobody to blame. As we write this book, we feel that the harmattan may finally be over and the skies are clearing up. We are certainly much older now, so we know that life itself is the most worthwhile experiment, provided we remain alert and creative. The fact is we had a rather ungrateful and ambitious job to do in 1985, through unchartered waters. An original school for performing artists! A very vague and risky brief indeed... Worse, execution needed to be on behalf of performing artists of Africa. It has taken me personally 25 years to get to this point, when the reader may hold a book made simple that presents the facts, opens up the album of an extended-family from all over and gives a chance to the actors as well as witnesses to record their hopes and excitement... Everything being governed by time, it is also right that the unanswered questions are addressed in a frank and direct manner for the average reader of the 21st Century. But then, what's the point of giving a voice to performers, organisations, sovereign countries and academics if it is not to point in one direction for the future? This time, I shall quote the Chinese wisdom which says that the dog may have four legs but it heads in one direction only.

One generation later, having explored extensively the multifaceted issues, I may confidently conclude with this book that the *Foundation* (FACE) is the best vehicle and *African Centre of Exchange* (ACE) the final

Daniel Labonne

destination. First, we need to feed 'the dog' - and money has been the most damaging issue and calls for drastic measures. The *Diamond Theory* can be trusted as a road map. The Castle Arts, in Bulawayo, will always remain a point of reference to establish that Utopia is only a steep mountain to conquer. In fact, Castle Arts points towards the ultimate outcome of training and 'empowering the performer'. Each African city ought, one day, to have its own Castle Arts. Finally, the concept of *exchange* is not magic; but it is a tool for cross-fertilisation and a method of giving value to disregarded arts forms while reaching out to larger audiences. Yes, the harmattan is clearing up, Professor, and the future is finally looking brighter for Africa... Should the performers step in and begin the dance that empowers?

Let us call to remembrance (see Part Seven) what the observers and partners, from North and South, had to say about this unique experiment in the field of the performing arts in Sub-Saharan Africa. Among them some, like Louis Akin, passed away; others have betrayed; many were sad to see those who dared to dream sink into oblivion... The bottom line is this: Africa has been robbed of another 20 years of creativity and development through the arts. Do I have to mention that I have never been paid for the services delivered during decades of what may still prove a determining experiment in the cultural development of a continent? But it was never a one-man band. It would be too long for me to thank here, all those who deserve a mention in this vast enterprise. Chapter Five of the book is a tribute to supporters, participants, enablers and hopefully, the photo album will be a supplement to set the records right.

Dr. Issa Asgarally has kindly accepted my challenging invitation to venture out of his area of expertise: to write a preface about performing arts and about the Africa region. I thank him for that. We do connect on the philosophical plan: interculturalism - his area of expertise - ought to take many forms and wars must be avoided, not won. Monique Pin first read the reduced version of the book and encouraged me to publish it as a history document; Gail Hill and Floryse Dubarry proof-read the finished product and the latter translated the prologue from French. This book would never have come together without the indefectible support and love of my wife, Sheila, who through thick and thin, always thought that nothing in our creative life together would ever match the ACTPA Project in Zimbabwe, as managed by ATEX in London. I must also thank my two sons, Pascal and Nicolas, who have undoubtedly suffered from the energies invested by their father into a collective dream, depriving them of the time and affection they deserved when they were younger.

Finally, just as Africa is a crying reality, the African performer is no abstraction. To make sure that this book does not sink into an ocean of assumptions and vagueness, I have requested a man and a woman to watch over the reader from beginning to end. I am inviting Sotigui Kouyate and Myriam Makeba, two remarkable performers who lived and died as artists and dignified Africans to inspire the work of FACE as, hopefully, this book paves the way for a brighter future.

NOTE 1: 'Daring to Dream' must be attributed to Monique Pin who read the pictorial report and immediately came up with this alternative title for the book.

NOTE2: translated from French. page 11, Introduction 'Mes Etoiles Noires.' Lilian Thuram. Editions Points.

NOTE 3: The Harmattan is a dry and dusty trade wind that blows south from the Sahara towards the Gulf of Guinea. West Africa is affected by the Harmattan between November and March, when the temperature may drop to 3% Celsius.

Daniel Labonne

PORTRAIT OF THE AFRICAN PERFORMER
Sotigui Kouyate

Photo by Esther Kouyate.

Sotigui Kouyate (1936-2010) a monumental performer who always claimed to be African first, a traditional Griot next, then a stage and film actor. He insisted upon his plural identify as a Guinean, a Malian and a national of Burkina Faso. He graced the stage of the globe, in Paris with Peter Brook (Mahabharata), in the UK, across Europe, Asia and America. His films include *Little Senegal* and *London River*. When I performed as an actor with Sotigui Kouyate in Canada, under the French director Claude Regy, I used to call him 'La Tres Haute Volta' (The Very Tall Volta) to refer to the former name of his country, Upper Volta, so tall was his tree-like body and his uniquely chiselled face. But it was his big heart and remarkable modesty combined with exceptional talent that kept Sotigui Kouyate close to his roots while he gave a uniquely touching dimension to every character he played. He remains a living example of the humanity, the depth and fascination of African performing arts.

Daniel Labonne

PART 1

The Past

Backdrop to a Dream

Daniel Labonne

To all the individuals whose photographs appear in this book, we express gratitude for their kind collaboration. We do hope that the book is fair to them.

THANK YOU

On behalf of the ACTPA Project, on behalf of the many performers who have benefited from the experiment, I extend my sincere and total gratitude to those organisations that have financially contributed to this meaningful project between 1985 and 1991: the African Centre for the Training of Performing Artists.

THE ACTPA PROJECT (1985-1991)

SPONSORED BY:
SIDA - The Swedish International Development
Authority
The Ministry of Education and Culture of Zimbabwe
UNESCO
World Decade for Cultural Development (UN)
The Government of Mauritius
The Government of Zimbabwe
DANIDA - The Danish International Development Authority
The Commonwealth Foundation
The Rockefeller Foundation
DSE, Bonn
FINNIDA - The Finnish International Development Authority
NORAD - The Norwegian International Development Authority
Sydney Black Foundation - UK
The Ministry of Foreign Affairs of Holland

And
The Labonne Family

Thank you to the other organisations which have brought other forms of support, directly or indirectly. I extend my thanks, on behalf of artists, on behalf of Africa in search of a sustainable development.

IN CO-OPERATION WITH: The African Cultural Institute (ACI);
          The Organisation of African Unity (OAU)
          The International Amateur Theatre Association (IATA);
          The Union of African Performing Artists (UAPA);
          Goldsmiths College. University of London;
          The City University - London;
          ACCT - L'Agence de Co-operation Culturelle et Technique;
          The British Theatre Association - BTA;
          Arts Council of Zimbabwe;
          British American Arts Association;
          DATS - Denmark;
          Swedish Dramatic Institute;
          British Council (Mauritius Office);
          Air Mauritius;
          Air Zimbabwe;
          Bulawayo Chamber of Commerce.

PROJECT MANAGEMENT: ATEX - African Theatre Exchange (UK)

THE ACTPA PROJECT IN BRIEF

Title of Project: African Centre for the Training of Performing Artists - ACTPA

Objects:	To train performing artists and trainers from all over the African continent according to needs using an innovative process of Exchange. To give substance and meaning to cultural development in the Africa region.
Purpose of ACTPA:	Centre for research, Education and Exchange devoted to the study and practice of all aspects of African Performing Arts; Data Bank on African Performers and Live Arts; Headquarters of the Inter-African Theatre Company; Activity Centre for Union of African Performing Artists - UAPA.
Founder:	Daniel Labonne, researcher and theatre practitioner from Mauritius, Resident first in Côte d'Ivoire, since 1985 a UK resident Founding member, Vice president and Treasurer of the UAPA; Cultural entrepreneur and director of ATEX Project co-ordinator on a voluntary basis from 1986 Artistic Director of the Pilot Project from 1988-1991; Evaluator of the project from 1996 to 2001 with the University of London; Author of the 'Diamond Theory' and founder of FACE in 2012.
Initiator:	The Union of African Performing Artists (UAPA) set up in Zimbabwe in 1984 by individual performing artists from 17 African countries who 'through their voluntary commitment accept to unite in a concerted effort to work for the promotion of African Performing Arts'... The UAPA ceased all activities in the early 1990s.

Project management:	From 1987 to 1992: ATEX - The African Theatre Exchange, a company limited by guarantee registered in Britain.
Origin of project:	A school project was made official in the course of a colloquium on African theatre organised in Stockholm in April 1985. ACTPA was first given its name by Daniel Labonne in a brochure, written and produced for the UAPA and published in Denmark in 1986.
Host country (pilot)	Zimbabwe
Opening of ACTPA:	**September 1990 ACTPA at Castle Arts Bulawayo.**
Training on Offer:	ACTPA Diploma Course, a one-year course ending with an inter-African theatre production Short Courses bearing on - A specific skill useful to the performing artist -The role of the performer in Africa (Theatre for Development) - National or Regional Needs (Courses on request) - Specialist training (Theatre Directors) Roots Diaspora Course for artists of the African Diaspora wishing to reconnect with their Roots A Diaspora Course for non-Africans wishing to learn from Africans in Africa
Target Intakes: trainers	African performing artists, directors, technicians,
Languages used:	English, French and African Languages
ACTPA PILOT:	AFSYMWORK in Mauritius (1988) ACTPA at Castle arts (1990-1991)

Daniel Labonne

PARTICIPANTS TO THE AFRICAN SYMPOSIUM WORKSHOP (AFSYMWORK) CAME TO MAURITIUS FROM THE FOLLOWING COUNTRIES

AFRICA	REST OF THE WORLD
NIGERIA	UK
TANZANIA	FRANCE
SIERRA LEONE	BELGIUM
MADAGASCAR	DENMARK
CÔTE D'IVOIRE	FINLAND
MOZAMBIQUE	SWEDEN
BURKINA FASO	USA
SENEGAL	
GHANA	
ZAIRE	
ZIMBABWE	
CENTRAL AFRICA	
SOUTH AFRICA	
MAURITIUS	

PERFORMING ARTS FORMS TREATED AT THE AFRICAN SYMPOSIUM WORKSHOP (AFSYMWORK) IN MAURITIUS

KOTEBA	DRUMMING
AFRICAN RITUALS	WRITTEN AFRICAN DRAMA
THEATRE IN EDUCATION	THEATRE OF THE OPPRESSED
THEATRE ANTHROPOLOGY	THEATRE FOR DEVELOPMENT
AFRICAN BALLET	DANCE DRAMA
GRIOT ART	MUSICALS
STAGE DIRECTING	RITUAL THEATRE

Course 1: September 1989:   DIRECTING A DANCE DRAMA IN
CONTEMPORARY AFRICA (9 weeks)

Course 2: April 1991:   LUCY & ME - Anthropology and
Performing arts (13 weeks)

The 3-year pilot project was interrupted after year 1, when the school was abruptly deprived of agreed funding, without any formal explanation in 1991. The Castle Arts in Southern Africa was abandoned and ATEX in London stopped all operations.

THE ACTPA PROJECT IN PHASES

ACTPA Build-up:

Phase 1 lasted from May 85 to December 86 - 19 months for a pre-study which included various missions to Zimbabwe, to Canada, to Cameroon, to Ethiopia and Tanzania... Daniel Labonne moves from Côte d'Ivoire to take up employment in the UK. ATEX is set up to provide a structure to the co-ordination, to raise funds and to protect the fledgling project.

Phase 2 started in January 1987 namely with the writing and circulation of the ACTPA Guidelines by Daniel Labonne, in which are defined the parameters, rationale and scope of the project. ATEX takes charge of the general co-ordination of the project. An agreement is reached with Zimbabwe whereby the newly independent African country will host the centre.

Phase 3 provided a working structure for the project while widespread support was sought and obtained worldwide, namely in a ground-

Daniel Labonne

breaking Round Table meeting in Paris in 1988. More field study in Senegal, Zimbabwe, Ghana, Togo, Côte d'Ivoire, Sierra Leone, Gambia...

Phase 4 The African Symposium Workshop (AFSYMWORK) brought together training specialists from all over Africa and the world in a comparative study to test the feasibility of the ACTPA Project in Mauritius. The exercise established the management skills of ATEX.

ACTPA Pilot Project:

Phase 5 came about with the Castle Arms, when the Zimbabwe government entered in an agreement with ATEX and offered facilities to accommodate the training centre in Bulawayo. The Castle Arms was renamed Castle Arts, then furnished and equipped by ATEX. We conducted the selection of resource persons and hiring of staff before intakes were transported, accommodated and trained in ACTPA at Castle Arts.

Phase 6 the Pilot Project lasted from 1990 to 1991, when the centre became operational and successfully delivered two training programmes.

The ACTPA project stops all operations and Castle Arts is deserted when funders cut off the supply of funds in 1991. The interrupted programme leaves the project coordinators with debts...

Phase 7 The host country, Zimbabwe, issues a statement of appeal for ACTPA at Castle Arts to continue. To no avail.

Post ACTPA:

1 year producing reports and setting the accounts right, organising the archives of the project, steering the project clear of controversy. One last visit to Stockholm by Daniel Labonne proves unproductive. Self-financed work.

Daniel Labonne lobbies old and new partners to repair the damage done to a promising project and the loss for Africa. Self-financed work.

1992. ATEX tries to diversify its activities by providing services with ATEX Consultants. ATEX sets up the *World Africa Foundation (WAF)* which is never launched. Daniel Labonne conceives *The London Africa Show* to salvage the Castle Arts and the experiment. To no avail.

1993. 'The Other Side of the Dream' a book written and illustrated by Daniel Labonne fails to find a publisher. The ACTPA Project is formally dead.

1994. The UAPA has ceased to exist and has fallen into oblivion while Zimbabwe slowly falls from grace with the international community.

In 1995, a first evaluation is conducted as Daniel Labonne collects feed-back from the African artists from across Africa who took part in the ACTPA Pilot. Self-financed work.

From 1996-2001, Daniel Labonne undertakes an academic evaluation of the project with the University of London (Goldsmiths College), as a private post-graduate student. Self-financed work.

In 2002, Daniel Labonne is granted an MPhil degree for his research. The long study is entitled *Development Through Creativity (An Experiment with African Performing Arts).* The University considers that the project may then qualify for a new beginning and a viable future.

10 years later, Daniel Labonne writes the book EMPOWERING THE PERFORMER to pave the way for a new departure, based upon a body of research dating back 25 years and personal continued investment. The book includes the pictorial report from 1993.

ACTPA Revival:

2011: FACE (Foundation for Arts, Creativity & Exchange).

THE APPEAL OF THE HOST COUNTRY

1. <u>Successes</u>

ACTPA as a living project is now proudly a year old. During this short time, it has already vindicated the reason for its birth and survival by way of two successful training workshops which were encapsulated in the performance productions named "FOOTPRINTS" and "LUCY & ME."

FOOTPRINTS and LUCY & ME have made ACTPA a success story, a reality indeed an invaluable asset in the promotion of authentic and African theatre. These two productions brought together several eminent African theatre trainers and performers from fifteen African countries and these men and women from different cultural backgrounds forged a new language which defied all barriers of communication - a new culture of common identity. The cultural identity of Africa and, in particular, African theatre was made a reality. ACTPA became a fact and was no more a dream.

These ACTPA initial successes derive from the sterling management work of ATEX, under the able and committed leadership of Mr. Daniel Labonne. Through ATEX, the aesthetic energies of African performing artists were successfully harnessed and, in the process of cultural contact and exchange, produced a new African performing artist who has confidence in his past and future.

On the financial side of the ACTPA project, the international donor agencies for this project deserve our highest commendation and applause. Without their faith in and commitment for any meaningful development process to take place, these first two international training programmes of ACTPA would not have come about. The host country, Zimbabwe, has made everything possible to make ACTPA a success. It has provided the venue, the Castle Arts in Bulawayo and all the logistics to hold the two international workshops, "FOOTPRINTS" and "LUCY & ME."

2. Problems

The first year of ACTPA as a three year pilot project to establish the parameters for a permanent ACTPA Programme, has met with one major problem or mishap which was the disagreement of views within the UAPA executive board. From what we could glean from outside, the real problem seems to have been the UAPA itself as an institution. Who is UAPA in terms of country representation? Failure to have a clear answer to this vital question, in our view, was the cause of all the problems of ACTPA - the bad publicity aimed at it. The critics of ACTPA tended to dwell on theoretical issues which time can only resolve.

The role played by ATEX has been questioned as if to suggest that nothing should have been done at all to make ACTPA a reality. Even the host country has been criticised for the manner in which it has handled the project vis-a-vis ATEX. The fact that two partners (ATEX and the Ministry of Education and Culture) had entered into a contract to make ACTPA a reality is not conceded. To say the least, this is mischievous and unproductive. From the very beginning, ACTPA management process had been a subject of interest to both ATEX and the Ministry and an option had been made for evolution and programmed gradual development to take place. Thus, discussions on how to improve/develop the management system of ACTPA have been taking place and are now at an advanced stage and therefore the critics of ACTPA have therefore no valid base to stand on regarding this aspect.

3. The Future of ACTPA

An agreement has been reached between ATEX and the host country (Ministry of Education and Culture) to transfer ACTPA management task from ATEX to Zimbabwe. A consultative meeting will be held to

Daniel Labonne

finalise/establish the new administrative set-up. What it boils down to is that fund-raising and receipt of funds and their disbursement (management) will be done by the host country and ATEX will be left to provide ACTPA Training Expertise wherever this is required by the ACTPA executive management board.

A strong appeal is therefore made to all well-wishers and the international donor agencies - for them to give their full support to ACTPA, both financial and moral support. Especially those donors who have provided funds for the first phase of ACTPA, we appeal to them to continue with the work so that what has been so far achieved continues to grow in strength.

Failure to receive tangible financial support from donor agencies will certainly mean the death of ACTPA as a project at a time when **Africa needs ACTPA more than ever before. ACTPA as a project is at the centre of development for the Region of Africa. As a project for the World Decade for Cultural Development, ACTPA fulfils all the four objectives of the decade and as such deserves all the support** of the United Nations funding agencies.

Zimbabwe as the host country of ACTPA, lends its full support to ACTPA and with its new role as overall manager of the project sees an even more exciting future for ACTPA within the last two years of its experimental life.

In conclusion, we want to again thank all the partners who have made ACTPA what it is now. We assure them all of our continued support of this innovative and ambitious project for Africa and we hope many more will become partners in this great project.

Signed: MR M. G. MACHINGA
Deputy Minister of Education and Culture, Zimbabwe
Harare, 25 October 1991

THE APPEAL OF AFRICAN PERFORMERS

MOTION OF THANKS AND APPEAL BY PERFORMING ARTISTS AT CASTLE ARTS
AT THE END OF THE 13-WEEK COURSE ORGANISED IN ACTPA AT CASTLE ARTS,
BULAWAYO, ZIMBABWE ON THE THEME "LUCY & ME"

29th July 1991

We, the undersigned, performing artists of Africa having been informed, selected, transported from our respective countries to Bulawayo, Zimbabwe, are pleased and grateful for the exceptional opportunity to travel, to be accommodated in Castle Arts, to be trained and to train, to work creatively with colleagues from other African countries, to exchange experiences and experiment, to discover new forms, new techniques, new skills and new cultures, to further our professional training, to enjoy the status of a respected artist in an atmosphere of freedom and creativity, to learn about video techniques, scriptwriting and anthropology, to participate in an original production, inter-African by nature, international by status.

Together with our specialists-trainers, we wish to express our sincere undivided gratitude to the Government of Zimbabwe, to the funding agencies who have financially contributed to this course, to the population of Bulawayo, to the staff of Castle Arts, but more particularly to ATEX, the project managers of the project, for their efficiency, their discreet but effective support in all circumstances.

As LUCY & ME becomes a successful stage production our special thoughts go to the artistic director and Doctor Brahane of the Museum of Addis Ababa.

We are thankful for the efforts of ATEX to keep the training free and accessible, opened to all Africa, but we have also been constantly aware of the financial difficulties of the project; As we have been aware of the

Daniel Labonne

destructive undertaking of people who have been trying to sabotage this exceptional project.

As we feel privileged to have been among the first to benefit from ACTPA at Castle Arts, we wish to place the following appeal, in our own names, on behalf of our colleagues at home, and in the name of younger Africans who MUST be given the same opportunity for training and production work.

We appeal to Funding Agencies to continue and increase their support to the ACTPA project and to Castle Arts that requires to be better equipped and staffed.

We appeal to Our Governments to support actively the present efforts of the Government of Zimbabwe and the project managers, ATEX;

We appeal to ATEX to continue to service the needs of ACTPA at Castle Arts and the development of African performing arts together with all other committed organisations. May the artistic standards and the essential professional management of ACTPA never be dropped.

We appeal to those who through ignorance or interest are threatening the progress and development of the project so they should try to understand that we would all lose (with Africa!) if ACTPA were to fail.

We appeal to the Non-African Governments and International Organisations to do more to understand the problems that we Africans have to confront and to evaluate fairly the promise of solutions contained in the concept of ACTPA and to provide financial as well as material assistance to the project.

We Appeal to the OAU, UNESCO, to the Government of Netherlands, to Finnida and other Scandinavian agencies so that our collective creation "LUCY & ME" be toured in the near future with the assistance of ATEX.

We appeal to well known artists and the press to help the promoters of the project to establish ACTPA at Castle Arts firmly for the benefit of the majority of performing artists and the development of Africa through the arts...

Signed by the international trainee-participants and residents at the castle arts for the course "lucy & me." Zimbabwe, 29th July 1991.

A.Zewdu	Ethiopia	S.Abubakar	Nigeria
H.S.Kiros	Ethiopia	D.Lumumba	Nigeria
N.A.Sowah	Ghana	K.Bernard	Tanzania
S.Torgbede	Ghana	P.Lwanga	Uganda
L.Ndlovu	Zimbabwe	P.C.Tilikunkiko	Rwanda
I.Chiyaka	Zimbabwe	L.Green	Zimbabwe
K.Khuluma	Zimbabwe	W.Stobart	Zimbabwe
E.Phiri	Zimbabwe	J.Chari	Zimbabwe
N.Bare	Zimbabwe	S.Mwangola	Kenya
Alassane Dakissaga	Burkina Faso		

Daniel Labonne

THE CONTEXT OF THE EXPERIMENT

To better understand the ACTPA experiment and assess its full impact, one has to place the project within the framework of the 'World Decade for Cultural Development (1988-1997), proclaimed by the United Nations.

Development understood at its most basic form applied to humans implies an evolution, not only from childhood to adulthood, but a comprehensive growth that transforms the adult into a responsible agent, actively engaged into the complexities of life, willing to contribute to the destiny of one's community. Such evolution of the individual can be measured in social, cultural and economic terms. That is where education and training matter. The most elementary form of training is the one given by the mother to her child, as she guides him, step by step, until he reaches full maturity as a human being.

This general understanding of training placed within the context of cultural development may be applied to a child, to a country or to the artist. In Africa more than anywhere else, the role of the performing artist may prove determining within the process of development. That is one of the early findings of this experiment.

In all training processes, trust and hope matter equally for those at the receiving end. Then, it is a matter of know-how and experience for those who need to transfer knowledge. The crucial issue of *need* points towards what skill is required as a means to achieve an end. Planning and organisation brings all these factors in an effective interplay. From point zero, each factor was gathered in the build up of the ACTPA project. The golden rule was the constant check that each measure taken was related to needs. The Union of African Performing Artists (UAPA) needed a purpose to justify its inception and raison-d'être. Africa needed a different approach to training its performers after decades of unfruitful trials, since political independence. Another fact of significance: the

ACTPA project had initially been a one-man band and, yes, the project remains the brain-child of one man. Criticism has tended to question what is common and natural to all human projects - he who is best equipped and knows the way takes the lead. But the pictorial report (*see Part Six: An Album For History*) will demonstrate that there has been an ongoing concern to make sure that there was always a plural input for what remains a unique project.

Perhaps the utopia component that generally underpins artistic work has been wrongly applied to the tough issues of development. At least, I had the excuse of attempting to act on behalf of a multitude of entities and sometimes conflicting interests. Such is the nature of a vast continent with infinite variety. In addition, in Africa, the performing arts are also vastly complex. We had no choice but to service the cause of the performing arts and somehow make it work. That was the challenge. To achieve so much in such a short time was no easy task and to come up with some spectacular results ought to have brought us some credit. Instead, we were blamed by our peers, punished by the same partners we had carefully persuaded along years of hard work. The money raised and promised to serve the many was withheld or diverted to serve less deserving causes elsewhere. More than a disappointment to me, personally, the demise of the ACTPA Project was a tragedy for performing artists of Africa.

What cannot be taken away from me is the fact that we did manage to set up purposeful structures that responded adequately to needs. To date, there is still no equivalent to ATEX to service the image of Africa and manage transnational cultural projects. Where is the equivalent of the Castle Arts, as a high place of artistic excellence for African performing arts? This is said without disregard for the latest efforts and initiatives across the continent. About training strictly speaking, I have proposed with ACTPA a fairly original method - 'the horizontal method' to be considered as one of the main axis within 'the process of

Daniel Labonne

exchange.' That method did not develop overnight but grew from my earlier work in theatre during 20 years before ACTPA. With or without Castle Arts, the method remains valid.

With or without the UAPA, performing artists have a right today to claim what had been devised to assist them and fulfil their needs for original and purposeful training. The method only begs to be further experimented and developed. I have suggested in recent academic work, that it is possible to envisage a new form of performance with African arts that could be called 'exchange theatre.' By demolishing the structures, by starving the project of vital funding, by attacking the serious researcher, by nipping in the bud a promising artistic blossoming, incalculable damage has been done. But we kept the accounts right up to this day. Personally, I have never given up on a job that remains related to needs. A million times more than personal interest, it is a matter of giving the performing arts of Africa a second chance because, twenty years later, the needs remain unattended. But the experiment has also demonstrated that aid, development and governmental strategies have proved mostly counter-productive. I have come to the conclusion that enterprise remains the most viable approach to long-term progress.

From our vague resolutions within the UAPA to the imposing reality of the Castle Arts in Bulawayo, the road has been bumpy and full of obstacles. Such a state of affairs may be common to all pioneering work... Many would cynically add that, in Africa, all roads are rough and bumpy... That may be the case, but the Castle Arts may well remain for a very long time a strong symbol, a benchmark in achieving the potential of African performing arts. In Africa, by Africans and for Africans.

Of course, we do recognise our mistakes along the way and we have certainly paid a heavy price already for some poor decisions. We must however recognise that in all experiments, mistakes are inevitable. Actually, they are most revealing and an integral part of the whole. Ultimately, difficulties and risks should never reduce the merits of the efforts invested along the way or the positive outcome at the end of the road. This book places the facts with hindsight so that the reader may determine, in a historical perspective, the real potential of this experiment.

As the Deputy Minister of the host country sadly points out, some had gone as far as to pretend that nothing ought to have been done... Such poor judgment can hardly be explained, unless one finds a political motive in preferring under-development and inaction! To some extent and for a number of years, it has been rather easy to blame the vehicle (ATEX) or the style of the driver (the project co-ordinator). The objective observer will remember that the experiment was breaking new ground, without any road map from the past. With hindsight, it must be stressed many times that the efforts were required of me on a personal level and progress has been recorded thanks to essentially *voluntary* action. Remember: the project took off from point zero. More importantly, I was simply granted a moral carte blanche to take the project ahead... As the dust settles after twenty years, the same applies today: I am taking yet another initiative towards meeting the same initial objective.

Observers will have had the time to check on alternative ventures that are comparable to ACTPA at Castle Arts and compare with what actually had been achieved in only one year of activity in 1990-1991. One statement of fact: one does not eliminate the crying needs of performing artists by closing down the Castle Arts. It remains undeniable that the ACTPA project first materialised thanks to ATEX deliberately operating in the rich North, then with relentless momentum, grounded all the efforts at the Castle Arts, south of the African continent. How unimaginable can that be? A castle dedicated to the arts deep in Southern Africa? This book reports with the authority of photographs and with the sanction time, that real performers from some 15 African countries have experienced the reality of a home for the rudderless performing arts of Africa, caught in a limbo for so long... What the trainees and specialists did during the days and weeks spent in Castle Arts was most productive. Records have been kept in written form and in video films. They actually tested the process of exchange and, on a daily basis, followed the tailor-made training provided by the African Theatre Exchange (ATEX). Both trainees and specialists were transported, accommodated, given the tools for creative work and paid during their entire stay at Castle Arts.

The World Decade for Cultural Development is over and nobody seems to care. Yet, with the ACTPA Project, diverse and unrelated cultures have engaged in the most creative manner; artistic forms of expression, isolated for too long, have been exchanged to allow rewarding fusion to generate a new creativity full of promises and vitality. That might just be one way of shifting the minds away from anger and conflict. Ironically after the demise of ACTPA at Castle Arts, Zimbabwe, then a most deserving host-country soon plunged into war and famine... Fate or immaturity? It pertains to others to conduct their own analysis of history or politics. After twenty years, my job could just be to echo the plea of African performing artists: what on earth have you done to our castle?

To the extent that there have been enough benefits on record for those who have had the good fortune to live and work at the Castle Arts, in Bulawayo, either as trainees or trainers recruited by ATEX, we shall keep the satisfaction of having done nothing more than our duty, as a fellow performing artist and as a researcher.

The first draft of this report dates back to 1993. It took the shape of a pictorial report to prove the point that many have been involved along the way; that with some scientific claim, the project has built up a graduated momentum that led to FOOTRPINTS and LUCY & ME, two inter-African productions. Where Theatre for Development had been isolating the artist and frustrating micro communities, the 'exchange process' restored human creativity in a development process that places the artist at the heart of a feasible cultural development. The proposed process aims for measurable impact at macro levels, namely through cross-cultural education and economic outlets. Today, in the 21st century, the need is pressing to pick up the pieces of the experiment and pull the most precious findings of the experiment from underneath the rubbles. By publishing this book which accounts with facts and pictures, with testimonies and frank explanations, the issues of a unique experiment, we are once again merely completing our duty. That same duty that kept me busy, safeguarding the archives of a precious project and later, evaluating both process and findings at Goldsmiths College, University of London.

What exactly had been the terms of reference from the outset? My job was to devise ways and means to undertake the study of a theatre school project valid for the performing artists of Africa; then, I had to demonstrate the originality of the training on offer, in terms of both methodology and finality; it was expected that a host country would be found; more importantly that the funds would, somehow be found. I did all of that, I am pleased to report. There were many witnesses, some very enthusiastic spectators (*see Part SEVEN: What the World Had to Say*) and yet unsuspected numbers of beneficiaries. For the record, it was agreed that I would need to deliver results within a pilot period of 3 years - from 1990-1993... Were the results too strong and compelling in 1991?

We are today in 2011. ACTPA at the Castle Arts has fallen out of all agendas: another failed effort to be blamed on a chaotic order of things associated to the battered African continent. I have personally given 10 additional years of my life to evaluate this unique experience. From the practice of the comprehensive experiment has evolved a theory - the Diamond Theory. In 2002, with a post-graduate degree, the University of London has indirectly granted me a new licence to try something new, more realistic and feasible. In 25 years of ongoing work, I may only hope that I have modestly contributed to a better understanding and increased exposure of the unsuspected potential of the performing arts in Sub-Saharan Africa. As expressed in the special resolution of the Ministers of Culture of the African Union, in 1990, maybe with my fellow performing artists involved in ACTPA at Castle Arts, we have managed to give substance and reality to the World Decade for Cultural Development, as proclaimed by United Nations.

Just as Africa cannot afford to rely on short-termism, African people cannot be reduced to a mere open field for more experiments... Their living forms of performing arts remain one of their most vital treasures. The needs of the performing arts in Africa have long exceeded the vagueness of intentions of a regrouping of artists in 1984. It was a useful step in the right direction. Yet, some failed to understand the point of an International Scientific Council which I set up in 1985 to give our artistic project a broader appeal and a more solid grounding. It is the same scientific rigour that must apply to the decades of trial and error, leading on to a revised vision for the future.

With this book, as I respond to the yet unanswered questions, I am confirming that what used to be called the ACTPA Project remains a unique project that refuses to be relegated to nightmare scenarios. The issues are much too vital for entire populations and tens of millions of young people. The crucial role of the performing arts in the development of sub-Saharan Africa will only make sense if the right strategy demonstrates the full relevance of this applied research. The pilot project is over. Cultural development cannot be limited to one decade, either. Lessons have been learned and history has moved on. In the 21st century, Africa, as a continent of 54 states, is more confident thanks a maturity borne out of more trials and errors, experienced in various fields, other than arts and culture. The global village seems more ready and anxious to rely upon viable strategies. New partnerships are being created as technologies are challenging humans to confirm their uniquely fundamental creativity. This experiment claims that, in the global village, Africans certainly have a brand new role to play.

Nationalism, internal wars or external invasions are unlikely routes to write the history of modern Africa. By reaching out across borders, languages and cultural differences, there might be a more exciting story to tell. Together. Such a story, as in FOOTPRINTS and LUCY & ME, might be about the art of survival, oral traditions and fundamental human attributes translated into a new artistic language. Who best to trust for this self-exploring, self-revealing undertaking than the performing artist of Africa?

In the last century, we dared to dream. Today, we must dare to engage in a serious and long-lasting enterprise resting upon a solid foundation for permanent structures that would benefit Africa and its peoples. First, with this book, people of good faith ought to be allowed to make sense out of what we really mean by 'Empowering the Performer.'

PART 2

Unanswered Questions

About a Unique Experiment

To accomplish great things, we must not only act but also dream;
not only plan but also believe.

Anatole France

Daniel Labonne

This mysterious photography was taken when I discovered a map of Africa carved out naturally on a sidewalk on the streets of Harare. Notice that even the island of Madagascar is adequately positioned east of the continent... I invited my Ethiopian colleague, Debebe, to stand by with his trainers and cast a friendly shadow... We were trying to convince newly independent Zimbabwe to avoid the mistakes of older independent African states and welcome the ACTPA Project on its soil.

ARE YOU A DREAMER, DANIEL LABONNE?

If I were, then I must be a rather conscious dreamer. Being an artist and a poet, I recognise the importance that dreams occupy in perceptions of life. Dreams are helpful in that sense that they are the safest means of escaping the prison of existence. First, one is trapped into the physical structure of a body, with its physical characteristics. At birth, everyone lands on a bed of circumstances that will determine one's early awareness and condition the rest of one's life. Such circumstances can become the bars of one's cell, unless one is able to dream of a means of escape. I was born on an island. The islander always dreams of a lost continent and aspires to reaching out beyond the natural sea borders. Awareness of these 'prisons' opens the only window where one is allowed to aspire to freedom: dreams. Yes, I am a dreamer. But one has to qualify the dreamer. In my case, while I am able to dream, I would next shift my dreams into a different zone of consciousness, where I may for example write about it. More importantly, I believe I am able to manage a dream until it is fleshed out and translates into reality. That is the privilege of the artist, especially the theatre artist who may not undergo out-of-body experiences, but on the contrary, internalises multiple life-story experiences by escaping one's personal circumstances, to embody other people's circumstances in a staged dream. But beyond the theatre artist, I suppose there is a Capricorn and Aquarius meeting-spot in my make-up: I do dream as an Aquarian but the patient, wilful strive of the Capricorn is a stubborn adventure. In the end, the dream becomes reachable. You may say that I am a dreamer with a purpose. The best dreams are those dreamt collectively.

WHAT DO YOU MEAN BY 'DREAMS DREAMT COLLECTIVELY?

It means that, for instance, the African Centre for the Training of Performing Artists was a well-formulated dream, as well as an achievable dream. It means where there is collective dream, there is a will; and where there is a will, there's a way. It also means that the term 'dreaming collectively' has a connotation familiar to African thought.

Daniel Labonne

Finally, I cannot forget that the theatre is essentially the organisation of an alternative universal vision, boxed in such a way that society is invited to share a collective dream.

WHAT IS YOUR DEFINITION OF DEVELOPMENT?

We should not forget that every living organism operate at cellular level. The term 'development' cannot be restricted to the modern economic meaning and reduced to statistics. Well-being and self accomplishment must be part of the equation. Applied to Africa, a more holistic approach is dictated by the history and the cultures of the populations directly concerned. Nothing is static in life. At cellular level, a living organism has a beginning, an evolution, ultimately an end. What is true for a plant, a mineral or an animal applies to humans and human societies. Development is therefore a process, both unpredictable and open-ended. It tends to be irreversible for living organisms but reversible for civilisations. Ultimately, development seems unique for every civilization. What is common in the development of all civilizations, past, present and future is the unique creativity invested by a society engaged within a process of development. One could claim that, so far, circumstances or policies have failed to tap into the creativity of African peoples south of the Sahara. Brain drain keeps diverting individual creativity and potential leaders to underpin other cultures, sometimes through emigration, often through inadequate education. Contrary to other civilisations, war and looting are not an option for Africa and Africans. History has demonstrated, from the Romans to European colonial conquests that development tends to be boosted through invasion, occupation and exploitation of appropriated possessions. So what are the real options for sub-Saharan Africa? This study describes an effort to provide an answer.

WHAT IS YOUR DEFINITION OF THE PERFORMING ARTS?

Performing arts are generally understood to embrace acting, music playing, dancing, singing, miming, story-telling, circus arts; plus the technical and managerial support required to deliver these live arts forms. But we need to go beyond personal experience and cultural perceptions. My own personal background is the theatre and the European concept of the theatre flows from Ancient Greece. Today, the most popular form of performing arts in the world is pop music sustained by the media and firmly rooted into the economy of rich countries, because nearly everyone listens to recorded music and songs. Once, I described some religious rituals as practiced in India (and Mauritius), as traditional forms of performing arts. It would be fair to embrace all these considerations in attempting at a definition of performing arts. It may be difficult to obtain universal agreement on any definition, but once you attempt at teaching the arts and training performers, broad agreement must be sought and obtained. Performing arts in the context of this project embraces all forms of cultural representations involving a performance, a performer and an audience, away from immediate reality but happening as part of the inner life of the community. Such representations push the group rituals towards the arts. Having said that, the term 'Performing Arts' is evolving very fast. I shall mention four trends to be reckoned with. First, the notion of 'performance' has been borrowed from the actor's delivery to embrace any live talk, generally tallied to fit within the taste of an audience, tuned to a television culture. Tone, content, sound bites, timing, eye contact have all been transferred from live performing arts to television delivery and audio-visual journalism. Secondly, the capacity of the actor to perform convincingly has been recuperated by power seekers, including politicians and corporate celebrities. The theatre game is under attack, if we consider the art of the theatre director is being aggressively claimed by the PR specialist who is highly paid to watch over the image of his client, the 'performer'. Communication techniques and timing and expected impact are often calculated in terms of sales or votes. Thirdly, the phenomenon of Reality Television has taken a direct jab at the art of the theatre actor: no script, no plot, no training, no artistic appeal. The direct impact of television is challenging the raison d'être of drama, while the spectator is being invited to give in to laziness and find pleasure in being mere

Daniel Labonne

'voyeurs' as the performer pretends to enjoy the exhibition of self. The fourth trend is found in the spectacle of sports, especially football. Given the popularity of this global show, which attracts millions of spectators gratified with comments over the 'performance' of both the team and the individual 'performer,' the football game has long entered the field of performing arts. There might be an additional meaning of performance attributed to the rendering of machines. For example, when one refers to the 'performance' of a computer... To teach performing arts nowadays require a revised appraisal of the world we live in. Ultimately, the performer cannot ignore all these trends. But there lies a new challenge of remaining stubbornly human by keeping the arts closer to the living and recognising the value of performing arts in various societies, especially in Africa.

WHAT IS YOUR DEFINITION OF AFRICA?

The first answer is rather obvious: it is the second largest continent on the planet, with eleven and a half million sq. miles. It is also the place where even the scientific community has agreed that humanity first appeared on African soil. For those who believe in God, Africa must have necessarily been a chosen place for God to create man. But if we look at the treatment that Africa has suffered in recent history, and if we also consider the natural calamities that affect the continent, then the African continent has either a mystical function, or else, it has heavily suffered human or divine injustice. Whatever the case, I do not agree with any doom-and-gloom view of the continent and its people. It remains the cradle of mankind and it is likely to remain the last continent afloat when all others would have self-destruct. Already, African land is being once again speculated over to feed the growing populations that, elsewhere, have irreversibly damaged their own soil and given in to greed and waste. Before that, the underground minerals of Africa have made some nations powerful and wealthy while these natural resources have brought misery to local populations. How can we forget the precious contribution of the Black continent in terms of manpower during the centuries of African slavery, to develop newly conquered territories? European Colonisation has damaged the African continent in many ways. My definition of Africa is more than geographical, precisely because it is the origin of all humanity and, later, the sons and daughters of Africa have taken the milk of the motherland to feed other nations, far away from the continent. Have you noticed the difficulty for the average person to sub-divide Africa intellectually? It is as if it is both unnatural and impossible a task to break up the magical entity of a unique place on the planet. Now, just consider the three syllables A-Fri-Ka. There is a musicality unmatched in the natural rhythm of the sounds, like very quick successions of an able drummer who leaves you numb and powerless. But the name is unthreatening: it feels and sounds like a welcoming chant that work both ways: the sometimes unconscious call of the child calling for a faceless mother, a mother who remains both physical and subliminal. Inversely, it is the call of the same mother calling back ALL its children towards Oneness. Africa has managed to remain total and undivided in spite of all. That is the unique characteristic of motherhood. Africa still keeps enough secrets to start humanity all over again, despite the arrogance of its ungrateful dispersed children. Egypt, in the North of Africa, was the first civilisation although, today, the youngest civilisations pretend that they have lost their memory and he who shouts louder deserves more credit.... In spite of the painful past, the curse of ignorance and the confusion of the present, Africa remains the keeper of the original flame and, in my view, it still holds the key to the future. To that extent, Africa is ageless with untested potential. The continent ought to be better explained, better understood and a lot more respected, while its cultural and economic potential is unlocked.

WHO IS GOING TO DO THAT? EXPLAINING AFRICA AND GIVE IT MORE RESPECT?

First, only Africans themselves could be educated and motivated to open-up, to develop the right medium, to master the right skills and engage into a new dialogue with confidence. Both creatively and

Daniel Labonne

collectively, as damaged trust is repaired and restored. That points towards the performing arts. Whereby the need for a new function of the theatre and the performing arts.... That also points towards the right conditions and the time to reflect, create and deliver. In the 21st century, universities cannot do that, because their function and their mode of operation as their expected results are pre-determined. Imposed models of civilisation are sometimes useful, but, they can be boring, often misleading and they have failed to motivate Africans. To a large extent, real freedom is the freedom to dream. One needs enough space to dream out what sort of civilisation one wishes for oneself. Both individually and collectively.

WHAT IS SO SPECIAL ABOUT THE ACTPA PROJECT?

First, its inception. The fact that at a given time, in one given place, a given group of actors from all over the continent met and agreed on a specific course to follow. Equally special is the fact that powerful witnesses, like UNESCO, were present to salute the coming about of that collective wish to be trained differently. That other organisations like the International Amateur Theatre Association (IATA) immediately sponsored the birth of the idea of a school was exceptional. Later, as a project, its journey from dream to reality also became quite special. It was not a classical project, from top to bottom, with power and money to drive it forward. Instead, it was a bottom-up project, from a wide range of practices and a very broad geography. It was initiated not by members of the same practice, as in a traditional trade union, but a gathering of mature practitioners and academics aware of their common concerns for the arts and the need to stop relying upon others for solutions. The ACTPA Project reflects a rare form of maturity, in this respect that it is not the expression of frustration, neither is it a call for aid or assistance, nor is it a request addressed to national authorities. It is above all the realisation that only a fresh beginning in peaceful ways, through the creative virtues of the performing arts may hold some chances of delivering a more balanced individual in Africa. It is then the refusal to consider the continent as being poor in such areas as song, dance, rituals, symbolic representations and purposeful community performance. On the contrary, the world could learn from Africa the art of dance, the culture of celebration and the ability to survive.

HOW IS THE PROJECT DIFFERENT FROM OTHER INITIATIVES ELSEWHERE AND TO WHAT EXTENT IS IT SPECIFICALLY AFRICAN?

The way it came about and the brief that was gradually handed down to me. That is different, with hindsight. There is something very African about the way the whole project took off. As you know, in Africa, your word is a million times worth a legal contract. There was no hard binding resolution, no contractual agreement, no paperwork. Instead, consensus gently shaped up the resolve and started shifting responsibility around. In reply to the responsibility that was placed upon my shoulders, I had to devise ways of honouring the collective trust. Consensus is a very cultural dimension in African culture, possibly the biggest obstacle to democratic principles. Democracy favours majority rule over minority wishes. Decision traditionally flows slowly from the agreement between elders in Africa. Unless and until consensus is first attained towards decision is reached, no real action follows. That is possibly one explanation for slower development: cultural consensus sometimes stalls action.

HOW DID CONSENSUS WORK IN THE CASE OF THE ACTPA PROJECT?

First, there was a major achievement: the Union of African Performing Artists. The coming together of theatre workers from different parts of Africa, from both the stage and academia, luckily brought about the resolve to form an organisation - the UAPA. Never underestimate the rare coming together of French-speaking and English-speaking performers who have been kept in separate linguistic blocks since colonisation. The place of this meeting: Harare, Zimbabwe, the youngest of independent African nations. The sponsors were different compared to the former colonial shepherding factor: a strong Scandinavian presence, namely the International Amateur Theatre Association and the then Secretary General of the International Theatre Institute (UNESCO), Lars Malmborg, a Swedish director with an opera background. The project was born within this happy triangle formed by newly independent Zimbabwe, the rare Scandinavian presence in African arts and the maturity of the African theatre workers at this international conference. I was well placed to understand the mindset: I was also acting as interpreter between the French-speaking and English-speaking representatives at the conference. Exceptionally, there had been two weeks of field work prior to the conference, so that the harsh realities of grass-root Africa prevented any inflated ego or linguistic quarrel to prevail. More than vague recommendations were required. The times demanded serious resolve and the means for responsible action. After all we were one generation away from the Independence years of African nations. Just as the latest child nation of the Independence, Zimbabwe deserved a better chance to succeed. The UAPA was set up by the Africans, present in 1984, who decided to expand the concept of cooperation beyond theatre, in order to embrace a broader, more African definition of 'performing arts.' That new definition was going to prove either an asset or a serious constraint, as the project began to evolve. In the background, the days of discussion and experimentation on development had raised awareness about the absolute need to prioritise and articulate a clear workable resolve for progress.

BUT THE TERM 'PERFORMING ARTS' HAD ALREADY BEEN WIDELY USED. IN THE US, FOR EXAMPLE.

Yes. The US has had to integrate and recognise the substantial input of Afro-Americans in the form and content of American music, dance, theatre and film. Americans needed to take some distance from the European definition of theatre and introduce some crucial distinctions. That process actually bears some lessons for others who aspire to develop a cultural identity and a vibrant form of expressing it. The term 'performing arts' spells out an American perception, within the context of their own understanding of cultural development, at a given time of their history. By the end of the 20th century, it was the turn of Africa to review existing concepts, including the American experience. That is why, in my evaluation of the project at the University of London, I was encouraged to dare create a new word to express what early forms of theatre and performing arts may mean, in African terms.

WHAT IS THE TERM THAT YOU HAVE COINED TO DESCRIBE AFRICAN PERFORMING ARTS?

Drumma. It is almost too simplistic and it only begins to address the fundamental needs. Because we are dealing here with complex issues, simplicity may be the shortest route to clarity. *Drumma* describes forms of performing arts that preceded ancient Greek Drama which has given shape to modern theatre. The term also points towards the survival of the drum in all cultures, from the beginning of human communication. It points directly to the key role of drumming across Africa, as a religious, social, psychological and existential accessory. Finally, I refer here to the modern form of African dance-drama in which, like an orchestra, the drum accompanies the narrative and every twist and turn in the drama unfolding in the theatre. In magical terms, only the drumming allows for the drama to unfold. It is the constant source of energy - the electricity - that sustains the action. The drum is not only one instrument, but one early sound, one fundamental ability to accompany the human voice and establish the rhythm for music and dance. It is about harmonised messages and sharing of experiences. The universal representation of drums up to the drum kit in modern westernised music making, may be a lasting common heritage of the earlier African ancestry of mankind. Drama has become a highly sophisticated form of expression in the civilised world; *drumma* underpins the whole process of staged representation without categorising culturally what remains a precious human mode of expression for the socially aware and intelligent creature who evolved from Africa. *Drumma* heals, unites and restores the memory across cultures and races, across borders and a history of division. It ought to assist in telling the true story, the whole story, and nothing but the true story. A poet once said that it only takes one drum for Africa to wake up. What he meant was probably that, thanks to drumming, time is contracted and humanity is magically brought together to the A of early beginnings, without over-simplifying the drama of existence and the saga of the ongoing development of humankind to this date. *Drumma* is more about time, story-telling and the concern about an inclusive reality than it is about a particular human group or cultural identity.

HOW IS *DRUMMA* RELEVANT TO THE ACTPA PROJECT?

It responds to a fundamental need: to give a name to a phenomenon that is ignored, downgraded, considered as folkloric. In reality, it has remained vital to most communities. In my own research, it is one of the direct results of the ACTPA experiment. It also recognises a common reality across Africa: the omnipresence of the drum and the art of drumming. It restores the possibility of negotiating new ways between African societies to seek for common factors, and resist to the risks of new fractures and painful wars. Finally, it heralds ecological values between nature (the tree trunk), the animal world (the stretched hide), human aptitudes (the skilful hands of the drummer), intelligence as expressed by coordination of the ears (attention to the other through creative sound), on a philosophical level, the need to fill the big void (namely with woven sounds of the beating heart amplified in space), the call towards other levels of consciousness (the dead and the gods) and the fusion of all these elements into unifying art forms. Adequate education begins with identifying existing needs. The first production resulting from the ACTPA at Castle Arts was described as a Dance-Drama. The term is awkward and a mere attempt to reassure the non-African English speaker. The ACTPA Project is above all about the adequacy of education so that development becomes an exciting self-motivated adventure for the Africans. Telling the African story is the next challenge. *Drumma* responds to the basic needs to understand how to begin to address a two-pronged challenge: 1. setting up the right school that might lead to 2. telling the untold story of Africa and Africans. The process of healing a fractured culture and a damaged memory implies finding a common language capable of articulating creatively a shared experience through a vital catharsis. Development only occurs when there is life and a will to live. Finally, it is above all a matter of telling the African story to fellow Africans and to the younger generation on the continent. *Drumma* is intended to feel and listen to the pulse of a silenced continent. The phenomenon has existed in various parts of Africa in micro communities. I also coined the term '*drumma*' to circumscribe the cultural specificity that Africans have given to varied forms of performing arts, including storytelling and ritual. The point has always been two-pronged: bonding and catharsis. To that extent, in Africa the arts have remained for too long inward-looking. But the word I have coined is outward-looking and projected into the future, within a development perspective.

BUT THE 'SILENCED CONTINENT,' AS YOU PUT IT, MUST BE ATTRIBUTED TO THE CULTURE OF SECRECY OF AFRICANS...

Yes, there is a culture of secrecy. But that is true in many cultures. Do we really know what and who determine the policies that govern the world? Isn't secrecy more about religion and rituals in all cultures, from the Egyptians to some western fraternities of the 21st century? If secrecy is particularly valued in African societies, we must simply acknowledge it as fact. Then, we need to decide whether secrecy equals bad, therefore to be rejected as the colonial powers have done. Or is there a need to revisit and reassess together with the guardians of traditions, how best to treat and retain the most useful practices from the past? There are serious factors that affect health, ecology, environment, social cohesion which are all valued in modern civilisation. In the context of this research, all we are claiming is for the African performing artists to be empowered through adequate training, so they may negotiate, first, by tapping into the wealth of oral tradition and performance, then, by

Daniel Labonne

formulating creatively what is the best way forward. The fundamental rule is not to be judgmental, either about the current world order, or the thousands of years of African culture.

HOW TO DO THAT? HOW TO NEGOTIATE A THOUSAND YEARS OF AFRICAN CULTURES?

One way of doing this would be to find a way of inviting the guardians of traditional performing arts within the walls of a modern training centre. In terms of knowledge and practices across Africa, the authority is not in modern universities, but among the elders. Is it right to reject that wealth of knowledge at a time of global uncertainty? Can Africa afford the luxury of casting away indiscriminately oral tradition, for example? Should Africa commit cultural suicide by forgetting the thousands of dances practised by communities, for the sake of what is called progress? All we are saying, to paraphrase John Lennon, please give arts a chance. The way to peace flows through the arts. In Africa, the last chance before irreparable damage is done would be to empower the performing artist to act as mediator and transformer of culture, with a real chance of impacting upon the education of the young and development of individual countries.

DID YOUR SPONSORS UNDERSTAND THAT ASPECT OF THE ACTPA PROJECT?

No, I do not think so. I found out when I decided to place a picture of a traditional dancer on the cover of the brochure for inauguration of ACTPA at Castle Arts, in 1990. Somebody asked me whether I was trying to promote 'tribal culture?' I realised we are dealing with irrational fear and fundamental ignorance about Africa, grass-root Africa. If that is the case, who best than the African performing artist should reassure and educate? For that to happen, one needs a new kind of training, a methodology that enables what I have called 'vertical exchange' between modernity and tradition, in the most creative way. Initially, the exercise is one of building trust, whereby the need to complete the cross with 'horizontal exchange' among fellow Africans from all parts of Africa.

TELL US ABOUT THE EARLY DAYS OF ACTPA... THE GENESIS OF THE PROJECT.

First, the UAPA engaged a dialogue with Swedish and Danish organisations that committed their early support beyond a punctual conference in Africa. Two names must be mentioned there: John Ytterborg, secretary general of the IATA and Martha Vestin, a theatre director from Stockholm. Both individuals deserve much credit for their early listening ear and their ability to see African initiatives blossom. The UAPA voted a programme of action and training was found to be the most potent area in which to invest the concerted efforts. While we conducted field work in Africa, I personally had long discussions with Martha Vestin about the inexistence of adequate training. Further discussions were held, first in Cameroon, next, in Stockholm, where a memorandum was signed to confirm that, yes, training would be the focal point of this new understanding about the needs for training performing artists. The Stockholm Memorandum confirmed the 3-party agreement involving African artists (UAPA), Scandinavian parties (the sponsors) and Zimbabwe (the eventual host country for a project). It was about setting up 'An African School of Theatre.' This very vague idea slowly evolved to gel into a clearer definition. It took a session of work which I conducted personally with new friendly organisations in Denmark, (DATS and IATA). The first series of intense discussions led to yet another meeting in Zimbabwe, involving a reduced number of committed well-wishers from the 3-party understanding, earlier in Stockholm. The definition was spelled out to me and formalised in a report: the school of performing arts would 'respond to existing needs' from across Africa.

Daniel Labonne

WHAT EXACTLY DOES THAT MEAN? THIS QUESTION OF NEEDS...

It means it is not about somebody's great idea imposed upon a continent of 1 billion people. Nor is it, for once, another attempt to reproduce what the rich countries of the North have developed for themselves. It cannot be driven by ideology. It means that if schooling so far has not delivered in Africa, it is the adequacy of schooling that must be questioned. It means that those who hold the answers have possibly never been asked the right question. Scientifically, it means that there must be a method of testing the research by allowing the communities concerned to respond whether their deeper needs are being addressed. In engineering terms, the new part must fit in and allow the system to function better. Development is a journey and it is one that takes a people all the way towards achieving its own potential. The real need for the people of Africa is Development.

WHAT NEEDS ARE WE TALKING ABOUT?

Cultural needs. Somehow, the new school had to lead towards cultural and economic development. From my limited experience, African peoples do not live from bread and water alone: they need to sing and dance. Life only makes sense when it is sanctioned by the right dance. Celebration and mourning, birth and death, success and setbacks are all good reasons to dance. Where is the structured training programme that caters for this fundamental need to develop such a specific cultural trait? Why not try to convert this special aptitude to practice performing arts into an economic advantage? What is the place reserved in the schools in Africa for self-development through the arts? Why should you be surprised that poor leadership remains endemic in Africa, if the child is not allowed to follow a culturally meaningful course of self-development? René Descartes write 'Je pense, donc je suis' (I think, therefore I am). That fundamental premise of western civilisation has led to a type of schooling which has delivered a restrained, controlled, thinking personality and a system of schooling which is almost entirely devoted to one area of the human body: the thinking head. Responding to the needs of Africans necessarily means a more integrated approach to life and training. I would like to be able to push my research until it becomes possible to affirm that, for the average African, it is 'I Dance, therefore I am.'

THAT IS A PHILOSOPHICAL VIEW. LET US GO BACK TO THE AFRICAN SCHOOL PROJECT. HOW DID THE PROJECT TRANSLATE INTO A CONCRETE SCHOOL IN AFRICA?

To understand the course followed by the project and the ongoing research that remains valid today, one must never lose sight of this concept of needs. The other constraint came from inception of the Union of African Performing Artists (UAPA) itself: the union was pan-African with founding members from South, East, West and Central Africa. In a word sub-Saharan Africa seemed to want a school that would be as inclusive as possible. The third issue was soon going to prove determining: who is going to pay for the costs of researching, establishing and running a school? Anybody in his right mind would have run away from such a vague, improbable dream. It was fraught with risks, given that Africa has long been a gaping wound in need of all the basics, in terms of water, food, shelter and medical care. What were the chances of advocating for the performing arts as a need for survival? I decided to take on the challenge and it took me a good part of 15 years of my life.

WHY SHOULD THE ARTS BE GIVEN ANY SORT OF PRIORITY?

Because you cannot develop a people against their will. Because development is first about education but not necessarily about school only. Because all the resources to assist Africa have been geared towards economic, military and political development. Because Africa is a broken continent and, so far in Africa, education leads to a broken personality. Because the core issue is about adequacy of education. Performing arts should be considered an asset on which to build the personality of the young African.

Daniel Labonne

WHAT MADE YOU A QUALIFIED PERSON TO TAKE ON A PROJECT LIKE ACTPA?

As an actor and theatre director, I had spent years researching new training methods for a Mauritian theatre before I joined field work research in theatre for development for another five years. In the mean time, I had been a consultant for the African Cultural Institute based in Dakar. I did work for the Francophone agency (ACCT) more than once, namely in Niger. I had been a member of the jury for several years for the Interafrican Playwriting Competition organised by Radio France International. An earlier regional project for a production workshop had been submitted, approved and implemented in West Africa in 1981. I was fully qualified to take charge of a project that involves research, training, negotiating skills and creative ability in 1985. Aged 35 and a father of 2, I was neither a beginner, nor a madly ambitious man when I decided to accept to take on the challenge of managing the ACTPA project. What must be stressed is the fact that there was never a job description, nor a fee attached to the job. Let us look at one specific qualification: I had been elected vice-president and treasurer of the Union of African Performing Artists (UAPA), to refer specifically to the terms of reference that led to the additional responsibility of taking the project across totally uncharted waters.

WERE YOU LIVING IN MAURITIUS IN 1984?

I was at the time an entrepreneur, living with my family in Cote D'Ivoire, in West Africa. That means I was self employed and I was relatively more free than my UAPA colleagues to engage into whatever was involved in promoting a common dream for a school of performing arts. As an actor, I had worked both in Mauritius and abroad, for the stage and television, with a high, in Quebec. My work as a director had taken me to staging avant-garde theatre and modern interpretations of classics. In terms of research, I may mention two aspects of my earlier work. First, my first visit to Africa took me to Senegal, not for any theatre work, but because I was researching direct teaching techniques of unwritten languages, with specific regards to Kreol in Mauritius. For five long years, I conducted an applied research in the theatre, covering all aspects of theatre practice. The research was self-financed and involved providing appropriate solutions to objective problems affecting the practice of theatre in Mauritius: training the actor, the use of local language, the stage treatment of poetry as a preferred language by Mauritians, the staging of traditional Sega to tell contemporary life, the question of aesthetics and quality in theatre work, the key question of national identity, marketing issues for plays, how to break up the racial divide encouraged by official policy.... In the process, the theatre was being used as a sort of social service, delivering a task that neither the school, nor literature, nor the media, nor politics was delivering at the time.

THE QUESTION OF NEED AGAIN.... WHAT WAS THE THEME OF YOUR EARLIER THEATRE WORK IN MAURITIUS?

The broad title given to this research was *'What Theatre for What People.'* It led to productions and public appreciation of the outcome of the research. Later, more interaction with fellow African theatre workers had been granted to me in a one-month seminar, organised in Abidjan. My research took on a different direction with Theatre for Development as experimented in Zimbabwe, in 1984. It just happened that I am bilingual and was able to assist the 'exchange' between English-speaking and French-speaking Africans during the field work, that gave me a real insight into the differences and similarities between the two language blocks and whatever was common to the African concerns in both groups. Those who benefited, among both participants and sponsors, found in me the best person to take on the early tasks of seeking consensus over a school that would address the needs of African performing arts. Finally, when I was personally offered a contract to teach drama and to do some theatre directing in the British theatre, I moved to London. I decided the opportunity was providential towards promoting the school project from the renowned square mile of 'theatre land,' in central London. The sheer negotiation work and the

Daniel Labonne

communication issues involved in convincing richer countries and 53 African countries was likely to stand a better chance, if conducted from London. But the most determining factor, besides my adaptability, was the fact that the whole project was actually coordinated thanks to voluntary work. There was no money to be earned. I knew it from the outset and decided nonetheless to become a facilitator so that the dream expressed from fellow Africans may shape up into concrete reality.

COULD YOU CLARIFY THE LEGITIMACY OF THE PROJECT?

Legitimacy became one of the early issues with serious implications. You know the saying 'Beggars cannot be Choosers. Yet, there you had a group of theatre workers from poor countries which hardly had a structured theatre practice, without any mandate for influencing matters in their own respective countries, daring to dream up a continental school to train future theatre artists and performers. Theatre unions or performing arts associations hardly existed at national level, in most African countries. The UAPA had decided to call itself a union and not an association. Was it because of an affiliation to the continental African Union? But it soon felt awkward as I set out to promote the ACTPA Project, because the general perception is that a 'union' implies an active trade and that the workers within such a trade decide to defend their rights and interest, as opposed to the owners and managers of the industry. Wasn't the UAPA putting the cart before the horse? I decided that the school project must be promoted precisely as the spelling out of good intentions and modesty, to guard against any perception of the mobilisation of some form of vain activism. In other words, we may be poor and underdeveloped, but you cannot blame us for wanting to learn, and learn together. More importantly, from each other. The dream was already threatened with toxic distrust, emerging from both international interests and from national ministries. The other aspect of legitimacy arose from the sort of tacit agreement about what is meant by Africa. That is an essentially political understanding that affects all matters connected with Africa. The decision-making circles understand different geographical areas linked to vested or ex-colonial interests whenever one mentions Africa. African governments generally have an order of priority which places food, shelter and education high on the list. Theatre and training performing artists fail even to appear on such a list... Stage artists who were found to be too enterprising or strong-minded occasionally find themselves censored or... in jail. If any money is involved, the question of control over such money is likely to cause concern about the legitimacy. All these questions had to be addressed, one way or another. The decision to promote the project from London only partly reassured. I decided that providing more information and consolidating the legitimacy of the UAPA was crucial to granting increased credibility to the ACTPA Project. The UAPA Brochure was produced to assist in this initial task. Some goodwill was earned, not without a streak of jealousy among fellow theatre workers and discomfort among powerful organisations. Suspicion also grew from another area: what was this pan-African project being conducted from Britain? I had to provide additional legitimacy to the ACTPA Project by setting up a British non-profit organisation for transparency and to boost the fund-raising. ATEX (The African Theatre Exchange) responded to the need for accountability and professional approach to project management.

WAS ATEX THE END OF YOUR WORRIES AS PROJECT CO-ORDINATOR?

Not at all. ATEX provided some protection to the coordinator who had to deliver while his operation remained transparent and legally grounded. ATEX responded to the need for transparency and professional credentials without jeopardising the 'dream' negotiating with a potential host country soon demanded guarantees about terms of reference. For a government to commit property and other forms of assistance, it is no easy matter. However, ATEX could attend to the task of providing some guarantees faster than UAPA, dispersed across the African continent. It was gradually made clear that the ACTPA Project was being managed by ATEX, but that the project 'belonged' to the UAPA. But then, how could a loose organisation like UAPA claim to own and run an institution, given all the human, practical and logistical considerations? The best solution was to allow reality impact upon the dream by making new friends and accept support from many quarters. There was necessarily a degree of improvisation and creative thinking. Flexibility and pragmatism dictated the way forward. In other words, allow concrete results to build a momentum for the project.

HOW DID YOU DO THAT?

I provided the intellectual back-up with a Guideline document and obtained additional international credibility to back the ACTPA Project. Thus, the International Scientific Council was set up in London to reassure all parties concerned, consolidate the foundation around ATEX and give a new boost to the 'dream.' ATEX succeeded in doing its job, only thanks to an ongoing campaign aimed at rich countries of the North and, in the South, at a maximum of African countries. An enormous task indeed, made worse with the fact that the project continued to depend upon voluntary work. All funding organisations insisted that they would finance sub-projects only. No allowance was made for administration costs. Not even a per-diem for the day-to-day work of a long period of 6 years, including the pilot project years at Castle Arts. The ACTPA Project progressed across choppy waters, thanks to unfailing willpower and a rather clever succession of sub-projects leading, gradually but surely, to the main project - the training centre in Zimbabwe.

LEGITIMACY MUST HAVE REMAINED A CONCERN THROUGHOUT?

Real legitimacy was only achieved when a host country invited ATEX to accept a venue and to conduct the pilot project on its soil. Prior to that, it took a special resolution negotiated by ATEX leading to a special resolution by the African Union who granted its full support, on behalf of all its member states. From being a vague dream of artists expressed by a fragile union, ATEX managed to place the project under the umbrella of the UN proclaimed Decade of Cultural Development. Another resolution from UNESCO cemented the base of international goodwill that allowed for the grounding of the 'dream'.

IS THERE SOMETHING ABOUT AFRICA ITSELF THAT MAKES PROGRESS DIFFICULT?

The question of legitimacy is linked to the key question of governance. The continent can hardly be considered a grouping of organised, independent nations. Instead, it is a fractured territory that has suffered violent and arbitrary splits. Those splits have been legitimised and are called borders. But these borders have so far caused more problems than solutions. Then, you simply have to read the papers, whenever Africa hits the headlights and you understand that Africa has consistently remained the object of covetousness from outside and chaotic behaviour from within. If one needs an example, there's the story of the failed coup in Guinea Bissau and the involvement of highly educated foreigners, well-trained mercenaries, multinational greed over Africa's natural resources. The situation in Côte d'Ivoire where elections have actually delivered two heads of states, both claiming legitimacy, reflects the arbitrary carving of states and the inability to adjust. Poor governance and corruption tend to be blamed upon African leadership exclusively. In reality, it is about a combination of poor education, the history of over-exploitation of African resources at the expense of the development of local peoples and a deeper cultural malaise.

THE REAL WORLD IS ABOUT POLITICS. THE PROJECT WAS ABOUT A DREAM...

But dreams matter and respond to a vital need. The arts are nothing but the ability to indulge into healthy dreaming while remaining awake. The human being is a complex creature and the mind needs constant massaging. The reality of a wonderful building has first been dreamt of by the brain of an architect. That is prior to impacting upon reality. At the

Daniel Labonne

other end of the spectrum, the Sphinx in Egypt stands as the lasting evidence that art survives long gone civilisations and their mortal politicians.

HOW DID THE ACTPA PROJECT MANAGE TO AVOID POLITICAL PITFALLS?

A project like ACTPA could not go ahead without the political will. And it was left to the coordinator of the project to find the arguments, the language and the logistical means to win the essential support. Worse still, co-ordination had the delicate task of reassuring every party that the enterprise was being scientifically conducted with the generous spirit of the arts. Polarised attitudes had to be gently tamed into adopting a more open approach to the arts. Decision-makers had to be literally educated into grasping the win-win situation that the ACTPA Project holds. The South does not have the means for ambitious projects; the North does not have the will to assist beyond basic needs of the South. These are realities that coordinating a project like ACTPA entails. English-speaking Africa needed to hear French-speaking Africa, and vice-versa. The older generation of Africans had to accept to sit at the table of the younger generation, and that is no small matter in Africa. Development is a concept fraught with trappings... Not to mention the power of money in the world in the 20th Century. Imagine steering a 'dream-project' among all these icebergs and monsters...

FROM A CULTURAL POINT OF VIEW, WHAT IN YOUR VIEW NEEDS TO BE DONE TO ADDRESS ISSUES OF ARTIFICIAL BORDERS AND POOR GOVERNANCE?

However risky the task, these issues had to be somehow addressed. Along the years of research, we proposed four ways to forge ahead. First, a process of healing is essential with respect to the persistent bleeding from the carving out of the continent. African performers ought to make it one of their duties to use their arts to address this need. Specialist training is required for that purpose. Secondly, an improved and original approach to education for young Africans may lead towards better leadership. Somehow, the performing arts ought to find a place in the schooling of young Africans. A third issue lies in the need to accommodate traditional value systems for an integrated form of development for Africa. Where universities have failed to deliver and traditional knowledge is self-destructing, the performing arts could be used. Finally, a process that activates a healthy south-south 'exchange' among African nations would certainly go a long way towards creating better conditions for peace and development. ATEX and the ACTPA Project, used in tandem, advocated that all these measures point towards economic benefits and peace.

IN THE CASE OF THE ACTPA PROJECT, HAS THE INITIAL PARTNERSHIP BETWEEN AFRICANS AND NON-AFRICANS WORKED?

It did for the first few years. The initial partnership required special attention. The loose agreement between African artists within the UAPA, Scandinavian theatre workers, development officers and Zimbabwean representatives needed to be consolidated. A cement was needed to build up a foundation. Any serious action required the engine that would take forward such a complex combination of interests. The engine and the cement became The African Theatre Exchange (ATEX). ATEX managed to deliver against all odds, by actually training performers from 15 African countries, while keeping intact the initial triangular partnership. Not less than 3 members of the steering committee of the UAPA were paid resource persons in Bulawayo, during the pilot project. The Swedish International Development Authority and Scandinavian agencies were persuaded to act as the main provider of funds. More importantly, the early resolve to implement the school in Zimbabwe was respected. The initial understanding had remained intact, but the ride had been bumpy... Perhaps, ATEX has been a victim of its own success.

Daniel Labonne

WHY IS IT THAT ACTPA AT CASTLE ARTS IS NOT IN OPERATION TODAY?

Precisely because of its success, more than its weaknesses. Just imagine: if only ACTPA at Castle Arts had been able to complete its full pilot programme of 3 years, and implement the school, it would be today in its 20th year of operation! How many original shows would have been produced? How many hundreds of performers from all over Africa would have been trained in choreography, setting design, event organisation, performing arts, development theatre or 'exchange' techniques? Perhaps, the school would have become self-financed for years already, thanks to its Diaspora Courses opened to non-Africans? Perhaps franchises would have been created elsewhere in Africa? Instead we must acknowledge a rather depressing reality... the sad African reality affecting some of the main players behind the early success of the ACTPA Project. Instead of hosting a unique centre of creative arts and delivering original products Made in Africa, for various reasons, Zimbabwe plunged into total chaos... What was intended to become a positive version of 'cultural development' and a model for Africa has turned into a nightmare...

HAS THE PROJECT BEEN LOST WITH THE DOWNFALL OF THE HOST COUNTRY?

Too many people have benefited and there has been enough transparency throughout for the project to have a future. I deliberately decided to place the evaluation into the public domain, by completing the post graduate study at University of London. The answer to your question is no, the project is not lost. This being said, there's been some scavenging to reckon with, once the project was starved of funds and the Castle Arts was unable to remain in operation. It is unfortunate that Zimbabwe sank economically and politically. But the dream for a pan-African school for performing arts is still alive. The need is there. The project would eventually be available, once there is an invitation from a new host country, once a safer form of funding has been found.

BUT HASN'T THE MAIN FINDINGS FROM THE EXPERIMENT BEEN RECUPERATED WITH TIME?

The best form of compliment is imitation. I know at least one very serious attempt to copy both the work and the logo of ATEX. The project suffered from the same curse that has plagued everything of value in Africa. From the healthy human resources exported over centuries for free labour, to the precious minerals exploited today for others to look beautiful and become wealthy. The prevailing attitude has so far remained unchanged: such resources are so precious that Africans would not know how to maximise their benefit... The principle of aid rests upon this attitude. When African leaders are coerced into corruptive behaviour and dispose of natural resources for their own benefit, the bad press is quick to point a finger. When the will, responsibility and ability are there for Africans to manage their own resources, no credit is given. On the contrary: somehow they are perceived as dangerous...

ARE YOU REFERING TO PERFORMING ARTS OR TO MINERAL?

Both have value. Both are precious. Both can be found in African soil. Cultural Development was precisely a concept of United Nations to underline the need to understand and validate the importance of both the economic and cultural. Together, they form an integral part of national wealth. There is a duty for the Africans themselves to pull themselves together in order to spur on their own vision of a manageable progress. The Performing Artists took on the challenge and tried, with the ACTPA Project, to show one way of processing their resources, in order to achieve progress.

Daniel Labonne

BUT WHAT HAPPENED TO THE MAIN FINDINGS FROM THE EXPERIMENT, BESIDES THE VERY CONCRETE REALITY OF THE CASTLE ARTS IN ZIMBABWE?

The less tangible findings from the experiment have been partly recuperated by vested interests that have tried to reproduce fragments of the ACTPA/ATEX successes. Significantly, there is at least one pale copy of ACTPA in Africa, reduced from a permanent training centre to a regularly organised and well-funded festival. The concept of 'exchange' has simply been awkwardly translated into the unattractive term 'market,' with no impact upon the development of performing arts, either on the quality or on the quantity of African stage productions. The years of data collection and purposeful negotiation of ATEX have been boxed into a rather academic body which duplicates more or less what university departments have been already doing. Squandered - again - are the efforts towards pulling together various resources in order to spark on and enhance development through creativity. The goodwill to develop training programmes 'according to needs' that lead directly to original performing arts products 'Made in Africa' have suffered a setback. The Union of African Performing Artists (UAPA), at the origin of the whole undertaking, has simply vanished, with it, the inability to act in a concerted and productive manner.

AND WHAT HAPPENED TO THE CASTLE ARTS?

Has the Castle Arts in Bulawayo been reconverted into Castle Arms, its original name from the independence years of belligerent Rhodesia? I did learn that physically, the building is still intact. But what is it being used for? I do not know. The most ironic of African realities can be measured with my own case: from coordinator of a unique training centre in Africa, for Africans, I had been reduced personally to conduct the evaluation of the ACTPA Project in a post-graduate study.... in London. In other words, from a provider of a unique service in training, I had been reduced to a paying mature student. There lies the paradox and the opposite of what was intended with the Decade for Cultural Development. My friend, Prosper Kompaore of Burkina Faso, many times a consultant for ATEX in the build-up to implement the ACTPA project was damning when he met me at Goldsmiths College: 'My friend Daniel has messed up his life,' he said jokingly. What he meant was I had apparently lost my sense of purpose and enterprise. He failed to understand how, at least, I was not a teacher at London University.

HE WAS RIGHT, WASN'T HE?

Of course he was. And that reality must not escape the study of African Performing Arts and the contradictions of cultural development. But time only will tell. Given the ongoing need to safeguard the findings whatever the circumstances if like the phoenix, the ACTPA Project rises up again under a new form, in a different host country with guaranteed funding and long term beneficiaries, every measure taken to keep the records and the findings safe would have proved worthwhile. So, wherever you are, my friend, I must reassure you: my life has been as purposeful and creative so far. Above all, even disguised as a mature student at the University of London, I have never let down those artists who once entrusted their wildest dream to me.

BUT THE FACTS STATE OTHERWISE, DON'T THEY?

The facts attest of the difficulties of Africa in the real world and the relative myth of development, so far. I only feel so sorry for Africa and for the performing artists who deserve so much better! But I suppose, there is what sceptics call 'African harsh realities.' Then, there is the ongoing dream of affirming positively and collectively the African experience. As long as nobody else is actively delivering the right training; as long as the productions 'Made in Africa' are not reaching out towards the millions of potential spectators across Africa, as long as exceptionally talented performers are still reduced to forgetting their own dances to learn in foreign universities, the need remains intact for a project like ACTPA. Castle Arts may have been locked up to stop the

Daniel Labonne

project, but the experiment goes on. Following my MPhil thesis available at the University of London, *Empowering the Performer* is yet another stepping stone in the same applied research.

DO YOU MEAN THE CENTRE WAS NOT ALLOWED TO OPERATE?

I mean that the project was starved of funding and the 3-year pilot project was stopped after the first two courses of the first year. No incident had marred the conduct of the first courses. The filmed document at the end of the first course demonstrates absolute unanimity about all the objectives of the project having been met. Both the international observers and the host country were using superlative language in praise of the work of ATEX and the achievement of ACTPA. Most importantly, the participating performing artists were elated about this firm grip over reality, with the Castle Arts, the 'exchange process' and the staged productions. I would refer to a document produced by the Utrecht School of Performing Arts with the long interview of Stephen Chifunyise of Zimbabwe and Francis Nii Yartey of Ghana, both resource persons who produced the dance-drama 'Footprints.'

WHAT IS THAT REALITY OF AFRICA YOU REFER TO?

Not everyone is happy to associate success with Africa. This is of a political order and I can't help it. The challenge had been upheld to establish an original school of performing arts in Africa, for Africans. Suddenly others wanted the credit. This is a human factor. No major incident had marred the pilot project at the Castle Arts after ATEX had levelled down all the obstacles leading up to the actual centre. Such a success had a price and, up to this day, I paid the price and was denied the credit. On record, ATEX remains a unique facilitator that would probably have done much better, had it decided to rely upon the private sector. But history has been made and no one may undo what had been delivered. The truth and merits will be restored by time. The considerable achievements of the ACTPA Project, jointly with the work of ATEX, are still available for posterity. There are many audio-visual documents to testify of the healthy achievements within this experiment. My recent MPhil thesis has provided another cushion of credibility. The written long study has opened yet another window of opportunity for the experiment to resume in due course. Possibly after I would have left the stage for good... At least, I have been able to stop a wonderfully positive human undertaking from being dragged into ugly controversy, terminally.

WHY WASN'T THE TRAINING PROGRAMME SIMPLY INSERTED WITHIN A DRAMA DEPARTMENT?

Because the objectives of the project could not be contained within existing institutions. The development issues, the artistic content, the south-south exchanges and the cultural complexities determined the course to follow. The African Centre for the Training of Performing Artists is a total experiment. The experiment was justified out of an agreed conclusion that existing practices in performing arts practices had not delivered. It was not a national issue, but a continent-wide concern. It was not about another school for career performers, but the right school for the right purpose in Africa. Was it going to be an institution, a building, a training programme to be inserted within existing drama departments? A festival? An occasional workshop? Early on, knowledgeable observers qualified the project as being 'unique and timely.' This qualification remains valid as I speak to you. It all boils down to these 3 little words 'according to needs.' Africa has been afflicted with unique drawbacks, including slavery, colonisation, debts, artificial borders, civil wars, corruption, bad press... to mention but a few of the man-made calamities. The continent's development had stalled from the 17th century and its history is widely unknown, hardly taught even in Africa. To address these cumulative negative effects, the continent requires a fair amount of healing, fresh sources of inspiration for goodwill to spring from the people, the means to develop with a fair chance of success, responsible and far-sighted government. To take a self-defined development to an improved standard requires bold initiatives, a positive vision, confidence that flows from a better image of the continent. The poor image of Africa requires urgent attention, out of Africa. The self image of Africa needs nurturing; it also needs the creative engagement of the peoples of Africa, from across the continent. Such a task cannot be done without the skills of the performing artist.

BUT THAT IS ALMOST AN IMPOSSIBLE TASK...

These are difficult times and the needs of Africa are such that initiatives must come from all quarters. One thing is certain: aid will not do, not aid only. Africans are also different to other peoples. One major difference is the enormous wealth of performing arts forms safeguarded along millennia. It has been a mistake to disregard the importance of such a wealth. It would be a mistake to cut off this cultural heritage in the search for economic development. It would be equally wrong to continue to train Africans to become strangers in their own land. Cultural development in Africa can't do without an input from the performing artists. Next, it can only have an impact with a focus upon an adequate system of educating the young. Somehow, the performing artist must find a place in the schooling of young Africans.

WHAT ARE THE SUBJECTS TO BE TAUGHT THEN IN ORDER TO TRAIN THE PERFORMING ARTIST OF AFRICA?

Obviously, there are the basic subjects, such as dance, drama, stage management, production techniques, acting, singing etc. The 'exchange process' has been demonstrated as a viable method in the ACTPA Project. But the African world view, modern image building, education systems, creativity, development studies are all subject matters that ought to be part of the training of performers in Africa. Why? Because live performing arts form part of the very fabric of society across Africa; they keep the community sealed together and they inspire and support every aspect of social life. Just as the amphitheatre at the heart of the city of Athens became a means of educating, entertaining and elevating the citizen, a modern African civilisation could remain an unattractive proposition to the average African citizen, unless the vision emanates from within the culture. Grafting external experiments and imposing ready-made systems only generate violence. They merely deny and ignore the strong roots and the complex heritage of African peoples. Forceful education systems and external models of schooling lead to mediocre forms of government, within Africa. Growing numbers of migrants wishing to join the model, out of Africa, only show the lasting damage done and the frustration.

HOW TO START ADDRESSING THE PROBLEM?

The United Nations may have many failings but they got it right when they proclaimed a Decade of Cultural Development in the 1980s. The ACTPA Project was precisely about that: devising original strategies towards achieving potential on national, regional and continental levels. Economic development is not all; nor does the economist hold all the answers. Not in Africa, at least. Who else then does? The ACTPA Project suggests that, specific to Africa, the performing artist may just be another key actor in triggering and achieving cultural development.

WOULD THE PERFORMING ARTIST THEN BECOME A PARTNER IN DEVELOPMENT?

At least a partner equal to the economist, I would advocate for Africa specifically. Train him/her to be effective and pro-active. Original methods of training are essential and I have tested out the 'method of exchange' that advocates a horizontal approach to knowledge. Until and unless there is regular and civilised exchanges between African countries, there will not be any fruitful exchange between Africa and the rest of the world. Finally, the performing arts must be re-assessed as raw material in Africa.

WHAT IS THE FINALITY OF THE PROPOSED TRAINING?

To equip the performing artists with the skills required, so that they are able to manage themselves and manage the arts in a modern world. The

Daniel Labonne

finality would be to train them into becoming entrepreneurs, teachers and communicators in development.

WHY WOULD THE REST OF THE WORLD CARE IF ONLY AFRICANS ARE CONCERNED AND ONLY AFRICA WILL BENEFIT?

We live in a global environment. A frustrated individual from the South will risk his life to reach and join the rich world. That is a sign of desperation and it is already the case. Modernity must become accessible to the African; just as the African must make a contribution to the modern world. The ACTPA Project at Castle Arts successfully integrated traditional arts with modern art forms and audio-visual techniques. One plausible reason to support an original school of performing arts is rooted in the objective needs of the time from a global perspective. Technology is already dragging the world in a new order and I suggest, from my research, that Africa may just have a specific function in this new world order, dominated by technology. That function consists of keeping mankind rooted culturally, so it does not lose balance as technology accelerates its momentum. This being said, the whole ATEX-ACTPA undertaking remains an applied research, specific to a time and a culture. The experiment would have delivered more and more results that would have been assessed, just as was assessed the first outcome of the training in 1990-1991.

WAS THE TERM 'UNIQUE' JUSTIFIED TO QUALIFY THE ACTPA PROJECT?

When I introduced the document entitled 'ACTPA Guidelines' to a group of experts gathered in London, in 1987, they came up with the words 'unique' and 'timely'. Later, an observer from a major US organisation spelled it out in those terms: 'But a school opened to an entire continent with an original training method does not exist anywhere else!' she exclaimed. I could have replied: so what! Instead, I was diplomatic and explained that exceptional needs require exceptional measures. The problem came to be felt later: was Africa going to be allowed to lead in anything positive and original? Are the powers that be going to support a cultural and artistic undertaking which had the potential of turning the cursed continent into a new champion of the arts? I tried to explain that this was not a world contest and we are not in a competition. Africa is not trying to overtake anybody! All I was doing was to weigh up the handicaps that have stopped the Africans from making a breakthrough, before suggesting there might have been a miscalculation from a cultural point of view. Possibly ignorance and prejudice have simply blinded the earlier players. Certainly, there is a culture of secrecy that has made matters worse for Africans. The difference was not to correct the mistakes for the benefit of others who would or would not write a new revolutionary thesis about 'black arts' or 'the lost continent rediscovered.' The approach was to push towards an EMPOWERMENT of the victims of misunderstanding and systemic underrating. The ideology of downgrading sub-Saharan Africans reached an apex with near madness and extreme cruelty in the system of Apartheid in Southern Africa. Thank God, common sense has since prevailed and Mandela restored some redemption to human intolerance. I must remind you that The ACTPA Project evolved prior to the end of Apartheid in South Africa. There was some additional meaning in establishing the centre next door, in Zimbabwe.

EXPLAIN THE WORD 'EMPOWERMENT' AS APPLIED TO THE ARTIST...

Such positive empowerment had been the case before in sports. It took the vision of a leader like President Houphouet Boigny to build a state of the art stadium and host the first Afican Cup of Nations in the Ivory Coast. Then, it took less than one generation for Ivorian footballer Didier Drogba to become the best scorer of the English football league, and the first to score at the opening match of the new legendary London Wembley stadium. Training at inter-African level is a viable route to empowerment. But then again, the difference is not to sell African talent to enrich the football industry in Britain, but to find the sensitive nerve

Daniel Labonne

that would wake up the creative spirit of a battered people in Africa. Development cannot be a race, won once and for all, by one group of nations or even one civilisation. Underdevelopment is not only about under-performing economies, tyrannical leaders and ethnic warfare. It may be about the inability to listen to each other. It has long been a nearly impossible task when one tries to trade across borders because of bizarre conventions and ex-colonial groupings... It certainly is a language problem as it has been a currency problem. While advanced nations are adopting a common currency and federalising their resources to survive, weaker burgeoning countries were struggling to manage national currencies in Ethiopia, Zambia or Ghana. I know nothing about economics but it seems to me that one cultural currency that is common to the whole of Africa is DANCING. So, why not develop dance, first to understand each other through shared dancing, then by understanding the world using dance as others use algebra? Finally, why not make a positive contribution by supplying a wealth of dances to teach the world how healthy it could be to dance our troubles away? Why not assist in the teaching of the young by teaching how intelligent the whole body could be if the head was not permanently crammed with bookish knowledge? But first things first, it is not about teaching others. It is vital that Africa finds its own terms towards achieving what UNESCO calls 'integrated development.'

BUT TRADITIONAL DANCING HAS BEEN KEPT FOR SMALLER COMMUNITIES AND SPECIFIC FUNCTIONS.

Does that mean that the African performer should simply ignore tradition and learn Shakespeare and Moliere? Should these traditions be allowed to die away in isolation and secrecy? Wouldn't it be wiser to consider these traditional forms of artistic expressions as 'raw material?' Already, in the first courses of ACTPA, it was proven that, within an appropriate training programme, a dance traditionally reserved for women could be revisited by men dancers, if it means developing increased awareness and empathy. Similarly, a shoulder dance usually attributed to a tribe in Ethiopia, could express restraint and teach the aesthetics of peace to Zulu warrior dancers. Drumming from Cote D'Ivoire may well fuse with the xylophones of Zimbabwe to create a new sound of music... Learning about the history of the Bantu people or the Dogon civilisation in West Africa may allow for amazing creativity, if the training process allows for increasing freedom and a broad vocabulary for creative work. Respect and curiosity lie at the bottom of the process of learning through exchange.

BUT WHAT DOES THE TRAINEE GET AT THE BOTTOM LINE? WHAT IS THE BOTTOM LINE IN THIS PROCESS?

The bottom line is as simple as basic arithmetic: if each of 15 trainees contributes 3 dances from his own cultural tradition, every dancer leaves the course with a total of 45 dances. One may begin by growing rich in dance currency, while developing understanding for fellow human beings. First, begin by understanding the other through intelligible movement. Share, discuss and compare their worldviews and their value systems. Sooner or later, trust the human brain to make sense out of the 'exchange' so that a healthier civilising ethos would emerge. What is unique about the ACTPA Project is the 'Horizontal approach' as opposed to the 'vertical approach' to learning.

WHAT IS THE 'VERTICAL APPROACH?'

The approach that advocates knowledge comes from above and elsewhere. From a superior experience which has placed the transmitter of knowledge definitely on another level. To access such knowledge, one must dispel all former communal knowledge collected from birth. Then, one must deserve the goodwill of the superior transmitter and pay the price to be gradually admitted to his cultural castle. That is the process imposed upon the African child who intends, one day, to go to university and occupy a job of responsibility. To some extent, he must accept to be purged of all traditional knowledge. As a reward, he is transformed into a pseudo stranger in his own land.

Daniel Labonne

WHAT IS 'THE HORIZONTAL APPROACH?'

The approach whereby the performer is no longer considered an empty vessel to be filled out with borrowed knowledge. Instead, the performer brings along his own baggage, containing his languages, his traditions, his dances, his dramatic practices. In the horizontal approach, he is invited to voluntarily engage in an exchange of skills and knowledge with a fellow performer from another tradition and culture.

DESCRIBE THE TRAINING METHOD.

I had devised a training method in my early research in multicultural Mauritius. The 'Atelier Theatre' decided that to respond to the systematic denials and negative attitudes that trapped the Mauritian identity, an original form of theatre would require a new narrative told in a new theatre form. The starting point was the living actor, considered a complete person and not 'an empty vessel.' The training method developed was based upon the study of differences and similarities and the careful recruitment of actors from different backgrounds. But key to unlocking the creativity within the performer was the conscious realisation that all islanders share the same limited space (the island) and the same time frame (now). More by fatality than by free choice. All drama emerges from these basic premises. The research delivered regular concrete results, each time with innovative productions. Later, the same method was adapted and applied to produce foreign plays. When I was invited to train actors in Europe, I transposed the same method and was able to teach 'From Story-telling To Theatre.' So much for the training methods...

HOW WAS YOUR EARLY EXPERIENCE APPLIED TO THE ACTPA PROJECT?

In the case of ACTPA, a different approach was adopted in this respect that the disparity and vast quantity of forms of performing arts from all over Africa actually became both THE RAW MATERIAL and THE STARTING

POINT. The training progressed on these two rails. There was no script pre-written in advance. Nor was it based upon improvisations. Imagination only came at a later stage, when mutual respect and genuine curiosity had enriched the full understanding of the other. The various socio-cultural experiences were assumed and acknowledged, never discarded. The performer was considered the holder and transmitter of oral tradition and performing arts forms. Neither a vessel first to be emptied (such has been the method employed whenever African actors are trained in the European tradition of theatre), nor a mere subjective affirmation of static forms and value systems, the performer is trained into developing an interest for the other practices from other cultures and other parts of Africa. A comparative approach to one's own inherited practices gradually evolves from discovery to curiosity, from curiosity to investigation, from investigation to teaching each-other. In the course of the 'exchange process,' critical discussions, analysis and practical training lead to a new aesthetic consensus. Obviously, experienced artistic directors oversee each phase of the training. Their job is to gradually develop a production project, borne out of the exchange that occurred there and then. The process is democratic and open, not devoid of risk. But each performer is made aware of the overall aim: to achieve personal and cultural development at individual level first, as a group of performers, next, in order to affirm the positive story of cohabitation. The method is based upon sharing respective differences, on a negotiated fusion and on mutual acceptance. It is a specific form of cultural development, using the performing arts and applied to Africa.

WHAT IS THE ULTIMATE AIM OF THE TRAINING METHOD?

Development is the aim, in the sense that it is a way of moving on from position of stalemate and isolation. Bridging the cultural gaps and healing the wounds from a painful past must be part of the aim. Devising an original approach to the treatment of live performing arts for a unique people would be the direct objective of the ACTPA Project. The ultimate aim is also to take the lessons learned to the community back home, after having performed the finished product to an audience at the Castle Arts. This is not about folklore and pleasing consumers of exoticism. This is more of an existential will to negotiate one's cultural inheritance on a micro and national level, with a tacit agreement to grow together, towards achieving cultural development measurable at a macro, trans-national level. There would ultimately be economic benefits to be drawn, along the line.

WHY WAS THE CASTLE ARTS THE RIGHT VENUE FOR THE CENTRE?

The Castle Arts was one of many venues proposed by the Ministry of Education and culture of the host country, once they had been persuaded about the merits and viability of the ACTPA Project. UNESCO delegated a consultant to support ATEX in the exercise of assessing the appropriate venue, while providing the essential guaranties to the host country that competent management was available and adequate skills would make the project work. The Castle Arts was right because it was the one single act that gave strategic and structural reality to the dream of a school. The venue was never imposed, but the deliberate choice by the visiting consultants, approved by the authorities in Bulawayo and Harare. An African centre needed to be grounded on African soil. The Castle Arts became a geographic reality which silenced all the remaining doubters. The Castle Arts was adequate because it provided enough prestige, ample space for accommodation, catering, rehearsals, training rooms, administrative quarters, parking and security. After 3 years, the ACTPA guidelines produced in London and approved by the International Scientific Council, had finally delivered the physical framework for the dream to cement into hard reality. It must be remembered that funding was scarce and ATEX had already excluded the construction of a school. The volatility of an occasional festival had also been discarded, in spite of the success of AFSYMWORK in Mauritius in 1988. Cultural development cannot rest upon a talk-shop where intellectuals and experts look after their own per-diem and regularly exporting to the North their latest findings in the South. To make the point, the dream venue had to emerge from the ground readymade. It is a major gesture of trust and foresight on behalf of any government to decide to make the Castle Arts available for the experiment to enter into its phase of practical experimentation. Zimbabwe deserves all the credit for the trust, the foresight and generosity. All the more, because they never backed out and encouraged ATEX to go further, after the official opening ceremony and after the pilot project delivered the first 'graduates' and the first two original productions 'Made at Castle Arts.'

HOW IMPORTANT WAS IT FOR THE LOCAL COMMUNITY AND THE HOST COUNTRY TO HOST ACTPA AT CASTLE ARTS?

South Africa, next door, was under the apartheid regime. Zimbabwe had to prove innovative and successful in the 1980s. The youngest African nation was full of optimism, rapidly healing its wounds from the war of independence, full of optimism. The Castle Arts had symbolic meaning for the city of Bulawayo, for the host country, for Southern Africa and for the entire continent. The government had confiscated the venue because the Castle Arms had been used during the ethnic conflicts, between the Shona and the Ndebele peoples. What a wonderful message of peace for all parties concerned, when the name replaced the word 'Arms' with the word 'Arts!' From day one, the mission of performers had been granted symbolic relevance at the heart of African realities.

ARE YOU SURE YOU CHOSE THE RIGHT HOST COUNTRY, OUT OF 52 AFRICAN COUNTRIES?

Zimbabwe was once the flag bearer of freedom and hope and not only for Africa. Bob Marley and Stevie Wonder were among the stars who signalled the symbolical importance of an independent Zimbabwe. The international conference of UNESCO which brought about the formation of the UAPA, was organised in Zimbabwe to salute the freedom and the people having won that freedom, after an arms struggle. Racial

Daniel Labonne

reconciliation was one of the major challenges facing the new rulers. Becoming a positive role model for neighbouring South Africa, under Apartheid was the other big challenge. All the support to the young independent country was needed. The ACTPA Guidelines stressed how important it was for Zimbabwe to avoid the ugly trappings of older sister nations in Africa: corruption, war, famine, debt... There was a message of hope to be created in Zimbabwe, to be flagged up for men of goodwill to take notice. The old rivalries from colonial days had left a rather shameful track record across the African continent. Performers from former British colonies were generally training in universities. These were delivering arts managers, more than creative artists. Africans from former French colonies felt a cultural pressure to turn towards Paris for improbable glory and success. As the old saying recommends: avoid pouring new wine into old casks. Zimbabwe was a brand new cask in need of novelty and potent ideas. Furthermore, the multicultural population of Zimbabwe could be engaged in a mutually enriching interaction with ACTPA at Castle Arts. After all, the performing arts are universal and cultural Africa had no other option but to be forward looking. The whole point of the Decade of Cultural Development, proclaimed by United Nations was to correct the course of development and clear the way for cultural understanding and peace. In that particular respect, the World Decade For Cultural Development has failed. Peace has been the greatest casualty and Zimbabwe must be seen another casualty.

WAS ACTPA AT CASTLE ARTS A CASUALTY?

Who knows why the project was starved of funding after such a promising first year? The consensus over Zimbabwe as the right host country for ACTPA, had long been sealed between the Scandinavian sponsors, the UAPA Steering committee and various Zimbabwe representatives. Whatever happened to Zimbabwe, its leaders and its people during the last decade is a matter for others to study. The least that could be said is that it has been a major setback, for the young nation and the continent as a whole. Is it a total coincidence that occult forces derailed the establishment of ACTPA at Castle Arts, soon before Zimbabwe plunged into bankruptcy, international disrepute and near famine?

YOU MUST HAVE BEEN SHATTERED THAT THE HOST COUNTRY PROVED UNABLE TO KEEP UP TO THE EXPECTATIONS?

I have nothing but praise and gratitude towards Zimbabwe, as host country of the ACTPA pilot years. I must remain modest and stick to the arts and hope, after the event, that possibly ACTPA at Castle Arts could have played a small role in promoting a better image of the host country. We had already trained a considerable number of Zimbabweans. It is a cheering thought that, thanks to the ACTPA Project, a cultural industry based upon original shows, the grooming of talents, the processing of arts products and - why not - a dynamic entertainment culture might have brought tourists or at least a capital of goodwill to unfortunate Zimbabwe.

WHY DID THE TRAINING CENTRE STOP AFTER THE PILOT PROJECT?

For financial and political reasons, I regret to say. A budget had been agreed with the funding and development agencies on the basis of training programmes over a period of three years. Funds were withdrawn after less than a year. The international consensus patiently negotiated in Paris at the ATEX Round Table was slowly undermined. Were the initial ACTPA results too strong? Was ATEX perceived as being too independent and too daring? Was competence in steering the 'African dream' becoming threatening? Was there an economic concern that ACTPA could drive away potential paying students from drama departments abroad? Was it petty inter-African jealousy getting the better of idealised African creative ventures? Is the fact that Africans are able to work creatively and deliver quality products for the stage and eventually for the screen, perceived as unwanted competition? Was it

Daniel Labonne

simply the fact that one consultant was granted too much power by the funding agencies to decide on the fate of the project?

ARE YOU SAYING THAT THE PROJECT MIGHT HAVE BEEN BROUGHT DOWN BY ONE MAN?

I do not know. Did this consultant use the power invested in him to demolish the work of ATEX and the deeper wishes of African Performing Artists? Following the pilot year 1, the host country tends to blame the Union more than anyone else. My own job was to steer the experiment through. It would be up to others to study the politics of southern Africa in the 1990s or the policy of the various agencies concerned by development. Suffice it to say that ATEX has done its job to the end, having researched and collected the evidence to this day. It was indeed the success of ACTPA at Castle Arts that caused the dream to crash, so soon after take-off. But you do not have to take my word for it: the feedback from trainees, resource persons and international observers remain on the record, so positive that I am convinced that the project still has a future. And that is what really matters. (*See Part Seven. What the World Had to Say*).

WHAT REMAINS OF THE ACTPA PROJECT AFTER 20 YEARS?

If I were cynical, I would reply that the objective needs that still beg to be addressed. I could say in poetic terms that 'the dream is still alive'. But let us be factual. The record of its successes under three different forms: a university post graduate thesis which was nothing more than an evaluation of the project after 10 years; 19 separate reports; the ACTPA Guidelines that maintain the relevance of an African school of a different kind; the Castle Arts Handbook; video documents testifying of the living conditions and training methodologies at the African Symposium Workshop, Mauritius, and at Castle Arts, Zimbabwe. The Castle Arts is hopefully still intact, with the plaque unveiled by Minister Fay Chung, at the opening ceremony of ACTPA in September 1990. The expression of satisfaction of ministers, mayors, observers are there for reference; the harmonious coming together of French-speaking and English-speaking Africans documented; the passionate feedback from trainees and the objective reports of the training specialists. Two plays were devised and staged at Castle Arts. Both the scripts and the filming of the productions have been stored for the record. The training method is there for me either to experiment further or to codify for research to be taken to another level. The project may have gone dormant, but the experiment has picked up a life of its own. How can we underestimate the living beneficiaries who have since returned to their respective countries? Development through creativity is likely to make sense in their lifetime work. So, the good work continues...

WHY WOULD AFRICA NEED THE ACTPA PROJECT TODAY?

Today, more than ever, training the performers according to needs would be better understood. Because the continent is beginning to lift itself out of the psychological and economic depression that has plagued the development of the 53 countries of Africa. New partnerships are bearing fruits as African leaders are acceding to another phase of independent thinking and South-South alliances are becoming a reality. The burden of debts has been partly lifted. Exchange is being experimented in commercial and geographical terms. New roads are making it possible for inter-African trade to develop and enterprise to flourish. Hopefully, we would have vaguely contributed in the awareness raising that has brought about major stage and film productions in the last 20 years. *The Last King of Scotland, Blood Diamond* and *The Lion King* are among the new material that, on the world stage, is telling the tale of Africa at least from a balanced point of view. Still, I cannot help feeling a little sad that a major stage or screen production has not emerged from sub-Saharan Africa, with African performers. But over and above box office success and Hollywood productions, the narrative according to Africans to fellow Africans matter more than ever. Africa is still acting like the beggar sitting on a sack of gold. It would be totally wrong to allow Africans to become consumers only, in the field of performing arts.

Daniel Labonne

WHERE ARE THE SIGNS OF SUCCESS ON THE ARTISTIC FRONT?

As I write these words, the Festival Des Arts Negres is happening in a new chapter in Dakar, Senegal. That is excellent news. Except that the last chapter of the festival happened in 1966! The dates speak volumes about how disruptive cultural development can be in Africa. The concepts of festival and folklore are risky and counterproductive. The needs of today are continuity, sustained training, reliable structures and ongoing production. Only regular inter-African exchanges and quality products will do. We are talking about a mode of exchange among 53 countries, a specific response to a unique situation. The means matter at least as much as the end. In the arts as in business, only success succeeds like success. There's also the advent of a commercial cinema emerging in Nigeria. This is great news and it shows that the arts stand a better chance if sustained by the private sector. Finally, the regional regrouping of countries, like the SADC, points in the right direction. But arts and culture must become one of the priorities for Africa.

WHAT NEEDS TO BE DONE NOW, IN YOUR OPINION?

Two big questions remain: has the World Decade for Cultural Development delivered for Africa and its population of one billion? Has a proper evaluation been conducted by the United Nations to decide to what extent the 53 countries have been touched by the campaign? The decade may be over, but real action will only be effective with bold initiatives along the years. At the heart of such action: the young and the need for adequate schooling. Cultural development still means that any self-formulation of an achievable development must spring from within the culture. Aid would not do, not only because it perpetuates corruptive practices and encourages dependence. On the other hand, immigration remains a desperate solution for the more fortunate. Africans need to be motivated to engage into a passionate adventure of creativity and self-revelation. The discovery of the African personality could become a passionately shared experience over a generation. Such a process would best be entrusted to performing artists of Africa. The continent owes that to itself; the African story must be told before tradition dries out and cultural desertification destroys the remaining reasons to grow together. The aim of cultural development is to become assertive nations, made up of confident individual contributors to society and to the world.

THIS IS AN AMBITIOUS PROJECT WHICH REQUIRES A SERIOUS THEORY TO SUSTAIN IT.

My research with the University of London has helped me formulate the *Diamond Theory* that offers a graphic presentation of the role of the performing arts, considered as a uniquely precious raw material, yet to be processed for lasting development in Africa. *(see Part Three: The Diamond Theory)* The ACTPA Project has delivered in more than one way: the Castle Arts is but a single materialisation of the dream. Once the theory is fully understood, there might be one day many castle arts, all over the continent of Africa.

COULD YOU SPELL OUT THE MAIN RESULTS FROM THIS VAST RESEARCH?

1. Firstly, the needs of underdeveloped Africa are so complex, that coordinated action does not necessarily have to await centralised policy. Initiatives may be as valid when they emerge from other sectors, like the voluntary sector. In the case of the ACTPA Project, the stage artists took charge of their own sector. What matters is the resulting positive change measurable in different ways, not necessarily economic from the outset.

2. Secondly, performing arts in Africa form a core of values that have been preserved. This heritage is a fact. Such preservation has multiple benefits, not necessarily for the immediate group directly concerned, nor exclusively for national purposes. Somewhere along the line, humanity at large has a vested interest in these forms of human heritage. But first things first:

Africans ought to process the performing arts forms of Africa within a strategy of cultural development.

3. Treating the performing arts in a training process leading to production can be conducted using an original method that excludes nobody, provided the concept of competition is replaced by a more generous concept of 'exchange.' In this respect, competition is cultural and 'exchange' must be seen as an alternative cultural factor.

4. Africa and major African projects cannot rely upon non-African sources of funding. Before any school or viable training programme may bear fruit, it is vital to devise an alternative means of funding. Through an independent arts foundation, for example.

5. In the 1980s, a lot of energy, time and other resources have had to be spent correcting the image of Africa. Curiously, in a strange order of priority, the rich countries act as if they were afraid of Africa. They demand to be re-assured first that Africans are serious and that whatever is being proposed is not a cultural threat to them. This PR exercise requires specialist attention and sustained funding, before any specific project. ATEX spent a lot of time responding to this basic need to correct the image of Africa.

6. ATEX responded to needs in terms of project management in arts and culture. Given the reduced period in the actual implementation of the training centre, the ground work of ATEX has proved to be immensely constructive, possibly more important than the training centre proper. Field study, technical and artistic research, delicate negotiations, fundraising, PR and project management are vital specialist tasks. These tasks provide the basic guarantees demanded by all partners but they are financed by nobody. All future undertakings like ACTPA are doomed to fail, unless the role of ATEX is recognised.

7. It may have been a mistake to entrust the funding of the entire venture to non-African development organisations. The facts

also demonstrate that there is a limit to North-South friendships. My own view is that the ACTPA Project would have a better chance of lasting success, if it had been possible to establish the centre as a self-reliant enterprise.

8. Regionalisation is definitely part of the solution for Africa. But, in the future, there is no reason for the ACTPA project to remain unique. There could very well be three to four different experiments, across the continent. That would only boost exchanges at regional level; regular exchanges require structural organisation.

9. The exchange process applied to training and what I have called 'exchange theatre' may very well deliver unsuspected results, in terms of quantity, quality and original aesthetics. In terms of cultural development, ACTPA could be to Africa what Hollywood has been to America.

10. There would be professional jobs available for qualified and experienced performers, like the resource persons who devoted so much loyalty and energy towards delivering results expected of them, in 1990-1991. The trainees who attended the courses in Castle Arts Zimbabwe will sooner or later testify of the validity of what had been invested in them... Has the training boosted their careers?

11. *Theatre for Development* does not have to exclude or down-play the creative artist. Nor does it have to neglect aesthetics. ACTPA was also a response to the scientific claims of Theatre for Development. Oral tradition has relevance today and poetry is present in African performing arts. Development has a better chance of working effectively for the uplifting of entire communities, provided performing arts are allowed to boost individual and collective creativity. But empowering the performer is a more valid strategy for Africa.

12. Who knows, in 2010, what Castle Arts in Zimbabwe would have been offering to the visitor in terms of display of costumes, musical instruments, dance practices, circus arts, dance-dramas,

Daniel Labonne

fashion shows…? A permanent show-case? A processing plant to polish performances and turn them into export products? An elite school of performing arts? A unique theatre and a museum? The experiment was interrupted but enough was achieved and records have been kept.

13. *Drumma* is but one neologism born out of the ACTPA Experiment. There would be many, many other original concepts…

14. The *Diamond Theory* is there to be investigated and tested as a valid analysis of applied cultural development specifically for Africa.

15. *'Footprints'* and *'Lucy & Me'* are but two productions Made in Castle Arts. In spite of limited budgets, the training managed to deliver promising productions.

Africa needs peace, provided the enormous wealth of creative energy is tapped into productively. To respond to the song-prayer by performer John Lennon, 'Please give peace a chance'… One way for that to happen, Africa needs to tap into its own wealth of performing arts forms and liberate the creativity of its peoples.

IN PROMOTING A PROJECT SUCH AS ACTPA, WHO SHOULD BE CONVINCED FIRST, AFRICAN DECISION-MAKERS OR THE RICH WORLD?

Both. And at the same pace. There is a crucial need for a master plan for the cultural development of Africa. My job was specific but it is done, although frustratingly incomplete. Having said that, it is most likely that the complexity of the issues and the legacy from the history of Africa, have carried the research way beyond the strict training and performing arts matters. Objectively, the needs beg for original responses. At the heart of these needs, independent funding allied to the enterprise spirit. It would take a campaign to convince Africans that on their list of priorities, the performing arts matter as much as health, food and shelter. As far as I am concerned, they do. Because you need a reason to live, the spirit needs its own nourishment, and the cathedrals and theatre buildings of civilisation always spring out from a dream. You may train the dreamer then call him an architect. Yet, it is the dream that matters.

WHAT IS YOUR MESSAGE TO THOSE WHO FAILED TO UNDERSTAND THE DREAM OF PERFORMING ARTISTS OF AFRICA?

It is in the interest of everybody that Africans be enabled to make a positive contribution to the world - in both economic and cultural terms. Such a contribution cannot be obtained by force, domination or accident. That was the case in the genesis of Jazz. Progress often lies at the heart of a dream. Nelson Mandela had a dream of a free South Africa and the possibility of racial equality. His dream survived 27 years of jail and came to fruition for the sake of many, including his old enemies. So did Martin Luther King die for his glorious dream of, one day, somebody looking like his brother - and your half-brother - could access to the White House. The current US president has materialised the dream of the human right champion.

WHAT IS THE MESSAGE TO AFRICAN LEADERS?

One reminder: the dream industry has propelled American values beyond the wildest hopes of its pioneers, thanks to the medium of cinema. And then, you need to know what you want? Do you want mediocrity and corruption to keep on depleting such a rich continent as Africa? Do you wish the world to deal with ongoing need for assistance and permanent beggars? Or do you want to motivate hard-working, creative peoples, willing and able to transform their own assets into honourable livelihood? Performing arts, dance and oral tradition must be seen as extremely precious raw material across Africa. Finally, the arts are the best answer to destructive and pointless wars. Our differences across the continent could be our best asset, provided we learn how to trust and mutually enrich from these differences.

Daniel Labonne

BESIDES TRYING AGAIN TO CONVINCE, SURELY, THERE IS A CLEARER CONCLUSION TO BE DRAWN FROM THE OVERALL EXPERIENCE?

One clear conclusion would be to empower the performer by pushing the enterprise spirit. Thus, the performing arts of Africa would develop all over the continent as small enterprise, creating jobs, supplying quality leisure, attracting tourists, complementing formal education. In which case, maybe the training ought to be private and non-governmental in the first place.

WASN'T CULTURAL DEVELOPMENT YET ANOTHER WHITE ELEPHANT DREAMED UP BY THE UNITED NATIONS?

Africa is NOT about aids and attending to a dying species: it is about life and the obsessive resilience of humanity to celebrate life for the miracle it remains in the whole universe. But the answer to your question is no, the World Decade for Cultural Development was not a white elephant. The initiative of the UN was right and worthwhile. It is a matter of freeing oneself from the straight jacket of economic ideology and the constraints of cultural prejudices. It is also about recognising that the WDCD was set out as a framework to focus upon a rather vague concept and mobilise resources into concrete, effective action towards achieving development that begins and ends with the welfare of the individual person. That is what the ACTPA Project has done: explore integrated development by focusing upon the diversity of cultures and the potential of arts forms in Africa. Should the curtain be drawn after a decade? The answer is again no. The issue here is development and the development of one billion people living on the second largest continent in the world.

IS THERE A LINK BETWEEN DEVELOPMENT, THE ARTS AND DEMOCRACY?

There was in Athens which brought about a wonderful civilisation. Why shouldn't it be the case for Africa? Both development and democracy remain in essence a PROCESS, not a result. It is the case for the developed world which followed centuries of a slow process to reach the current status. It will be the same for the developing world. Progress never stops and freedom does not have borders. But the rich and powerful tend to forget these fundamentals when they relate to Africa. It is a paradox if you force a people to be free, unless you define freedom according to your own terms and then lock that person up within your limited vision. In other words, by so doing you are imposing your own cultural experience. Nor can you, in development terms, force somebody to get rich. The need and the urge to be free or to get rich must spring from deep within, naturally or through adequate education, with a self-defined, perceptible path to follow. In the specific case of Africa, if I were to refer to my limited experiment, the performing arts constitute an unsuspected and totally underrated path. That cultural path leads to both development and democracy. Just as Euripides and Sophocles had a crucial role to play using theatre arts in the development of the citizen of ancient Athens, similarly the African performing artist of the 21st century does have a role to play to promote collective welfare and shared responsibility in Africa.

IF, IN YOUR VIEW, IT IS MORE A MATTER OF EDUCATING THE CITIZEN, WHERE PHYSICALLY IS THAT EDUCATION GOING TO BE DELIVERED IN AFRICA?

As the *Diamond Theory* indicates, either within the school where the trained performing artist may be given a role to play in the education of the young; or, in a purpose-built edifice (a *'drumma'*) at the heart of the city to reconcile the contradictions of tradition and modernity, to expose and explain the African philosophy, to learn about the vision from other African cultural perspectives. First, train the performing artist adequately, using the *exchange process.*

Daniel Labonne

WHAT KEY LESSON NEEDS TO BE DRAWN FROM THE ACTPA EXPERIENCE?

Africa is acting like a beggar sitting on a sack of gold. The saying is not from me. But from that superior African performer everybody nicknamed Sekuru (the elder) at Castle Arts, in 1990. His name: Louis Akin, former director of the National Ballet of Côte D'Ivoire. He had been recruited as one of the resource persons by ATEX. Sadly, Louis Akin died a few years later, reminding everyone that we all need to wake up, look the other in the eye and decode the dream. Before it is too late.

ANY HOPE?

Hope is the other meaning of the word 'Africa.' The images of despair, war and famine reflect the overall mismanagement that we are all guilty of, as humans collectively. It does not reflect the African spirit of resilience; it is but a manipulated image of the most optimistic people. Every single popular song played over the radio or from the latest IPod carries a legacy of the DNA of African performing arts. Look at any group of people across the globe celebrating and the manner they move to rhythm: somehow, Africa is calling and they are responding. They may not be fully aware of the origins of the hip or belly movement that swings them to the music. Let me take you back to the opening ceremony of the World Cup 2010 In South Africa. The whole programme is woven with African performing arts symbols, sounds, colours and movements. The symbols are meaningful and ageless; the opening words of the presenter are so simple: Welcome Home World. And yet it has taken so long and so many centuries of misunderstandings and suffering to get to these three simple words. To some extent, the ACTPA Experiment has fallen victim of misunderstandings. But the intentions were to welcome the world in and not to create a new cultural ghetto for Africans. I feel so proud that modestly, in my own ant-like way, I have tried to make a contribution towards getting, somehow, someway, to this major spectacular breakthrough for African sports and performing arts in 2010. The whole world was watching Africa. Therefore, yes, there's plenty of hope.

ANY REGRETS?

How could I have any? Of course, I was never paid during years of very challenging work, as I tried to manage a common dream into a tangible reality. But I have been fortunate to receive the minimum personal support and friendship to sustain my passion for research. Then, as a creative artist, I act upon my own drive. By and large, I have recovered from the trappings of bad faith, the climate of suspicion and the irrational fear. I certainly wish there had been plenty of funding for the training and many more productions from the Castle Arts. But again, as I watched the opening ceremony of the World Cup, the symbols were clear for me to read. Southern Africa was hosting the world for the biggest show on earth. That comforted me in the choice to give African performing arts a shelter, across the border from Johannesburg. If I needed yet another sign that it was all worth it and that, above all, I did not mislead the performing artists who placed their trust in me, the same opening ceremony supplied it. During the opening ceremony again, there were representations of huge footprints symbolising how humanity moved forward, from the cradle-continent towards its dispersed experiences. For your information, in 1990, the very first play devised and produced by the troupe with a cast of performers from all over the African continent, was entitled FOOTPRINTS... I refuse to believe this is a mere coincidence...

Where there is movement, there is hope and no place for regrets.

WHAT HAVE BEEN YOUR BIGGEST MISTAKES, AS THE PERSON IN CHARGE OF THE ACTPA PROJECT?

There were a few along the way. That is inevitable with a project of such magnitude. And then, what is an experiment if not a process of trials and

Daniel Labonne

errors? But no excuses, I would admit to four major mistakes. When the Castle Arts had been allocated by a host country to shelter ACTPA, perhaps I should have stopped, possibly get some legal work done, get the advice of the International Scientific Council... But then, I was under pressure from the funders to deliver 'a project,' not manage an organisation. Money was only allocated days before the take-off date of each 'project.' The other mistake which probably scared some among the funders in the North is the choice of the cover for the programme at the opening ceremony. I had approved the photograph of a traditional African dancing mask. Someone asked me whether I was promoting tribal culture... What I was trying to indicate was the 'raw material' that had remained stuck in time, frozen in a state of potential across a continent. The point is precisely to refine and modernise thanks to training. Was it wrong to entrust such a creative enterprise to development agencies with national policies and political interests? Probably, and we are now correcting this mistake. Perhaps the biggest mistake has been to limit the work of ACTPA to the theatre. The founders of the UAPA were all from the theatre and I am a creative artist from the stage. I have been an actor and a director before becoming a playwright. When I set up a body in London to assist technically in arts project management, I called it African Theatre Exchange (ATEX). However, performing arts spans over a wider spectrum than the theatre.

WHAT IS WRONG WITH THE THEATRE?

Nothing! I will always claim to be first and foremost a theatre artist. But I was in charge of a school project for the performing arts and I had to make it work. Therefore, pop music and fashion, for example could not be left out of the concept of performing arts. But to answer your question, the trap is this: there is a tradition of poor funding and ad-hoc activity in the theatre. The word itself conveys western values and practices that point towards kings, playwrights like Shakespeare and the glory of some languages. Performing arts in Africa will not develop along the same lines: there are no kings to commission genius works; the continent cannot afford to wait for the next Shakespeare; more importantly, the plurality of languages across Africa commands a different strategy for progress. The colonisers have done their best to impose their language from above. The result is what you see: confusion and underdevelopment. There must be another way, a more urgent and pacifying approach towards achieving progress, both in terms of content and form. I suggested the exchange process, to allow differences to meet and create a new synergy.

BUT THE THEATRE COULD BECOME AN INDUSTRY, COULDN'T IT?

Yes, of course. Although I dislike the association of the two words 'theatre' and 'industry' I was privileged to study at City University under John Pick who wrote the book 'The Theatre Industry'. I suppose I like too much the poetry of the theatre to concede the 'industrialisation' of the practice. But that is precisely the issue: cultural development in Britain and elsewhere has followed the trend of the industrial revolution. Everything, including the theatre has followed the path of the textile industry or the railway industry. It is historical fact. The history of Africa and the arts in Africa is radically different. The function of live arts in Africa has also been distinct, along hundreds of years, and the continent suddenly finds itself thrown into the 21st century. Can it wait for its industrial revolution and another hundred years? No. You will notice that the mobile phone has not waited for the earlier network of wired phones to spread across Africa. Different solutions for different times. Theatre remains a civilising process to be valued by all means and by all men. However, the assessment of the situation of the performing arts points towards a drastic and innovative measure in terms of cultural development across Africa.

ARE YOU AGAINST THE CONCEPT OF INDUSTRY APPLIED TO THE ARTS?

On the contrary. But we must agree on the term industry first. If 'industry' means quality and regularity in production, I am definitely for it. If it takes skills to be acquired through training, yes, I am for an industry. If it means an ever expanding market for an ever increasing number of spectators, I am precisely aiming for that. The global world is first a global marketplace and Africa cannot be excluded as it has been for so long. I am advocating precisely the INCLUSION of African performing arts, because it has been relegated and ignored for too long. That has not only alienated the African from the rest of the world, but it has alienated the African from himself, once he had followed education as we know it. Is there a better explanation for the failure in leadership across Africa? Action is required at the source and at the distribution point. Training matters, yes. But the right network to receive new performing arts forms matters as much. Such a network must be built across Africa. Not as an organisation with vague intentions as the UAPA, but a physically built network of venues that will make Africa proud and purposeful.

WAS IT ANOTHER MISTAKE, TO HAVE SET UP THE UAPA AS A UNION OF ARTISTS?

To some extent, yes. 'Union' is another term closely associated to an industry. The UAPA was in that sense placing the cart before the horse. Having said that, we had to start somewhere and we did. We needed a name and we called it 'union' perhaps to follow the cue of the OAU and recognise the need to bring an end to isolation. The other misnomer was to call 'artists' a group made up of at least 50% of academics. Academics argue and debate; artists create and make mistakes. I was the odd one in that sense as I combined a number of skills that my colleagues in the union failed to fully appreciate: creative artist, entrepreneur and researcher. This 3-in1 cocktail was a bit difficult to swallow. But I was serious about the task that was assigned to me in 1985 to set up 'a new school.' I also realised that there was here a real opportunity for progress and a widespread expectation for a breakthrough. In fact, the UAPA was dependent upon some form of outcome. But that could not be the main purpose: the survival of the organisation. Progress had to be directly related to needs, objective needs felt across the continent. I set out to research the situation in order to listen to facilitate the foundation of these needs.

A private room in the dormitory, inside the Castle Arts, Bulawayo. I had surprised an exhausted specialist soundly sleeping. For your information, each piece of furniture had been purchased by the project managers. The host country had offered an empty Castle so the project could be implemented in 1990. So? Was ACTPA just another dream turned into a nightmare for Africa? History merely repeating itself? Is the African performing artist condemned to impotence and sleep sickness? Or is it that ACTPA was an experiment which did manage to lay a sound foundation to sustain some long term structures with a solid grip over the realities of sub-Saharan Africa in a changing world?

TO REFER TO THE STATEMENT OF DEPUTY MINISTER MACHINGA OF ZIMBABWE, WHAT IS YOUR POSITION WITH REGARD TO THE UAPA?

I remain a proud founder of the Union of African Performing Artists as a responsible performer. Anyone who attended the theatre workshop

Daniel Labonne

conference held in Zimbabwe in 1984 could testify of my exhaustion. Why? Because I was doing two jobs: acting as a practitioner in the various sessions and acting as a translator interpreter. It was the actual translation of what performing artists from French-speaking and English-speaking countries had to say to each other that, in the end, prompted the need to form a union. The Union of African Performing Artists was founded thanks to my mediation between disconnected blocks. Following the formation of the Union, the very first action I took was to promote the UAPA and boost its credibility. I did it, first, by raising funds from Unesco and the International Fund for the Promotion of Culture; then, by travelling to Denmark in 1986 and with the help of Danish friends of the amateur theatre, the UAPA brochure explained and exposed the Union to the world. I held consultations but above all, I have worked as a theatre training specialist, so that I knew something about training. I realised that there was no training centre in Africa which delivers quality African theatre training skills. With the help of the Swedish director Martha Vestin, the case for a school of theatre was pushed through both to my colleagues of the UAPA and to the Swedish authorities. Each step of the way, UAPA members were involved. I welcomed the UAPA president several times in London, in my own house to further the objectives of the UAPA and the school. In ACTPA at Castle Arts, there were at least two members of the UAPA steering committee in each course. Let me point out: they were hired and paid for their services. It was clear to me that unless the UAPA had something to show, in terms of achievement, it would not grow and survive.

WHAT HAS HISTORY TAUGHT YOU?

History has proved me right. The UAPA has vanished because it has allowed the forces of division to demolish the achievement on which they could have sailed to make a difference. This attitude has prevailed for centuries to prevent progress across the African continent. There is nothing easier than to oppose an African to a fellow African. History has developed all the policies and techniques that break down communication and prevent collaboration. Development has long been anathema in the mind of some, once applied to Africa. South Africa is the best and painful example of separate development, so that the black African never finds the way out, having been locked up in a dark hole for so long. Regimes may change and political status may improve, but attitudes are harder to reverse. Do such attitudes have anything to do with the demise of such an innovative project springing out of Zimbabwe in the 1990s?

HOW DO YOU EXPLAIN THAT UAPA HAS LOST ITS EARLY FRIENDS AND SUPPORT?

It failed to back fully and unambiguously the ACTPA Project which had become its main pillar for the raison-d'être of the UAPA! The union also failed to broaden its membership base and its representation. Instead of championing its early involvement in Theatre for Development alongside the ACTPA Project, some union founding members gradually became negative and envious. I suppose there had been a fair amount of manipulation by powerful players. But your best friends are your neighbours, not those who occasionally come from far to offer you a ticket to a talk shop. Friends in deed are those who assist you in addressing your most urgent needs. Africans do not need favours, reserved for an elite. That is where there is and was disagreement. My position was made clear: Africa needs to find within its borders the motivation to grow and the means to pull itself together. Performing artists cannot behave as if they had a right to professional employment. Therefore, to some extent, the affiliation to a union had been fairly ambiguous. Either we were a group of activists - therefore running the risk of being perceived through the political prism - or we were mimicking the organised Actor's Union of the developed world - in which case we were placing the cart before the horse.

Daniel Labonne

WHAT EXACTLY IS 'THE HORSE' IN YOUR VIEW?

Training: devising the most adequate form of training for performers of Africa. Next, mapping out a way so that the performer may partake in the education of the young.

ISN'T IT DIFFICULT TO UNITE SO MANY ARTISTS FROM SO MANY COUNTRIES?

Of course it is. Because of the communication problems and because of the forces that have drawn up the gulfs between countries and between blocks. But the world has changed and the whole planet has become a huge village. We may say that the African gods are winning, in the sense that the original unity of mankind may yet prevail. But of course, technology will quickly take the credit. That's fine. But to come back to the UAPA, one of the damning problems was the fact that beyond differences in language or country or region, the founding members belonged to two types: the practitioners and the academics. An early debate emerged between modes of perception of the arts. For example, the academics longed to meet other academics from elsewhere to yet expand over theatre for development. As a practitioner, I was among those who longed to create together and share the stage with fellow performers.

YOU SAY PERFORMERS, YET YOU MEAN THEATRE?

You are right. That is one last distinction that affected the UAPA. We came together in a meeting organised by UNESCO, ITI and IATA in Zimbabwe. Inevitably, we were all individuals committed to theatre arts. At least we could immediately realise that to apply the theatre to Africa would restrict the perception of what the artists of the continent do and express. We needed a term that was possibly more vague but more inclusive. There, we were right: 'performer' is a more appropriate term in the English language. But in my post-UAPA research, the term performer itself is slipping beyond the focus of our action. We need new terms. But let us first empower the performer, so we may all understand the real issue before we argue over the right terms.

WHAT THEN WOULD YOU SAY TO THOSE WHO MAY STILL CRITICISE YOUR WORK TODAY?

I would simply say that I am possibly the only surviving founder member of the UAPA still believing in the ideals set out in 1984. My work is nothing else but the lasting promotion of African performing arts. Any serious observer will discover that before the formation of the UAPA and decades after, I have been forging on with the need to train the African performer adequately. My 'Diamond Theory' places the performer at the heart of cultural development in Africa. I am today confidently pushing the agenda of a UAPA founder-member when I advocate the Empowering of the Performer.

HOW DO YOU EXPLAIN THAT YOUR OWN WORK HAS OUTLIVED THE UAPA?

Perhaps because I am also an entrepreneur. I was already a freelance creative artist as well as an entrepreneur when we founded the UAPA in 1984.

WHAT DIFFERENCE DOES THAT MAKE?

It makes a world of difference and largely explains the early disagreement within UAPA that the host country of ACTPA refers to. I do not wait for solutions; I create the conditions for the solutions to emerge. Not only do I dislike dependence and have been self-employed all my life; but, I take my inspiration from dramatists like Shakespeare and Moliere who were not only writers and stage workers of genius, but they were also managers. They had to manoeuvre among the hurdles and prejudices of their times. Yes, success matters. But above all, it is about maintaining the high standards of theatre arts and remaining loyal to one's spectators.

Daniel Labonne

BUT SHAKESPEARE AND MOLIERE WORKED IN ONE COUNTRY, CLOSE TO THE COURTS... NOT FOR AN ENTIRE CONTINENT!

Thank you for reminding us of the enormous difficulty of attending to the needs of a vast and bruised continent. Defeat and disease have become permanent features in the landscape. So the UAPA is no exception. Neither is unfortunate Zimbabwe. But the UAPA being extinct and Zimbabwe having imploded, most of the early findings of ATEX and ACTPA having been recuperated, was I supposed to deny Africa of what it deserves? Do I have the right to deny performers of a real possibility of assuming a role in the uplifting of their nations and continent? Am I supposed to give up in the face of adversity, bury myself in frustration and hide the precious findings away on my island? I am no pirate. To some extent, I am only keeping the UAPA flame alive.

ARE YOU GOING TO REVIVE THE UAPA?

No. One cannot give birth to the same baby twice. Performers of Africa will take a view, in due course. The reality is that not only the UAPA of 1984 is dead and buried. Sadly, some of its most prominent founders died. This is the 21st century and Africa cannot remain the graveyard of good intentions and failed projects. There is a time for everything. What is needed now is a culture of enterprise, cut off from the culture of assistance and dependence. This is the age for the African performer to move upstage, not to engage into unproductive campaigns and elusive seminars. This is the age to establish solid foundations and build lasting structures. This is the age for FACE.

WHAT IS THE FUNDAMENTAL DIFFERENCE BETWEEN ATEX AND FACE?

First, the times we live in. Then, the body of research has been ongoing and deepened during two additional decades. FACE takes over in 2011 where ATEX has left the applied research in 1991. ATEX had responded to fundamental needs in the management of a serious project. How do you enter into a contractual agreement with a sovereign government? UAPA did not have such a mandate. How do you accept property in trust? How do you guarantee the safety of citizens from a dozen countries over long periods of time? How do you negotiate on an equal footing with a minimum of professional credibility with major funding agencies? How to you lobby organisations like the African Union and UNESCO so that they both supported the ACTPA project as the Regional Project for the African continent within the context of the World Decade for Cultural Development? ATEX did everything that the UAPA was unable to do. But there is another delicate issue that has never been addressed: money. My family and I have invested so much money in the ACTPA project that ATEX could account for. Otherwise, I would be sending a bill to the UAPA which obviously, it could never act upon. The government of the host country was in the end full of respect for the work done by ATEX and all those who participated in the training programmes were grateful for the services that benefitted them on a daily basis. Nobody has been ashamed of what ATEX or ACTPA has delivered. But I never got the credit and there was nobody ready to pay for a job well done. However, the success of both ATEX and ACTPA attracted animosity that actually killed the enterprise.

WHEN DID ATEX CEASE TO OPERATE?

ATEX ceased to operate in 1992, when I had realised that ACTPA had turned out to be a much bigger project than most players had originally thought. I was in the process of securing independent funding for ACTPA and subsequent ventures of a similar scale. My lawyers were studying setting up the World Africa Foundation - WAF. On one hand, controversy raged fed by jealousy and political motives. On the other hand, I needed to attend to most pressing personal matters, like earning a decent living and raising my family. Some thought that Africa did not deserve such a jewel as ACTPA at Castle Arts. But the demise of ATEX did not eliminate the vital need for giving value to underrated forms of art, not to mention specialist input in project management devoted to the cultural development field in Africa.

SHOULD WE TALK MONEY?

Yes. I have always been willing to talk money. I have been self-employed all my life. All records about the ACTPA project have been carefully kept to date. Believe me; systematic accounting has spared me a lot of additional aggravation...

HOW DO YOU RATE THE FINANCIAL PERFORMANCE OF THE PROJECT?

It was a relatively cheap price to pay for an enterprise with enormous potential. In terms of what has been achieved, it was definitely successful, if you consider the constraints applied to arts, to priority areas in Africa and to non-event projects. But if you assess the project on its own merits, only £265, 000 had been granted by donor agencies. The full cost of the project was £620,000 to cover the field study missions, the various meetings and negotiation visits, the mini ACTPA in Mauritius, the requirements at the Castle Arts, the staffing of both the venue and the school, the training programme and the logistics of the training programme, plus the production costs for two original stage plays. This figure must be set against a budget for the 3-year pilot project that amounted to approximately £1.5m and £748,000 for year one. Now, if you consider the full financial report which was submitted to the main funding agencies in 1992, the project was actually left in debt and could have dragged the project managers into serious trouble. No viable enterprise can operate on an ad-hoc, hand-to-mouth allocation of funds. More tragically, management should be funded in priority, but I met a wall of refusal to ensure ongoing harnessing of the many issues involved in a school for an entire continent. In spite of the achievements, the project was abruptly starved of funds, leaving the management body and the key player in a very dire situation in 1991. Was there a case of breach of contract, as my legal advisers suggested then? Besides, not only was the funding allocated always a fraction of the total required, but the means to create revenue were made impossible by the timing imposed by the funds provider. The will to generate revenue was actually viewed with suspicion. In those conditions, failure is the only predictable outcome. I am hoping this book helps to educate the actors on both sides of development. Cultural development is not only about the poorer countries struggling with their own contradictions. It is equally about changing a culture of bad faith and cultivating chronic dependency by individuals someone called the 'development barons.' But there is no time for that. The real solution is financial independence and opting for enterprise.

WHAT IS THE REALITY THAT OBSERVERS HAD OVERLOOKED ABOUT THE ACTPA PROJECT?

Voluntary work and the readiness to invest the seed money without waiting for external aid... A number of facts have been totally underrated in the co-ordination of the ACTPA Project. They need to be spelled out for the records. First, I was a resident in Côte d'Ivoire when the UAPA was founded. In Côte d'Ivoire, I was self-employed and I earned my living as owner-manager of a family restaurant. Had I not been self-employed and free of my movements, probably the project would never have progressed so fast and in such a healthy way. Being a dedicated theatre worker, I believed in the theatre school project enough to decide to invest myself in it. I ended up investing myself and my own money. Another point: prior to the ACTPA project, I had travelled to dozens of countries already as a consultant in theatre arts, so that I already had a fair amount of know-how. The ACTPA project benefitted from the combined experience and the freedom of being self-employed when I was chosen as project co-ordinator.

Daniel Labonne

WHY WAS EVERYONE PAID AT THE CASTLE ARTS AND NOBODY PAID AT THE PROJECT MANAGEMENT LEVEL?

That is exactly the point. Given the precariousness of the financial situation in 1990, I decided to push for results in the field of training and production. Everyone at Castle Arts was paid and the training programme was entirely free at the point of delivery. In the future, it is not excluded that studies will have to be paid for, through a system of scholarships or sponsorship. Remember: the sponsors imposed the rules which limited their involvement to activities only, while no management costs could be incurred from their funds. In those conditions, how do you impact upon real lives and expecting communities? Development is a lost battle if each initiative is left without proper leadership and permanent reliable structures are seen with systemic suspicion.

WHAT ABOUT LANGUAGE? DOES IT MAKE A DIFFERENCE IN FUNDRAISING FOR AN AFRICAN PROJECT LIKE ACTPA?

Language is a tough reality in Africa. In a country like Côte d'Ivoire, there are 60 different languages. Cultural projects in Africa have tended to follow language affiliations. Language also determines the type of education and the content of schooling. Money tends to be negotiated among peers and people speaking the same language and sharing common interests. You are more likely to find a Nigerian doing business in London and a Malian doing the same in Paris. London and Paris know that and expect this order to remain unchanged. A form of cultural development is required for all actors to grow up... I am totally bilingual. Being born in Mauritius presents another advantage. The project could be pushed evenly across linguistic divides. I was able to convince the French speaking that the project was to their benefit. It mattered that the English speaking Africans understood that there was no threat to their interest and their practices so far. My own conviction was this: there is only one Africa. Why not make it work in a collaborative and creative way?

OK. BUT THERE ARE MONEY ISSUES IN MOVING FROM ONE COUNTRY TO ANOTHER. HOW DID YOU DO THAT?

By investing my own money whenever necessary! The critics have accused me of all sorts of sins... But what are the facts? I moved from Côte d'Ivoire to the UK at my own expense. I moved there with my family to respond to a job offer as drama teacher and theatre director in 1985. My work permit did not allow me to undertake international work on the cultural scene. I set up ATEX in order to reassure my new country of residence and offer myself a minimum of protection. Now ATEX needed a track record for itself in 1987. I was advised to broaden the base of support for the ACTPA Project, because there was uneasiness about the motive and legal base of the UAPA. Therefore, I personally financed the meeting of the International Scientific Council in London. The ISC killed three birds with one stone: it gave ATEX a track record for the authorities in the UK; it pulled another pillar to support the ACTPA project internationally; it gave me an umbrella as project coordinator. The main point is this: I had all this initial work done at my own expense.

DID YOU USE YOUR OWN MONEY AT OTHER TIMES TO PUSH THE ACTPA PROJECT?

Whenever the project required it - which was often - I contributed from my own pocket. If I was short of the amount required, my family would assist. That is the big secret behind the success of ACTPA and ATEX.

BUT ALL ACTPA REPORTS SPELL OUT THE KEY ROLE OF FUNDERS IN PUSHING THE PROJECT THROUGH?

That is because I have done my duty by giving them credit for their input. But what is the nature of this input? It was made clear to me that no money was going to be granted for administrative costs. Therefore, ATEX has never received any money for administration and ACTPA depended upon its daily work for years. There were a minimum of three members of staff at the ATEX office in London. I have never been paid one penny for my own expertise in decades of hard specialist work. My experience and know how was either totally voluntary or an investment, depending on the ultimate outcome. When I managed to persuade the Scandinavian agencies to work jointly to support a project, the rules were made crystal clear again: money will be made available for projects only. In other words, limited amounts of money for punctual events, followed by a financial report relating to the use of funds.

BUT ATEX GAVE THE IMPRESSION OF BEING ACTIVE AND OPERATIONAL ON A FULL-TIME BASIS?

ATEX was extremely active and working overtime, such was the demands of an ambitious project, such were the risks of failing the increasing hope that was raised each step of the way. The explanation is simple: I had to oil the financial system throughout, while I gave the project a momentum with a series of activities. I had to abide by the rules: events only would be funded.

BUT HOW DOES ONE PROMOTE A PERMANENT TRAINING CENTRE IN THOSE CONDITIONS?

You may appreciate the difficulty we faced. I had to build up the momentum in such a way that allowed me to educate every major partner along the way. I simply had to change a culture of sporadic assistance and punctual injection of funds that left no lasting effect after the event. How many more festivals does Africa need? Is development about a short campaign to raise awareness about AIDS? Is a seminar likely to change endemic problems? Once a good report has been produced about a wonderful meeting of minds, who really benefits from this report? Most of the time it is not the poor country in Africa; it is the organising body in the North which justifies its action to deserve more funding for itself.

WHAT ABOUT THE ROLE OF INTERGOVERNMENTAL ORGANISATIONS?

What is true of national organisations becomes worse, when one deals with intergovernmental organisations. That is particularly true in the field of arts and culture. Money is so scarce and the bureaucracy that prevails in these organisations is so self-justifying that no lasting effect is ever expected out of the use of money. That creates a state of paralysis. Underdevelopment becomes endemic and progress is impossible. Exceptions must be made for the role played by the African Development Bank and its very effective role in the economic sector. There are a few other regional organisations which have grown in strategic importance since the ACTPA Project. Unfortunately, there is no awareness of the importance of culture and the arts in the development process within institutions like the ADB.

YET, A PROJECT LIKE ACTPA DEPENDED UPON OUTSIDE MONEY?

Unfortunately, yes. Development had become a system which is self-contained. That I discovered as I managed the ACTPA Project. Money is earmarked for events; events rested upon a guest list, including participants from the South; the press reported about the hype of one day or a couple of weeks; the publicity justified the raison d'être and renewable funding in the coffers for the organising body, generally in the North. There is nothing wrong with such a system. Except that it creates dependence; it builds the illusion of empathy and solidarity; it intellectualises the meaning of progress. Sadly, it is in fact a condemnation to permanent paralysis.

DOES THAT EXPLAIN THE MISUNDERSTANDING AMONG THE MEMBERS OF THE UAPA?

Partly, yes. If you are employed, say in a university in Africa, you are on a salary. But then, you are always on the look-out for the next opportunity to travel and network. The funding thus made available locks the

Daniel Labonne

academics within the same system. If the best minds of Africa are spoon fed during a career without real means to finance life-changing research and without the money to invest in lasting structures, where is the progress? My colleagues of the UAPA were right to criticise me in that respect: I was depriving them of the fun of going to meetings and seminars. But my job was clear: I was expected to service the needs of practitioners and find an alternative approach to the arts in Africa. Training was the issue. So far we had agreed. It was left to me to sort out the remaining issues. How? What? Where? How much? Who pays?

WHY DID YOU DECIDE TO WORK WITH THE SCANDINAVIAN DEVELOPMENT AGENCIES?

Because they were Scandinavians and Scandinavians had hardly any track record as colonisers in Africa. Because they were development agencies and we were dealing within the framework of cultural development. Because we had found early allies to whom we owe an eternal debt: John Ytteborg, the Norwegian secretary of the IATA, Martha Vestin, the self-motivated Swedish theatre director, and Bo Karre, a wise older man at the end of his career in the Swedish International Development Authority. The ACTPA Project would never have made such inroads had it not been for such real friends in deed.

BUT THE FUNDERS REMOVED THEIR SUPPORT AFTER YEAR ONE, DIDN'T THEY?

That remains a mystery to me, to this date. Why? No clear explanation had ever been given to me. But I suspect that friendship has a limit. This limit lies where political interests begin. And then, it is so easy to divide when so many are striving for a chance of survival. What is true in nutritional terms applies to funding in other fields in Africa. But perhaps my colleagues of the UAPA bear some responsibility in this damage to their own school. The analysis of the host country, in the statement by Deputy Minister Machinga after funding was withdrawn, points a finger towards irresponsible behaviour and immature attitudes. Hopefully we have now all grown up to learn.

IS THAT TYPICAL OF THE ARTS WORLD AND IS IT TYPICAL OF AFRICAN ATTITUDES?

Neither. There are basic human issues here. Africa is not used to innovating where rich countries have never treaded. Occasional tickets to a seminar is what most have been accustomed to and suddenly there were hundreds of thousands of pounds voted for a permanent structure. A venue for an event does not compare with a castle in Southern Africa. The success of the ACTPA project became unbearable. To some extent, that can be understood. That such a success is attributed to one man obviously has the consequence of turning all arrows to point at one target.

WERE YOU PERSONALLY A TARGET?

From the stings I have felt, I must admit that I suffered more attacks than I have been granted credit. Perhaps that explains partly why I had to take shelter in the academic world of London University. While some shared the remains of a defunct project in 1991, performers of Africa plunged back into the state of failure and depression again. I concluded that the job was far from being over. The withdrawal of funds only meant that the early partners had done their utmost but they did not want the project to succeed for whatever reason. A different approach was required, whatever time was required. Other sources of money had to be found. Because there was one clear damning issue to be addressed and that was MONEY. Unless the right money was found, there was no lasting prospect for either Africa or development. Never mind the traditionally impoverished world of the arts...

WHAT SOLUTION HAVE YOU FOUND OVER THE YEARS?

Money has to be found within Africa. The performing arts have no other alternatives but to become self-sustainable. Better still, performing arts

Daniel Labonne

must be turned into an asset. Therefore it is essentially about creating revenue. But first, never again allow any external tsunami to demolish the fragile shelter of performers and drown the first pearls extracted from the deep end. Set up a foundation and secure one's own money for the long term. But I am no sorcerer and the key word here is 'enterprise'.

WHAT IS FACE?

If you look at the anxiety in the appeal of the host country, the rare resolve of the ministers of culture of Africa in the OAU/AU and the optimism of the observer from the US (see appendix), you will notice the insistence upon the need to capitalise on this unique experiment in a near future. Permanent structures are the next step so the experiment does not remain another white elephant. The last twenty years have shown that permanent structures will not emerge on their own, like mushrooms after the rain. FACE is the ultimate response to the need to take up the challenge of collecting the means to an end.

FACE combines the objectives of each of the major responses to needs from the 1990s. ACTPA at Castle Arts was also about providing much needed structure to *live arts*, central to African living; later, my academic evaluation was entitled 'Development Through Creativity:' with ATEX, 'exchange' had proved central to all the progress registered in this unique experiment, both within the training methodology and in the pragmatic measures required to ensure progress. The missing base that cripples any lasting progress is obvious: unless funding is both adequate and independent, projects like ACTPA are doomed. We just have to wake up to that hard reality. FACE is thus an awakening that draws the energies and resources first towards financial security with a foundation. The foundation will serve the arts, creativity and exchange, as applied to African cultural development.

WHAT ABOUT THE LEGITIMACY OF FACE?

FACE is a company limited by guarantee under UK law. The Foundation is picking up the pieces of a wrecked initiative and this book is a refusal to back down while the facts point towards success and significant development. Millions of people are indirectly concerned. It is a duty to find the right solution, legally and otherwise, to overtake the teething problems and to forge ahead. The initiative must be seen as a brand new undertaking, in 2011, only to be measured by the success of the enterprise in the future. The appeal of the host country had fallen on deaf ears; the initiative of individual performers in the UAPA had been treated with suspicion and mistrust; the work of ATEX had been shamelessly recuperated by powerful entities, left, right and centre. The only option left is a private initiative with different, reliable partnerships. ACTPA is dead, long live FACE! One of the first steps would be to appoint a board of trustees to establish fresh and lasting legitimacy.

IS ENTERPRISE THE ANSWER?

20 years ago, ATEX had been accused of being a private initiative. That is exactly what it was, in order to fulfil the many technical and logistical tasks within a project like ACTPA. You will find in the 1991 statement of the host country, how pleased they had been to deal with ATEX which actually provided the right response to their concerns as a partner state. Obviously, the fund providers cut off their financing because they refused to acknowledge the effective partnership between ATEX and Zimbabwe. The Deputy Minister called this attitude 'disingenuous.' Not only the results demonstrated the validity of the working arrangement, but the partnership actually became the foundation that ensured the experiment was on course towards a permanent centre of excellence. The technical know-how in training matters, on one hand, had to be matched with management skills of a high calibre, on the other. Just imagine what would have happened if all the funds had been diverted from the objectives of the project or if a major scandal had occurred during the pilot years! Suspension of funds would have been justified in

Daniel Labonne

such circumstances and the press would have splashed out another failure of irresponsible Africans! You do not punish competence and dedication! You do not repudiate to ruins and decay such promising and concrete results towards blossoming cultural industry!

HOW TO PREVENT THE SAME MISHAPS FROM OCCURING AGAIN?

First, by doing what Africans have always managed to do: survive. Then, by being crystal clear from the outset about the nature of the new enterprise: what the performing arts of Sub-Saharan Africa require is a school of excellence. The model set out by ACTPA at Castle Arts points towards artistic excellence in a pan-African approach. Finally, by daring to confirm that ATEX had been right and that was the only way forward to establish an independent centre. After the demise of the pilot project, my attitude had been to justify my action and defend my loyalty towards performing artists of Africa. The pictorial report (*see Part Six*) demonstrates fully how I managed to get the founding members of the UAPA involved at every single stage of the experiment. But the ACTPA project proved a thousand times more useful than the UAPA. That is the hard truth to reckon with. The concrete reality of the Castle Arts meant sheer business rules had to prevail. The reality is that the pilot project was abandoned, starved of funds deliberately and the Castle Arts was allowed to return to oblivion. That is an unforgivable mistake. I personally decided to invest another 10 years injecting fresh momentum in the experiment academically. Not only was every single word of the ACTPA Guidelines in 1987 written by me, but I fully assume responsibility for setting ATEX to deliver the services that secured ACTPA and Castle Arts. Today, I must modestly acknowledge what the former host country called 'the sterling management of ATEX.' Because I am not ashamed of what had been accomplished and I have given so much for so long, I must assume full responsibility as I set out to approach a new host country. I must do so as an entrepreneur.

DOES THAT MEAN A PRIVATE VENTURE?

It means that a host country requires guarantees and it will only trust a track record plus the sheer ability to deliver. Only a private venture will do. Since we are dealing with the arts, the independence of artists remains a component. Cultural development cannot depend upon aid and external assistance. On the other hand, impoverished governments have other priorities to attend to. That is the key conclusion from the earlier experiment. What is then the alternative? It must be income generating and self-sustainable.

WHAT IS ACE?

ACE is the African Centre of Exchange. ACE is the permanent centre which will deliver the specialised training to performing artists, based upon the findings of the earlier experiment. Like ACTPA, it will be open to performers from all over Africa; training will be delivered with a clear purpose: equipping the performer to play his role as mediator between tradition and modernity. Either in the education sector delivering knowledge and skills to the young or as an entrepreneur generating activities and jobs in the African city. Trainees would be taught in the major languages spoken in Africa. In Castle Arts, Bulawayo, English and French were used all the time and that contributed to breaking down a huge barrier between Africans for too long locked out into artificial blocks. That is in itself one key exchange factor. In future, we have been advised to teach and use Portuguese.

WHY PORTUGUESE?

Consultants of FACE have recently paid an informal visit to Mozambique in a fact finding mission intended to determine the best host country for the permanent African Centre of Exchange. Portuguese-speaking Africans cannot be left out of the training process. We have also been advised to keep the permanent training centre in the Southern Africa region. There are other countries which are being studied as appropriate

Daniel Labonne

hosts for ACE to prosper as a regional training centre of excellence. The Guidelines originally recommended that, among other services, the permanent centre delivers courses in its language laboratories. An empowered African performer ought to speak and write several key languages. The laboratory may be opened to external language students who would pay, thus assisting ACE in becoming self-financed. Together with the new host country, it will be decided whether ACE will charge for the specialist courses to performers.

WILL ACE BECOME AN ELITE SCHOOL?

ACE will not be an ordinary school delivering cheap diplomas. The wishes of the performers, the recommendations of the AU ministers of culture, the challenges of cultural development all point towards a much needed transformation that delivers growth and quality. The skills and techniques that performers require can only be delivered by the best teachers and artistic directors. These need to be paid as all the other staff as demonstrated in the Castle Arts. The trainees need to be accommodated, fed, and equipped with tools for their education and personal development. All this cost money. That is why FACE is being set up as a foundation to secure the adequate and renewable funding. Exchange will also operate at other levels, namely through a North-South partnership linking creatively towns of Africa with cities in the developed world. But once a business-plan will be approved by all parties, it is possible to envisage a system of sponsorship for each student. What is absolutely clear is that the situation of most African governments is such that any expected contribution would be limited, possibly to sponsoring one or two students from a given country.

WHAT ARE THE MOST LIKELY PARTNERS IN ACE, THE PERMANENT TRAINING CENTRE?

As shown with the pilot project, ACE is intended to be a pan-African training centre devoted to devising pragmatic solutions to cultural development with an impact in both the education and economic sectors. As such, it is expected that major regional organisations within the African continent will show a commitment. Consultants from FACE have begun a series of consultations with major regional banking organisations. If, for instance, the African Centre of Exchange is set up in the Southern Africa region, together with the new host country, FACE would certainly approach both the African Development Bank (AfDB) as well as a major corporation present within the region. The Southern Africa Development Conference (SADC) would not wish to be left out of such a promising venture. A grant that secures the early years would be most helpful but a loan would depend upon the final business plan. Television would sooner or later benefit from the outlet from the training programmes. As such, they are natural partners in ACE. Will the cultural development message be heard? Whatever the case, support to FACE cannot be limited to means and partners in Africa only. We have shown that in our work in the pilot project. Africa is not an island and it should not act as if it were. Take it from the islander that I am. FACE has devised a plan that would assist in raising the profile of the continent. That is part and parcel of the task ahead. The choice of the Castle Arts was a pointer. Across Africa, there are multinationals with a vested interest in a peaceful and prosperous continent. These are the natural partners of the foundation and its proposed enterprise: ACE. But following the visit to Mozambique, it has become clear that should Mozambique express a clear interest in hosting the permanent centre, Brazilian partners might welcome our initiative and be invited to play a key role in our south-south cooperation. Performers from all over Africa would feel totally comfortable in a close partnership with Brazil. Most interestingly, a reciprocal exchange could also benefit Brazilian performers... (*See Part Four. The Future: FACE*)

IS THERE A RISK THAT ACE BECOMES AS DEPENDENT AS ACTPA AT CASTLE ARTS?

Not if FACE succeeds in attracting corporate sponsors. Not if ACE generates diversified activities with its cluster programmes that generate revenue. Initially, the aim must be breaking even. However, we must not shy away from the challenges ahead. In due course, a successful ACE would be adapted and reproduced in one or more African cities of Africa. Once it is clearly demonstrated that the training, the production and related services are profitable, it is more likely that the venture will become attractive to entrepreneurs and other host countries.

HOW DOES THE AFRICAN CENTRE OF EXCHANGE (ACE) PROVIDE MORE OPPORTUNITIES TO THE PERFORMER?

For the exchange between fellow Africans to be creative and dynamic, the experiences of the past 50 years must become familiar to the performers in order to develop a plural and inclusive view. That view is currently non-existent and the former colonial powers still manage to keep the performer wandering along very narrow corridors of opportunities. Time has shown that, in the process, the performer loses his purpose and seldom achieves his full potential. He remains second best. The most talented continue to choose exile or they are chosen to enrich the culture of others. Cultural development needs to offer a better option that reconciles the contradictions of contemporary Africa, while opening new avenues of understanding and peace. Theatre and the performing arts can be trusted to achieve that. We have demonstrated just that during the pilot project. But the crux of the matter will be in the sustainability of ACE as an enterprise. That means that ACE will offer services that are not on offer elsewhere. Then, the products of ACE will reach out to broader markets across borders. That is the most obvious meaning of 'exchange.' But ACE itself is expected to evolve as a concept, at a later stage, when architects will be invited to assist in developing what I have called the 'drumma' at the heart of the African city.

SO, ARE YOU ADVOCATING A FRANCHISE SYSTEM?

In time, why not? The first rule is to make the master plan work. Our approach has always been the entrepreneur's. Castle Arts materialised and delivered results precisely because the host country felt it could trust the management of the project. There would be a contradiction in terms, if we advocated the empowering the performer, while you train him into becoming dependent and unproductive. The finality of training the performer of Africa is for him to be in a position to help himself before he is able to help the young and assist his country. The most reliable route to achieving that is enterprise. What is true for the performer is equally true for African countries. The performing arts are plentiful and fully understood. Yet, they are untreated and so far neglected. Just as in Castle Arts, the African Centre of Exchange will look closely at means and ways of processing the raw material available across Africa, so they may generate meaning and value for Africans. If the results can be demonstrated as positive, there is no reason not to imagine a second and a third ACE in other parts of this vast continent. Exchange would take yet another practical meaning with a play produced in ACE in Southern Africa which may be taken on tour to West Africa or East Africa.

Daniel Labonne

PART 3

The Diamond Theory

Determine that the thing can and shall be done and then, we shall find a way.

Abraham Lincoln

Daniel Labonne

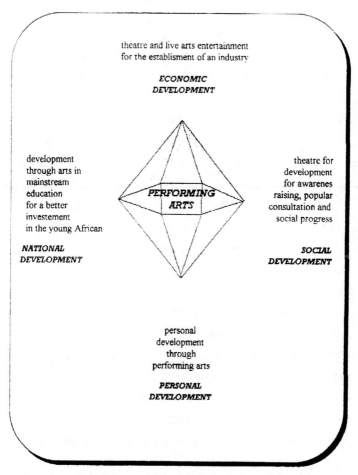

THE LONG TERM BENEFITS OF INTEGRATING THE PERFORMING ARTS
IN THE DEVELOPMENT OF AFRICA

Note: the theory had been developed within the context of my post-graduate study at the University of London. Today, I would replace the word 'National' by 'Educational'; I would also prefer 'Self Development' to 'Personal Development'.

FROM PRATICE TO THEORY

DEVELOPMENT: A PROCESS OR A GOAL?

The term 'development' generally applies to living organisms that are never static. On the contrary, they undergo a constant process of internal and external transformation, synonymous to what we call 'life.' Thus, a child goes through a process of cognitive and physical development, which never fails to always amaze the observer, especially during the phase of adolescence. Just like human beings, societies evolve through a series of transformations and register progress. Both society and the adolescent, undergoing development, require some form of training, if not systematic education. Two characteristics have led to the widespread use of word 'development.' First, the spectacular transformation that has affected the traditionally agricultural rural societies and turned them into, industrialised urban agglomerations. That internal development in rich countries of Europe and North America has led to the world order, as we know it today, dominated by a multitude of products, ongoing research founded on scientific knowledge, global trade and the ever-growing power of money. The second characteristic of 'development' is to be found in the assumption that the modernised, industrialised societies have become an ideal to be followed. Thus, the state of 'underdevelopment' in which newly independent countries in the 1960s, have been categorised. Up to the late early 90's, a concerted effort, more or less linked with the existence of the United Nations and its principles of Human Rights, has led to a division of the World into two economic leagues: the so-called 'developed world' which groups a small number of countries, on one hand; on the other hand, 'the developing world' encompassing the vast majority of the human population grouped essentially within countries of Asia, South America and Africa.

Daniel Labonne

Cultural Development seems to be a two-fold concept. First, it implies that culture, as the comprehensive and organic system that holds together a society and each individual in it, must be developed. Such development would ensure that both individuals and society enjoy increased freedom, become adequately motivated and are gradually equipped for progress. Secondly, a fulfilling development can only be achieved when it is fully in tune with the cultural values and systems of a community or a country.

The proposition that development is an aim to itself, essentially measurable in GDP and IPC is being challenged by the attitude of the populations, ultimately destined to benefit. Culturally speaking, they often fail to see the point of achieving what is expected of them and - that is the problem - they view development as yet another world order imposed from outside upon them. The model from abroad is invariably sold to them by a breed of expert know-it-all, if not occasionally by local intellectuals trained into ways, foreign to tradition. Persisting under-development stands as evidence that the divorce between this new class and tradition has not been rewarding. Political leaders, often emerging from the midst of this new educated elite, seem powerless, when they are not simply corrupt. Nowhere better than in Africa can this failure of development policies be measured. As we advocated the case for a school for the performing artists of Africa, (inside-in cultural development) the concept of 'structural adjustment' was being forcefully imposed on the ailing economies of Africa (outside-in economic development). Since, all parties, including the inventor of the concept (the World Bank etc.), have recognised the failure of 'structural adjustment.'

Development in Africa has failed to deliver, possibly because it was a poorly disguised neo-colonial form of assistance, with quick-fix methods, wrapped in guilt and good intentions. Somewhere along the line, there have always been the carefully projected calculations of bankers, seen today as the very masters of the development initiative. The Third World debts provide the evidence, as a painful reminder of this situation. The main motive has been self-interest. Development is far from being totally negative, however, as something had to be done in favour of the colonised countries, after the Second World War. They were offered political independence and aid, that is, financial assistance and expert guidance. Political manipulation, one-sided trade agreements, and cultural mimicry form part of the package deal, imposed by the rich on the poor. The point must be made, in the context of our study that bankers and economists are traditionally against novelty and creativity. Their concept of development rests upon a concept of cultural superiority felt, historically, by richer nations, which simply disregarded the real needs of those who are supposed to benefit from development. These needs relate to more than money to be earned and bread to eat. Development has been stifling the creative powers of the individual within the societies concerned. Dependence, corruption and debt form, today, the legacy of the old concept of strictly economic development.

Africa exercises hardly any control upon the terms of exchange in the dealings the newly independent states have to conduct, in a modern world. It merely suffers those terms and submissively obliges, namely with repayment of debts etc. it may also be argued that forceful changes have been repeatedly imposed upon the continent, throughout the centuries. The common factor in most exchanges with Africa: economic, legal, political and cultural coercion, as a side effect. As a result, the populations of this continent have been humbled to merely awaiting some form of external (spiritual?) change of fate. In the meantime, the various countries struggle to maintain survival levels of existence. Most are busy reimbursing personal debts, while the produce of their labour contribute to paying back of national debt... In the meantime, strange calamities like aids strike Africans in their millions. Should we be surprised that entire populations no longer believe in their own abilities to pull themselves out of the black hole of poverty and depression? Nor

Daniel Labonne

do they trust fully yet another new concept, imported to Africa, presumably for the benefit of African populations. Disillusion reigns supreme. And yet, a close study of the culture of Africans reveals a powerfully resistant fabric, which has braved all sorts of dangers along the millennia...

What observers have witnessed may be a form of fatigue combined with a profound feeling of helplessness and mistrust. Africa is becoming increasingly aware of its own inability to attend to the needs of internal governance while responding to the challenges of rapidly evolving economic, environmental and technological conditions, worldwide. To use imagery from boxing and sports, 'the repeated blows have damaged the spirit.' Above any political or economic consideration, there is the combined effect of cultural and psychological damage from the violence suffered along the history of Africa. Internally, under-funded educational systems are transforming young people into consumers and are producing an elite, ill-equipped for much needed leadership, in times of hardships.

One should not look in the statistics of economic achievements among African states to find reasons to hope, to rejoice or to dance. Nor are prospects of a better future either clear or promising. There is a likelihood of making progress only by focusing on their inner nature (i.e. the culture) of the man and the woman of Africa. Only by recognising their ability to believe in their own survival through a particular cruel adversity over the centuries and by tapping into their powerful creativity expressed through their wealth of songs, dances and laughter that the resilience of African peoples can become a source of revival. Only through more exposure to African art forms will such strength invigorate new generations of Africans, equip them to take up the challenges of development. Somehow, across Africa, optimism has never left African performing arts. Paradoxically, the African personality remains a wealth of laughter and joy...

There is no clear will, yet, of the richer nations to share with poorer populations of the South. Competitions remain fierce and the focus is still placed on the economic and political power. How, then, could the young African gradually overcome the sequels of the various forms of continued violence inflicted upon African peoples? How to overcome 'the artificial factor' recognisable in artificial borders, artificial leadership, artificial education, artificial linguistic groupings... What is left to the Africans to explore for their own immediate and long-term benefit? How to counter the temptations of exile or despair? I sustain the performing arts might hold one answer to those questions.

Development has come to mean material possessions, abundance of choice and political control over the sources of wealth. These modern values have been erected as an ideology for which people are ready to fight and die. The hard choice has been made clear for poorer countries like those of Africa, to either accept that model of development or run the risk of being branded ideological enemies. The penalties during the Cold War period were often costly. But adopting the ideology is no guarantee of achieving development. From an African point of view, a number of questions came to be raised: is the modern concept of development a matter for compensation for damage done before and during colonisation? Is development instead a form of inspired Judeo-Christian charity or cold calculation? Is it instead a system, which aims at effectively transferring technology and financial assistance, from North to South? Instead of being measured essentially in economic terms, should not development be assessed in terms of social cohesion, effective leadership, healthy populations and flourishing creative art forms? Assessed with these criteria, there is little doubt that development in Africa has failed.

It is essentially a problem of adequacy, in the method, in the pace and in the objectives of development. What was required was more a comprehensive definition of what a happy life could mean for a specific

Daniel Labonne

people. Such a definition can only be valid if it comes from within the community concerned and expected to achieve the goals of development. Development is now defined as process, no longer as an aim. The human being is being placed at the heart of such a development process, instead of the economy. Therefore, success can only be measured in terms of long-term human fulfilment, not short-term profitability. Man - and not technology or economic performance - is now seen as the 'engine and the very purpose of development.'

One must yet again, reduce the concept of cultural development to fit within the arena suitable to a necessary dialogue over the untapped potential from within a specific culture (African culture) by focusing over a specific social agent (the performing artist). Such an arena was outlined and made available for research and experimentation when the United Nations promulgated the World Decade for Cultural Development (1987-1996). To that extent, this research pulls vague statements and theoretical wishful thinking about cultural development, towards applied popular measures placed, thanks to adequate training, within the reach of specific societies.

HOW MANY AFRICAN CAPITALS HAVE A NATIONAL THEATRE BUILDING?

I wish the means are made available through FACE for in-depth research into such areas. Not many, is the incomplete answer. Although a number of countries, like Ethiopia and Senegal, have had a national theatre company. National ballet companies of Côte D'Ivoire or Guinea have had their days of glory to be studied in future courses of FACE... There are hardly enough theatre buildings to receive the plays which are produced within the average African country. The former colonising powers have kept a strong influence upon the type of theatre practices and taught in what used to be part of their realm. However, short-sightedness and poor investment have failed to point the way towards palaces of civilisation, comparable to the Manaus Opera, in the Amazon region of Brazil. On the African continent, productions made-in-Africa seldom travel across borders to be performed to other audiences. Although the average African remains a committed participant in live arts and a keen spectator indeed, he is unlikely to attend theatre performances. The economic question would be another area of study, because one needs to afford the entrance fee to see a show. Professional theatre only becomes viable if the structural and economic frameworks have been put in place. The reality is depressing: African performers hardly meet without the sponsorship and arbitration of a rich non-African country. There is pressure for plays to be first written before they are allowed to reach an audience; that practice is unnecessary to the extent that the performer pertains to the oral tradition and the audience is often hardly literate. The recourse to the playwright could not be bad in itself. Unfortunately, the subordination of the live arts to the written format attributes exaggerated importance to the written language, a weapon in neo-colonial power games, yet a key development factor.

Under the pressure of such strategies, the training of performers in Africa tends to push the practitioner towards adopting academia and the closed world of universities. In turn, the university tends to push the best performers and their work away from the natural environment and their communities. Training tends to be ad-hoc and short-lived for the African performer. Language divides (along the lines of francophone, English-speaking countries) have channelled theatre work towards enriching the French language or the English language first, before the communities concerned may even access 'their' own plays, before they may enjoy their dance-dramas, first-hand. Funding problems, as in every other sector of development tend to remain a cancer that kills slowly the creativity as they keep driving the best African artist to opt for exile... Mental exile first occurs given the inflow of information and the influence of the media; physical exile often follows, in the case of the most talented. Cultural exile insidiously works its way through the

Daniel Labonne

methods of training performing artists according to Stanislavsky's and Lecoq's methods. Most damaging is the finality of training intended to lead to professional theatre within a fully equipped building and an Equity card for the theatre worker.

In the case of the African performer, either a gap is created between the audience and the performer, or the latter, out of his own success, is driven out of the cultural matrix. Such forms of exile reduce the effect of the arts. They affect the communities concerned with another form of poverty: mediocrity. Exile may result in the end to unsatisfactory artistic careers and miserable lives for the performers.

Yet, in Africa, there is neither a lack of talent, nor is there a problem of poverty in performing arts tradition. Audience participation to live arts constitutes an asset in the cultural life, across the continent. A wedge has been placed between the performing artist and his audience, largely because of inadequate education. Even what is known as 'theatre for development' may be seen as part of that wedge. The performer is being systematically left aside in the theatre for development process, leaving the 'stage' to pseudo experts in development and undergraduates free to manipulate 'data' from the vulnerable communities. Surely, it is a good thing that the audience participates actively in their own-life drama. But they do not realise that they are being reduced to mere sources of information for academic analysis. Even the presumed direct action from the community can become a source of risk, because in Africa, governments tend to be paranoid about power and control. In my view, it would take strategic action, independent funding and constant experimentation, to reconcile artist and audience in Africa, for the benefit of 'development.' Development matters. But man must come first and arts cannot be subordinated to either propaganda or economic diktat. In Africa, the development game has been pernicious, so long that statistics add up and education is channelled through the imported models of university departments. The African cultural fabric remains delicate and unique, to the point that systematic transposing of foreign experiments does not necessarily pay off. Using the communities and their art forms without providing in return the gratifying effects of learning and catharsis amount to a disservice. Both the arts and the public end up losers. Redress would require a revised status to be attributed to the performing artist of Africa. That cannot happen without adequate training, preferably in a highly specialised school, eventually through a transformed educational system.

THE 3 R'S PHILOSOPHY

It is possible for African performers to be trained in Africa, by Africans, for the development of Africa. Could such training in the process discourage self-imposed exile and reliance upon aid? There might be a new training method emerging, more adequate than traditional methods if not western methods training for performers. I have called this method the Horizontal method... That is the method experimented at ACTPA at Castle Arts. This method could lead to varying forms of Exchange Theatre, as a characteristic of African performing arts, as opposed to other practices elsewhere.

From there, springs a new philosophy for cultural exchange. So far, the practice of exchange is rooted in colonial days and rests upon notions of conquests, trade and power. From the experiment, exchange may now be defined as a two-way process in human relationship that rests upon three principles: *Reciprocity, Respect and Responsibility*. From my research, African performing arts represent a potential wealth (the Diamond) so far ignored, downgraded, devalued, or hidden. Only Africans themselves can do something about it, but everyone may benefit in the long run. Specific attention and technical know-how could turn the potential into an asset for each country concerned and for the African continent. In very concrete terms, results from the treatment of the performing arts in the context of Africa, would eventually work their way up to bear a positive impact upon education, as well as other sectors like tourism and external relations. To get to that conclusion, a number of guiding principles had been applied and the particular history of the experiment had dictated both its long-winded process and its ultimate fate. Yet, lessons had to be drawn from the experiment.

Structural problems require structural solutions: so ATEX in London and Castle Arts in Zimbabwe were the most appropriate forms of response to needs. A specific predicament requires specific analysis and original response: training the performing artist in Africa has so far been patchy and leading to little development of the arts. Performers have generally failed to play their full role in the uplifting of their respective communities, after their training. Now, cultural development sets out a Decade to initiate innovative approaches so that Africans may have a chance to find their own solutions. We set about undertaking this experiment within the parameters described above. The process remained unwavering: from practice to theory. Finally, implied in the concept of cultural development as tested within a time frame and constrained to a particular region, is one golden rule used to measure the outcome of this study: inside-out solutions are preferable to outside-in solutions.

Development does feel like a bumpy ride. Let us simply summarise what we had to go through. Over-politicisation of issues; misconceptions and racism; jealousy and corruptive practices; the unfortunate habit of reducing the poorer nations to fighting for crumbs; over-intellectualisation of very down to earth considerations; competing if not condescending attitudes of academics vis-à-vis artists; constant diversion of objectives along the way under the pressure of diverging motives; distortion of facts to downgrade all matters African; recuperation of the findings from a serious experiment by third parties; permanent money worries due to inconsistent funding; human issues resulting the above and leading to new problems and perpetuating old ones; shortage of staff to address real managerial issues. There is obviously no precedence for projects qualified as 'unique'... Irrespective of all these pitfalls that some may qualify as typical on African soil, the experiment points to a new function for the performing arts within a development strategy. Such a strategy first attributes a unique place to the performing arts, in the exclusive case of Africa. The figure on page 137 also equates to a reinforcement of the cultural dimension of development.

EXPECTED BENEFITS FROM A PRACTICAL APPLICATION OF THE DIAMOND THEORY

I would have been in a more comfortable place, had the 3-year training programme been complete. If foreign trainees could have attended the Diaspora course, as recommended by ATEX, the viability of the training centre would have become more obvious. Had the dialogue with the host country been encouraged, rather than sabotaged, the Castle Arts could have taken other initiatives in the related fields of dance or even fashion. If the unity of purpose, as patiently built by ATEX up to the Paris Round Table, had not been misrepresented, divisive tactics would not have provided the ammunition to the enemies of the project. If... Responsibility does not stop with difficulties. We had to make sense out of whatever phase the experiment had reached.

The Diamond Theory suggests a win-win situation is possible. My brief was about developing a service for performing artists, for Africa considered as a specific cultural entity, considered in its vastness, inclusive of populations with distinct features, languages and practices. The question was from the outset a real challenge: how could development be boosted from the roots upward, in a cultural reappraisal of the circumstances of an entire continent? In training terms, how to innovate without mimicking what had been practiced already in drama departments, out of Africa? The answer can only be both technical and strategic. In other words, one cannot train only the performers without educating the decision-makers. Finally, what is the point of training, if the purpose of that training is not made clear from the outset? That is precisely what the Diamond Theory encapsulates for posterity: a comprehensive approach is inevitable for lasting impact.

Some basic benefits from the Diamond Theory could be thus summarised.

Performers in Africa will understand better their potential, their function, their rights, and their responsibilities. The development process applied to African societies can somehow be boosted with new dynamics, from a new base. Knowledge about performing arts and their practice may thus be collected, enriched and better shared among fellow Africans, first. Development workers in general will find their task somehow facilitated, namely through an increased participatory role of the populations concerned, through the mediation of performers. Human development and progress generally result from needs identified and addressed, from increased understanding of the sum of differences, as inequalities are reduced and new conditions for peace created.

Young people in Africa can only benefit from integrated education and economic development that takes into account the cultural component as mediated by a friendly performer-educator. Future generations anywhere would be made to benefit from increased accessibility to (and widespread knowledge about) what is today an underrated heritage from Africa: Performing Arts.

HOW THE DIAMOND THEORY APPLIES TO CULTURAL DEVELOPMENT

- Cultural development can only work when development is both acceptable and achievable, ensured of the full adherence of the individual and the wholehearted participation of the populations concerned.

- Encourage exchange among Africans, first; between Africa and the world, later.

- Establish means and ways for Africans to meet so they may discover, compare and creatively treat their differences.

- Seek solutions from within Africa and aim for self-reliance for Africans. The arts point to the best method to achieving this.

- Focus upon one common language understood by all in Africa: Performing Arts.

- Respond honestly to the need for adequate training of performers (in Africa); let them in turn assist in the need to review and improve the role and status of Performing Arts (in the world?).

- Address creatively the peripheral difficulties, common to development projects. For that there is a need to balance out the excessive credit attributed to the economist.

- Allow the performing arts in Africa to develop, in such a way that Africa may use its heritage to formulate an original vision and adopt the most suitable approach to an integrated form of development, on the model of India or China;

- Know yourself better - whether or not you are an African, whether or not you are a performer.

- Train the performer adequately so that he may bring a meaningful contribution to the education of the young African of the Twenty-first century.

Daniel Labonne

Why ACTPA remains a training concept for the 21st century

Based on the early findings of the comprehensive experiment, including this evaluation, not only is there a case to resume and continue ACTPA at Castle Arts; but a broader approach is possible and recommendable. Three target groups have been identified in the Diamond Theory.

1. **Train the performer**

   To explain Africa and its cultural forms;
   To bridge the gap between North and South;
   To develop Exchange between African countries using performing arts as the vehicle;
   To teach non-African popular art forms of live performance;
   To educate the young African.

2. **Teach the average person**

   (Both in the North and the South);
   The arts of dancing;
   The love and immense potency of his/her body;
   Fitness with a meaning and purpose;
   A minimum of creative rituals and practices as old as the earth;
   The uniqueness of humankind through its cultural experiments.

3. **Train the young**

   To master the language of performing arts as much as other languages;
   Not to disregard his body and its creative capacities;
   Not to forget or to reject the performing arts heritage;
   To develop through dance, "a sound mind in a sound body";
   To reconcile dance culture with formal education;

To actively learn how to collect and exchange dances for all occasions;

To assist in re-educating the world against inertia and passive submission to technology.

There is fresh demand made upon Africans to get their act together. The new circumstances governing the world at the end of the Twentieth century (end of cold war, increased possibilities for sharing, global communications) impose upon Africans that they sort out their differences and come up with imaginative strategies. Past efforts have been wrongly left exclusively to politicians, when terms were not dictated from outside the African continent. Nevertheless, complaints and accusations are neither effective nor adequate. It is also clear that all new solutions sought from outside are bound to be political and self-serving. Unless the development of a people is essentially a political affair, there is an objective expectation from Africans to set out their priorities, to bring out the strengths in their natural resources. Everyone knows diamonds are a well-exploited resource. Nobody from the North or the South would question the value of the hard stone. Just as the diamond, performing arts in my view constitute one of the valuables of Africa. From this recognition, it is a matter of devising new methods of finding an adequate method of processing and harmonising the many facets of performing arts. Just like FOOTPRINTS demonstrated at Castle Arts in 1990, it is possible to produce an innovative, exciting performance resulting from the fusion of many dances, originating from many parts of Africa. It is about time that such a new harmonised form of expression is brought under the limelight as it bestows upon its creators their real value. The deeper the quest, the darker the tunnel, the more valuable the diamond. If not for the buyer, at least for the rightful owner.

Daniel Labonne

FROM UTOPIA TO PRAGMATIC MEASURES

Such a dance will not be a dance of 'political unity' that has proved to be a necessary Utopia, in post-Independence Africa. Instead, it might well be a dance made out of the woven choreography from various cultures across the borders of the African continent: the unified version of multiple voices. To get to that point, five measures are proving necessary: (i) multiply the opportunities for Africans from various parts of the continent to meet among themselves, without external interference and imposed agendas; (ii) make it possible to have a fresh look at old forms of performing arts; (iii) allow these live forms which are so varied and multiple to be freely exchanged, just as books are exchanged in a library; (iv) create a 'school' that would allow for the experimental efforts of such a process of 'exchange' to be explored and developed; (v) devise the most appropriate form of funding for such a school, until lasting results are obtained.

Because of television and video, the image has already started to impose itself upon the model. Human behaviour is being shaped first for fiction, leaving the individual in society to adjust accordingly. This is a result of past trends of development. The process is unstoppable. What is required is to re-establish an essential balance. In the developed world, for instance, a child is more likely to attribute authority to what TV says, rather than to listen to daddy. Virtual reality is already invading everyday reality. There is a need for a new and intensely physical experience to balance out the mental stress of a world dominated by technology.

History, guilt, and prejudice have prevented such an innovative physical total experience. Going to the gym today or rushing to a house party at weekends are but symptoms of an increasing awareness of the imbalance. We suggest that Africa might have a brand new role to play in a stressful world. The African performer, in particular, may have much to offer, both in Africa and out of Africa. First, the terms of exchange must be revised, culturally speaking. That is what 'exchange theatre' has meant to do. That is what our experiment has attempted to undertake very openly. Perhaps, too openly, for it's always risky to try to please everyone... So let us restrict ourselves to the initial brief. From my research and experimentation along these long years, across this vast continent, I have found out that 'Exchange Theatre' could play a determining role for African performing arts.

It would have an invigorating effect on theatre and performing arts in general. The resulting effects may be comparable to what cinema has been, in the first half of the Twentieth century, for the emerging American nation. Cinema allowed American creative artists to take a lead in developing a taste for the particular living experience of new Americans, given their diverse origins and their many languages. Cinema was used as an art form to interpret the American story in a new and exciting manner. The creators focused upon finding a language and a narrative that enable them to make sense out of the life that was being invented there and then, with all its ups and downs. Cinema allowed for the development of a culture in the making, by treating it through the most adaptable medium, capable of expressing the creative spirit of an entire people, in tune with the age. Maria Ley reminds us in 'The Piscator Experiment' how Piscator conducted his experiment in order to add meaning and purpose to American theatre.

'Piscator's plan for the school was to create a new totality of theatre. The very name of workshop implies such totality. Not an academy of theatre, not a department of a university, but a training ground in which each member would be an exponent to the whole. Then everything would easily fall into place - the experience and talent of the teachers, the freshness and curiosity of students, Piscator's pioneering spirit, and the vigorous life of the American around us.'

Daniel Labonne

What the Piscator Experiment tried to achieve for American theatre, the ACTPA Experiment did the same with African Performing Arts - in search of a new school. Yet, three major differences: different times, different cultures, different needs.

This being said, just as in the Piscator experiment, only bold solutions will do.

The Future

So far, Africa has been acting like a beggar sitting on a sack of gold'.

Louis Akin. Choreographer. Ex director of the national Ballet of Cote d'Ivoire
Resource Person in ACTPA at Castle Arts in 1990

PART 4

FACE

Foundation for Arts, Creativity & Exchange

Daniel Labonne

FACE IS A LONG TERM SOLUTION

In 2012, FACE pacifies the entire process and buries all the acrimonies that have affected such a wonderful project as ACTPA in the 1990s. It is a new beginning on totally new terms. FACE picks up the pieces and goes straight to the point in a business-like approach. Enterprise is the best alternative to the begging mentality and dependence upon governments which are already overloaded with socio-economic priorities. Personally, I have never given up my work as a researcher, as a creative artist and as an entrepreneur. Twenty additional years of work have now been invested in the same field of research. FACE has put together a new package that will deliver spectacular results. Instead of waiting for funding, it will generate income in the mid-term. Set up as a non-profit organisation, FACE will invite on its board the trustees with the experience, the image and the goodwill to raise the sort of funds required for a lasting impact. FACE will raise money from corporations with an ongoing interest in a prosperous and peaceful African continent.

The truth is that Africa needs FACE. The other harsh reality is that the image of Africa needs serious attention and individual countries need professional back-up to undertake the required face-lift. The good work which occasionally comes out of the performing arts scene of a country fails to reach out for the huge potential audience across the continent. A pan-African marketing agent is non-existent. Finally, our experiment has demonstrated clearly that the surest way to prevent useful talent to choose exile and deprive Africa of much needed intellect and leadership is to expand the market while the quality of production is improved. Empowering the performer begins with training, then it should permeate through education and the overall cultural development of African peoples. The magic formula will not come from out of Africa. What Africa does not need is occasional talk-shops to intellectualise the problems. That is already being done in African universities. It is also unlikely that great plays and wonderful theatre buildings will be commissioned single-handedly like it was the case with royalty and noblemen in Europe, during centuries. There is a crying need for Africa to catch up with its own damaged past and pull itself out of cultural depression.

The African continent has already understood that, ultimately, it can only rely upon itself provided it manages its resources better, provided it pulls itself together and innovates creatively. Development in Africa will be unique or nothing. Definitely nothing compared to what has been done in other parts of the world. FACE brings together the ingredients that may give cultural development a concrete meaning recognisable by all, from within and from without. For those who may still dwell over past weaknesses, immature attitudes and political manipulations, FACE is an affirmation that, so far, the dream may have turned into a nightmare, but the arts are eternal and the performer is awaking from his slumber. More importantly, there is the main cultural trait of African people: resilience. But there are many other assets. There is a reserve of joy and creativity that needs to be tapped into. Just as precious diamond lies in the bedrock of the continent, precious cultural value has been preserved, namely through rituals and performing arts. The art of the Griot is fast disappearing under the assault of modernity and technology. The oral tradition requires urgent revisiting. Africa needs a hard long inward look in order to begin to live according to self-defined rules. For centuries, rules have been imposed from outside... Remedial action is still possible, but for that, the economist alone cannot be trusted again. This book suggests that the performing artist has a brand new role to play.

THE VISION OF FACE

FACE will have a two-pronged approach: first entrust the person, bearer of living tradition and renewable creativity. That is the performing artist of Africa today. Then, give a home to the performing arts of Africa on the model of the Castle Arts, in Bulawayo, during a brief but enlightening period of time. FACE advocates the empowering of the performer across Africa as a reliable strategy towards the affirmation of identity, a new sense of responsibility fed by a fresh determination to give an economic relevance to the performing arts. That relevance should take the shape of a structural presence at the heart of the African city. FACE carries another connotation: expect the best from Africa to be finally put on display. But the starting point is unchanged: training. However, we need to be realistic: unless the money is made available and for a reliable period of time, no lasting results will be there to show.

What about profit, will the suspicious development baron ask? Why not? Profit is more honourable than corruption or failure. Profit in the global world of multinationals can be pitiless and destructive. In our context of cultural development, it cannot be a dirty word if we mean business and pull away from aid. That is why as we set up FACE to plant the off shoots of the ACTPA Project into new soil and we are instructing technicians to look at the full potential of a school of excellence, leading on to a growing number of productions. Ultimately we need to look at the outlet and network for the distribution for such products. That implies a network of distribution. You know the old saying: you can't pour new wine into old casks. The new Africa in the making expects better from its performing artists. I remember what Minister Fay Chung said at the opening of ACTPA at Castle arts: *"The new Africa must use the traditions of Africa as well as the culture of the world to produce a unique and healthy vision of the future."* That is the challenge right here: a unique and healthy vision of the future. These words tally with my insistence from day one about finding out 'training the performing artist, what for?'

Africa needs 'a healthy and unique vision of the future.' Nothing else will do, not imitation of what the Americans, the Chinese or the Indians have done to develop their arts. Inspiration, yes. Imitation, no. No occasional festival with erratic display of folklore will do either. Content and method matter. Form, regular production and structured distribution are equally important. Quality and originality will have to originate from the raw material preserved by the communities across Africa. Impact and continuity are the criteria to measure real progress. It is about the future, no longer about a distant past, remember? So that uniqueness will have to take on the shape of a new performer, a new performance and a new venue for such a performance.

Healthy means life, as opposed to death, health as the opposite of disease. Hope as opposed to despair. You may even read ACE (the best and strongest card) as a counterstatement to the sad association of Africans to AIDS! Incidentally, development agencies rightly or wrongly support massively aids eradication programmes... We probably are not in the same business. Because arts is for the living! The training, the spectacle Made-in-Africa must somehow project these other layers of what Africans are about: a joyful and resilient people, focussed upon a vibrant and colourful celebration of precious life. But the Foundation needs to go further. Such a celebration of life requires a shelter of a unique kind. Therefore, just as Castle Arts emerged as a prestigious place out of nowhere which has provided comfort and status to the performer, a new building is required at the heart of the African city.

THE NEED FACTOR

FACE addresses a need not only for Africans, because the future that Fay Chung talks about is global and concerns humankind. Cultural affirmation matters to define and achieve a satisfying development. Cultural exchange has become global necessity for understanding, trade and peace. For those who may question the order of priorities, consider the following: the amphitheatres of Athens were not built when every citizen was properly fed and clothed. The wonderfully designed amphitheatres that have survived to this date did not wait until the economics were right and all the wars had been won. Nor were the cathedrals in the cities of the Europe built when every worker had a job and was a member of trade unions. The landmarks of great cities tell the tale of the civilisation that brought about the conception and building of these wonderful man-made monuments to life, self-belief and beauty. Amphitheatres and cathedrals must be seen as major achievements of cultural development of their times.

Daniel Labonne

Africa needs theatres more than cathedrals. Both concepts are cultural in essence and they both respond to profound needs of a people who, at one point of their history, wish to reflect over their existence and the purpose of life, from their own perspective. What exactly is the vision of the average African? How and when is such a vision likely to be expressed? First, it needs to be processed to become what Fay Chung calls 'unique and healthy.' Training, research and development are unavoidable in that process. ATEX has firmly advocated a basic rule to progress: unless Africans exchange regularly with other Africans, it is pointless to reach out beyond the continent. Exporting half-baked products and under-groomed talents to advanced societies has been a fundamental mistake, inherent of post colonial practices. A degree of coherence and quality will only emerge through inter-African exchanges. Paradoxically, uniqueness will only grow out of the multiplicity of forms and the plurality of languages and rituals. That is the premise of the 'exchange method.'

THE NEED FOR A LANDMARK

Exchanges between Africa and Africa imply a special venue for a very delicate purpose: to house and display the uniqueness of Africa. Yes, Africa needs to make up its mind about a two pronged need. First, how to preserve and process the huge variety of performing arts that communities have managed to preserve so far? Secondly, how to guard against the invasion of technology which is dragging humanity towards uniformity and accelerated rapports? But again, the challenge is neither negative nor defensive. It is about asking oneself this question: what is the landmark that the African city wants the visitor to see and explore that expresses the deeper meaning of life and the very soul of African peoples?

If there is no clear answer to that question in the present landscape, then FACE will boldly make a suggestion for the near future. 'Empowering the Performer' implies a physical conceptualisation of a venue that will become the focal point in time and space of the cultural development of Africans. Such a venue is not primarily about boosting the cultural industry, although the Diamond Theory acknowledges this modern necessity. The FACE theatre (or the 'Drumma') would become the place that gives value and recognition to the performing arts of each African country. The next function will be to allow regular exchanges between visiting productions that will inform the local spectators and foster peace between fellow Africans. Only the third function will offer the economic advantage of attracting and entertaining the tourist. In such a vision, the decision-maker and the urban planner cannot overlook the importance of giving a specific character to the development of the African city.

THE FUTURE AFRICAN CITY

By 2050, 50% of the Africa's population will be urban. In 2012, the figure stands at 38%. In *The Spirit of Cities* (Daniel A. Bell & Avner de-Shalit) , there is a recent claim that reverting to the early tenets of Ancient Greece may prove helpful as megacities attract populations of 10m or more. To counter the pressure for global uniformity led by technology and the Internet or to dampen the risk of aggressive national expressions, cities might grow into providing a different kind of belonging, as opposed to nationalistic considerations. That used to be the case in ancient Athens. My contention is that such positive attributes were fostered in amphitheatres, thanks to dramatic poets like Aeschylus, Aristophanes and Euripides. The dramatic teachings certainly contributed to the emergence of the early forms of democracy. Africa needs its own centres of entertainment where original styles might develop and genuine voices might be heard by the city dwellers. Democratic processes emerge from within a society at a given point of its own pace of development. The full expression of freedom and equitable sharing may require a completely different appellation that might even push the boundaries of current forms of democracy. In Africa, voices and styles

Daniel Labonne

are likely to be different to everything that happened before and elsewhere.

THE YOUTH IS THE REAL TREASURE OF AFRICA

Africa got close to 5% growth in 2011, exceeding predictions. In the last decade, Africa even has done better than Brazil and India. Half of trade in Africa is already on a South-South basis. Infrastructures remain a priority area for Africa. It is being predicted that for the first time since the industrial revolution, emerging nations are having a more determining impact than the developed world... But one factor signalled as a drawback is the poor quality of education across Africa. But the obvious remaining hurdles must be set against the real potential for development: Africa holds 10% of all global oil reserves, 40% of gold reserves and 60% of arable land.

More importantly, 50% of the population of Africa has less than 20 years. This can only be an asset in a competitive world. The education of the young must be improved to teach the young how to rely upon oneself, how to grow in confidence, how to trust his own environment and how to dare do things differently. Such a form of education would require the full involvement of the performing artists of Africa. Trained performers of Africa should find work in the schools of Africa. Enough damage has been done by allowing soldiers to train children at deadly wars, within and across borders. John Lennon may have died because he pleaded for peace to be given a chance. We must plead for the arts to be given a chance.

KNOW-HOW MATTERS MORE THAN KNOWLEDGE

Cheikh Modibo Diarra (president of Microsoft Africa) believes that Africans need to rely upon themselves... The habit of having big ideas that depend upon other people's money was yesterday's mistake in development strategies. To some extent, the ACTPA project has paid heavily for the same mistake. Modibo Diarra advocates that know-how matters more than knowledge for Africans in the 21st century. Know-how is the last step towards wealth creation. Utopia? Why not? Diarra is drawing attention and resources towards an industrial exploitation of the Sahara Desert to generate solar energy. I do understand his call. To hold raw material in one's soil is one thing; to treat and transform them is another matter. Just as the Sahara desert has been there for centuries, so have the performing arts in Africa. Africans need to look deeper and closer in their own backyard.

NEED FOR BETTER LEADERSHIP

Development, as imposed upon Africa in the 70s, may have dragged down the continent close to asphyxia. To mention but one symptom, development policies have forced the populations to cultivate exportable goods at the expense of their own needs. It is all a matter of restoring priorities towards restoring the adequacy of needs. How exactly do you do that? Education has a major role to play. In Africa, the arts are pivotal to education at family and community levels. They ought to be given a more central place in the school in Africa. A well balanced education delivers a well balanced person. The measure of poor education across Africa is not often recognised in the deceptive leadership. If Africans are to count upon themselves ultimately, their education must absolutely enhance their creativity and resourcefulness. Performing arts are so inherent in the make-up and modes of expression of the average African child that it would not be an overstatement to claim that leadership skills may depend to some degree upon tailor-made arts education, matched with knowledge and other academic studies.

THE ROLE OF INTELLECTUALS

Unfortunately, the continent has somehow mismanaged its intellectuals. Or is it the other way round? This situation is another sequel of poor education and excessive proximity with the former colonial powers which tend to seek indirect control over minds and resources. It is also natural to follow the example of those who have recorded success, just as it is fair to trust those one considers a friend. Yet, the much blamed corruption practices of African leaders stand as evidence that the intellectuals have failed to deliver. If another way must be found in the short term, any alternative approach is necessarily closer to home. Improvement will be achieved when the intellectual will cease to aspire completing his mental exile by leaving his own people and his own country. Even if the arts are not a panacea, they might certainly assist in restoring some balancing effect in an ongoing process. Not only in the schooling process, but later, in quality, home-grown and flattering artistic performances made available in the African city.

LET AFRICA EXCHANGE WITH AFRICA FIRST

What the economic analysis tends to overlook is the inherent weakness of the individual African country, due to historical factors. It is simply difficult to achieve much alone. African countries need each other. Some believe rightly that a number of the national prerogatives ought to be given up, in order to favour regional entities. If the rich and powerful are pulling resources, why should not fledgling nations pull their resources to survive and improve their economies? But as the doors of the citadel of the rich are closing up, there are two options left for Africa. Either, it grows faster by pulling together with the aim of dealing peacefully with the rich on an equal footing; or, Africans build healthier partnerships with emerging countries like Brazil, India and China. These partnerships are indeed the right thing to do, but as our experiment demonstrates, inter-African exchanges must be developed initially. There again, the arts may be a starting point to build bridges.

Asked recently about how south-south exchange could enhance solidarity, Taib Fassi Fihri, the Moroccan Minister of Foreign Affairs insists that a different form of exchange has become essential. *"It is out of question to remain stuck within a mind-set of assistance and assisted. That is even more so between developing countries. It is more a matter of sharing experiences and knowledge, in order to win together. That takes us away from top-down lesson-giving."* It comforts us to recognise in these words the discourse of our teachings at Castle Arts, in Zimbabwe, in the 1990s. What we then called the 'horizontal method' is precisely about avoiding the top-down approach to learning. The African predicament is so specific that it would be more rewarding to learn from each other. That may not be true for all topics and skills, but the performing arts have a different function and value across sub-Saharan Africa. And then, looking up to the achiever and mimetic practices have not delivered the development prescribed in the books. Better do things in one's own way, and as the Moroccan minister predicts 'win together.'

TECHNOLOGY, DEMOCRACY AND THE ARTS

And that takes us to reflect briefly about what has been recently happening in North Africa. There is a broader debate about democracy in the light of the recent events. The thirst for free expression of the young must be saluted. That is valid not only for individual countries or the North-Africa region, but for the times we live in and the entire world. In my view, technology has a stronger link than we suspect with both the volume and the nature of information. Technology is less concerned with communication as it is with control, markets and power. In this book, we are concerned about genuine human communication and the arts. The young have increasingly been considered a quiet consumer of fascinating technology. It is refreshing to witness a surge of humanity that reduces technology to what it is: a mere tool. Another factor has been downplayed by the commentators. It is the fact that young Africans are leading the way in voicing peacefully what they really want. Not so much protesting about political dictatorship or the price of bread, but, in the broader view against an unfair world. The unfairness in the existing world order needs to be addressed and leaders everywhere are not doing their best fast enough. The peaceful character of the revolutions in Tunisia and Egypt could be seen as a form of fatigue in a climate of extreme violence, in the name of one or another ideology. The young want peace and a decent life. Not abundance, luxury and frantic competition. Freedom does not have a nationality. It is not the cultural

Daniel Labonne

prerogative of a region of the world, certainly not a matter of race. Freedom and peace are human aspirations and the ultimate rewards of civilisations, including the Egyptian, the Persian, the Greek, the Roman and now the European. A final reminder from history: when democracy emerged in the city of Athens, it was not out of a vacuum, or the exclusive premise of enlightened leaders. At the time, leaders were mainly soldiers and invaders. Freedom and free expression were the main concern of the poet and the dramatist. Ideas and values were transmitted in plays; old beliefs were revisited on the stage. The arts were never dissociated from the civilising project. Africa, both in the north and in the south, should remember that the exercise of freedom requires an apprenticeship in a culture of free expression. The theatre and the practice of the arts are most effective in this educational process.

The continent represents 16% of the world population. Inter-African trade represents 10% of all transactions with other parts of the world. What is required is new opportunities and the will to explore these new opportunities. Human resources match natural resources on the African continent. It is a matter of shaking off confusion, more imposed than inherited. We need the arts to open the eyes of the peoples of Africa, so they may develop their faculties to debate and disagree, to immerse in catharsis or dance in solidarity. The reward of free expression and lasting peace lies at the end of this training process.

A LESSON FROM MICHAEL JACKSON

The performing arts inherently teach a lesson; that lesson needs to be taught to the young African. You Are Not Alone, sings Michael Jackson. You are not that poor, either. Provided, we may add, the means to exchange are made to operate. Far from being the dying child, you are the promise of humanity. Remember, you do have something to give to the world and the world has a right to expect your contribution. But the education you receive is so overwhelming with the advance of other high performers, so much stress is placed upon the economic version of life and the media are so relentless in targeting your time and attention. First, you need to learn to give to each other and develop a common language, an artistic and universal language. Based upon our earlier experiment, the older generation must give up the assistance mentality and create the conditions for creativity to be liberated. What does Africa have to offer? Africa has the ability to transform the handicap of a balkanised continent into an integrated whole, and to do so culturally first. Michael Jackson became more assertive when he wrote with Lionel Richie 'We Are The World'. The young African must be taught to fully assume his/her place in the 'we' referred to. The performer Jackson may have been raising the awareness of his peers who dissociated themselves from the poor and hungry. Now is the time for the poor concerned to show responsibility and grow up to take a rightful place among others as equals. What the FACE project stands for is fairly clear: out of all cultural factors, live forms of performing arts in Africa ought to be processed and integrated as a priority in the cultural development process. Performing arts in Africa emerge from the deepest layers of a conscious living experience and they provide unlimited growth potential for the next 50 years of development in Africa.

A LESSON FROM THE PAST 50 YEARS

In a diagnosis over the past 50 years of Africa, published in Africa 24 Magazine, this is what leaders of West Africa have to say. Independence was followed by a decade required to build a state and pull away from colonial empires. Trials and errors were inevitable. Then, there had been drought in Sahel countries, among other calamities, followed by a regime of imposed structural adjustment. Whatever the type of leadership and whatever the region, each African country was slowed down because of these factors. Industry had to take over some ground from agriculture; a vision of the future had to be formulated and tested out from year 0. The young nation tended to follow and trust the former colonising power. Yet, when the economic health failed to improve, it could not be exclusively the fault of the patient... When the political pupil failed to

Daniel Labonne

deliver, the former master used its powerful press to cast blame. One thing is now clear, after 50 years: *'the best remedy for Africa in this persisting situation of under-development is this: Africans must themselves invent their own tools to achieve development,'* says Aghatan Ag Alhassane, Minister of Agriculture of Mali. *'We are still on the look out to identify genuine landmarks of the African nations'* adds Desire Adada, the Benin Minister of Communications. Time being relative and the African situation being quite unique, it takes at least 50 years for each African country to have a good grip on all development issues. But the last word must be given to the honorary President of the African Development Bank, Babacar Ndiaye. *'I consider myself a citizen of Africa and Senegal is my village!'* That analysis from a technocrat who has touched the nerves of African economies, somehow tallies with our experiment with the arts. But is the analysis that drastically different? The last 50 years point towards the necessity to reduce nationalistic claims, to adopt a more modest approach at a national level and to seek regional integration in order to enable the (so far) handicapped child to take its rightful place at the table of a healthier and fairer human family.

INTEGRATION MATTERS TO AFRICANS

Paradoxically, more than a century ago, the continent had more or less been one integrated region, albeit with its earlier tensions and conflicts. It could be argued that the arbitrary split up of the African continent following 250 years of the slave trade had slowed down the development of Africa, long enough for other regions to seek and achieve their respective development and integration. It would be pointless to investigate intent; the time is also gone to pull out the blame card again. It is easier to acknowledge that underneath the layer of relatively recent awareness of being Nigerian or Rwandan, there is a strong cultural undercurrent which provides a silent conviction of being equally African. This two-tier identity felt by the individual African is astonishingly present in the attitude of those who have for centuries exploited the African continent: they tend to treat all black Africans as being one group, irrespective of their nationality, their physical distinctions and their cultural differences. Regional integration is therefore not only an economic necessity; in the case of sub-Saharan Africa, it amounts to repairing a damage done by history and restoring a cultural if not a natural order. The performing arts could expose to an audience of hundreds of millions how interesting their human drama has been, so far. Television will become in the mid-term an important player in the work of FACE.

CHEIKH ANTA DIOP AND NKRUMAH

Our claim is that a healing process for economies in Africa will also be cultural. In the 1960s, Cheikh Anta Diop restored a lot of truth about the role of Africa in the history of human civilisations. Thanks to his academic work, he invited the whole world to look differently at black cultures. He used Greek literature in his doctorate thesis to demonstrate that Egyptians were Black Africans. Therefore, the first sophisticated civilisation was African, geographically and racially. What Cheick Anta Diop did with his books and academic work was pushed inside the political arena by Kwame Nkrumah who became the apostle of panafricanism. Nkrumah was a child of the Cold War. So, is it a surprise that he sought to support his political efforts with Marxist theories? His analysis, in the independence years, was inevitably antagonistic. It was for him a matter of denouncing colonial imperialism in order to favour African unity. To some extent, the strength of his rhetoric has permeated the decades and cast a shadow of fear over what could otherwise be seen as a positive form of regional integration of the African continent.

In reality, everyone would have benefitted from integrated Africa capable of feeding its population and guarantee peace and security across the continent. New partners of Africa have rapidly taken the vacant seats left by those who had abandoned a divided Africa to its own fate, as they focussed upon their own problems and their own efforts towards regional integration. China, India and Brazil have realised the untapped potential of the continent and the paralysis in which Africa had

Daniel Labonne

been left, afflicted with natural and man-made calamities, weakened by poor governance and debt, stigmatised for endemic corruption and widespread disease. What Africa needs is genuine friendship from partners and trustworthy infrastructures. Our own experiment is distinct from the political analysis of Nkrumah or the revolutionary knowledge of Cheikh Anta Diop. In a much more modest approach to problem solving, we simply advocate that in all human undertakings, culture and the arts underpin all sustained efforts towards sublimating the worse hardships and the most precious of gifts - life itself. As a human group, possibly more than any other, Africans have taken a clear option in assuming an existence centred upon the celebration of cycles of life, the environment and social practices. Performing arts remains imbedded in the life of the community in these celebrations and rituals. Survival may have rewarded this cultural strategy. That strategy may just have to be taken further, to respond to the needs of the times.

AFRICA READY TO SHARE

In a world of mistrust and global surveillance, would it not be healthy to devise new methods of sharing our differences in creative ways? It seems to me that Africa is not seeking to save the world. Nor is it interested in conquering new territory. The facts demonstrate that the opposite is true. A saturated world is indirectly seeking new forms of refuge on African renewable soil. The practice of renting African soil to cultivate and guarantee food security to foreign populations is becoming a modern economic phenomenon. Is there any sign of a new war to reject this practice, while Africa can hardly feed its own children? Yet again, African generosity (some would say naivety) and readiness to trust (some would say gullibility) are being confirmed. It matters that Africans may peacefully devise the means to educate each other in order to develop a cultural coherence, to support and sustain their cultural development. As the world faces new challenges, there is a degree of urgency in allocating time, space and means for an untold story to unfold. The most trustworthy medium for that purpose is the performing arts. Ultimately, confidence and performance depend on this process.

FACE proposes to raise awareness widely and find the means locally to fulfil the need to liberate vital creativity in a development process that must positively favour and develop the generosity of African peoples who may have been underestimated or misunderstood. That is mainly due to the fact that nobody was listening and there has been a culture of secrecy. Nobody loses in the process, because it is not about competition, cultural superiority or snatching markets. It is primarily about allowing Africa to speak to Africa about Africa, until the discourse is coherent and, preferably, enjoyable.

To execute this very intimate operation, empower the performer.

Daniel Labonne

PART 5

For Africa, the Future is Now

SEEKING AN AFRICAN SOLUTION

A close observer of the decades of my own field study and artistic work in the theatre both in Mauritius and in Africa has long concluded in those terms: 'In what you have been doing, there is nothing wrong, except that you have been ahead of your time.' I accept this analysis as a handicapped person affected by foresight... Too much of it! In reality, my obsession with responding to needs springs from a deeper urge to be useful to my peers, or a frustration from earlier days as an educator. But the messenger matters less than the message. In the case of the ACTPA Project in the early 1990's, the message was about addressing real needs for real people. If people do not live from bread alone, in the case of needy African communities, what other need had so far gone unnoticed? It takes real time for a message to be clearly formulated and heard. It takes more time for vast territories to realise what they have in common and recognise the interface in their marked differences. The efforts were the more strenuous because it meant swimming against the tide, attempting reconciliation between arbitrarily divided nations. Not only because modern geography turned a Ghanaian into a foreigner to an Ivorian, although they may belong to the same culture; but the education inherited from colonial times tended to divorce the child from his forebears. There are vested interests in consolidating these relatively new systems while, with others, I was trying to build bridges and repair damages. Building bridges in Africa sometimes involves positive action within borders, as very different cultures might find themselves trapped within the same arbitrary borders. To a large extent, the political divide in Côte d'Ivoire in the 21st century must be attributed to this border system imposed a little more than 100 years ago.

But somebody had to do something, preferably with an African solution for a persistently damaging issue across Sub-Saharan Africa. By the time the 'Guidelines For an Inter-African School for Performing Artists' was produced in 1987, famine, wars, disease and debts were plaguing the continent. Leadership across Africa posed a serious problem although history is likely to find mitigating factors in the corruptive practices of investors. Human greed for power in the young states and fast regroupings in world politics were other factors. At the same time, technology and erratic economies left untrained leaders off balance. Time also matters in allowing a people to develop an immune system against inherited values and imposed order in a competitive environment. History may end up finding mitigating factors - hopefully in great drama plays! - For these African leaders who underwent the same inadequate education, then suffered the pressure of external politics and corruptive methods. To the outside world, the obsession of the press to show dying children and yet another corrupt villain from 'the cursed continent' certainly acted as a turn-off.... In such conditions, how difficult to project an optimistic vision and shift the focus over to the arts, from dying children to healthy Africans with a story to celebrate! But then, the question of need objectively dwarfs all other considerations. Only time will tell, I wrote in 1993.

TIME TO TELL THE AFRICAN STORY

Well, time is now telling and we seem to have reached the future. The signs are there that change is affecting Africa in the most unsuspecting positive ways. The Observer (20.02.11), Ian Burrell echoes the good news: *"The Economist revealed last month that six of the 10 most rapidly expanding economies over the past decade were in sub-Saharan Africa. Heading the list was Angola, transformed by the oil boom from war-torn wreck to the world's fastest-growing nation. The others were Ethiopia, Nigeria, Chad, Mozambique and Rwanda."* Unbelievable! Angola, fastest-growing nation in the world? Ethiopia, cleared of the horrific images of hunger-stricken children that left such a lasting impact on the minds? Rwanda, where only yesterday, neighbours were butchering neighbours? Suddenly, it is no longer the story of an exceptional success that confirms the depressing rule. No, writes the Economist, six out of ten rapidly expanding economies in the whole world are indeed from Sub-Saharan Africa. Time has been healing many, many wounds. But the healing process has only just begun and it is being measured in economic terms. However, the transformation is strong enough for the Observer to herald a warning in its title: IT IS TIME THE WORLD LISTENED TO NEW STORIES OUT OF AFRICA. Note the use of the key word 'time.' Note the warning to the world which had been obsessed for too long about a hopeless continent. Note as well the invitation to change both tone and content about what Africa really stands for. In the specific context of this book, let us retain the key phrase 'the world listened to new stories.' First, it is about a change of attitude on behalf of the 'customers of doom.' But, who is going to tell these stories? No doubt, both the Economist and the Observer are thinking about their own respective readerships. Beyond, there is the admission that the press forms public opinion worldwide and that such opinion has been deliberately damaging to Africa and Africans. I also read an admission that for too long, the stories out of Africa have been digging further "the gulf between the West's perception and the reality of modern Africa." In the context of our own innovative work in cultural development, it makes no doubt that any attempt to correct the poor image of Africa, or to suggest self-help schemes that were not dreamed of in foreign charity boardrooms were not welcomed.

From the early research done both in Africa and outside the continent, I would contend that the African story can only be told by Africans themselves. At least in an initial phase, if only because so many have tried to interpret their own limited understanding of what is in reality a complex kaleidoscope of 54 nations. The well-intended storytellers are often romantic; on the other side of the spectrum, both the journalist and the charity worker feed upon signs of death and decay. The despot and villain, from one African country or another, has been a long, sad soap-opera that has lasted for more than one generation. Africans themselves do share part of the responsibility, as there has been a failure to attend to the collective image of Africa and Africans in the world. One personality and one event have done enormous good in this sensitive area: Nelson Mandela towers the Kilimanjaro in everyone's perception. The last Football World Cup organised in South Africa has greatly

Daniel Labonne

repaired the image of Africa as a place worth respect and serious investment. So much for the world of politics and sports which produced a man of exception and one punctual event of global dimension! It is time for 'experts,' development workers, wild-life observers and romantics are given the seats of spectators, while Africans from all over the continent are invited to move upstage in order to reveal the deeper meanings of the long story of Africa.

Enter the performing artist, stage right.

THE PERFORMER, THE YOUNG AND THE ARCHITECT

The onus is on Africans themselves to assume responsibility and to take the initiatives, as we did in 1984 when the founder members from some 15 countries set up the Union of African Performing Artists. To respond to the challenge posed by the newspaper article, the buck stops with Africans to find original ways of formulating and delivering the African story. First among themselves, from Africans to fellow Africans, by devising the most creative approach to unique circumstances. That is partly what we mean by the term 'exchange.' It is both a duty and it is a challenge as put by IKENA CARREIRA of Azimuth consultancy, Angola: *"The challenge in Africa is to create."* She is not from the world of arts, but her remarks are relevant. She means that economic development is by all means crucial and more than welcomed. But again, it is about the whole continent and the whole person. It would offend nobody to describe the African continent as possibly the most 'holistic' of all continents. One is referring here to culture more than geography or industry. There is the uninterrupted, yet largely untaught history of Africa; there is also the unavoidable reality of the richest continent in terms of mineral and human resources. That is why the young prosperous Angolan woman is, incidentally, responding directly to a process contained in the title of my long study a decade ago, 'Development Through Creativity.'

Having survived human mobility, having suffered the slave trade, having outlived colonialism, having locked itself up culturally, having been bled by multinationals, civil wars and corrupt leaders, having resisted to moral and economic disintegration, having undergone discrimination then an ongoing bashing in the recent decades, having exported some of its best brains and talents, the continent is emerging finally from slumber and a sea of ignorance. Only an original approach, distinct from any mimetic recipe, would do. That is where our experiment with the performing arts points in a direction yet untested elsewhere.

The real story of Africa will be one of youth and unlimited energy, not retrograde attitudes and helplessness. First, reminds Sipho Moyo. Africa director of ONE in South Africa, it is about unlimited human energy: *"The real untold story about Africa is one... of the restless energy of Africa's youth - who make 70% of the continent's population.* " Imagine what such an enormous outburst of human resource on the ground could do, if matched with the mineral resources underground! Bono, the Irish performing artist and committed anti-poverty campaigner, is all excited about the African dawn after having witnessed such a long painful slumber. *"But (here's) the thing that excites me more in thinking about Africa's future - as the continent of the 21st century. It's one of the richest continents on Earth in terms of natural resources. If these resources are allowed to benefit the people above the ground, then they can pay for Africa's future."* Bono was being interviewed by John Mulholand. Again, without being aware of the experiment we conducted in the performing arts, Bono the performer and the South African Sipho Moyo are giving real meaning to my concept of the *Diamond Theory*. The fact is that times have changed and we have now entered the future of Africa, in the 21st century. Such an age would be meaningless if it were measured in dollars only. It would be rudderless unless it is accompanied by the real and full story told by performers, poets, architects. Unless the abundance underground is matched with lasting structures over-ground.

Daniel Labonne

ENTER THE ARCHITECT (stage left)

These structures would in turn shelter a cultural statement that, so far, has been stifled or muddled. The narrative left for too long to external vested interest and the introverted villager must finally find a deserving place in the limelight. Telling such a complex story from the early consciousness of humankind to the age of the mobile phone, may take an exciting number of decades. It would involve the full blessings of the guardians of the 'secret realm.' It would be meaningless without the creative energy of the young. Experience has shown that to depend upon central government or donor agencies foster misunderstandings and deliver white elephants. The performer as mediator has a key role to play in enabling the narrative to remain both authentic and exciting for the world to see and hear. Money will be a vital element.

Curtains up on FACE - Foundation for Arts, Creativity & Exchange.

NEW FRIENDS OF AFRICA

FACE is presented to the reader as a pragmatic approach to problem-solving. First, training and education provide the soundest foundation in the life of a human being by equipping the needy unprepared young person with the teaching enabling him to use a rod to fish with for a lifetime, to refer to a famous Chinese piece of wisdom. The Foundation would collect the active goodwill that favours an alternative to assistance and dependency. Money being a chronic problem, a monetary solution must be devised to address the issue and one has to begin somewhere. The focus must remain on equipping the young so that past mistakes may be avoided and the teething problems of young nations deliver their own lessons. But somehow, the arts in general and performing arts, in particular, must play a more substantial role in the formal education of the young. That cannot depend upon a single book or 'a unique experiment.' The interplay between arts, creativity and exchange supported with independent funding and expert guidance ought to ensure a healthier future for the young. FACE simply reconcile the various steps of the entire experiment: it was essentially about the vitality of performing arts as preserved and practised by Africans south of the Sahara; 'exchange' underpins both the method of training the performer and the key principle that may end the isolation of pseudo nations which have never been offered opportunities to discover or like each other. Finally, creativity is not only a vital human attribute; it is the most viable response to mimetic attitudes, emigration, poor leadership and the much blamed propensity to fall prey to the corruptive forces that plague Africa.

Another old English proverb is still valid: a friend in need is a friend in deed. Such should be the plain assessment of the role of China in the last decade or two across the continent of Africa. I am rather well placed to appreciate the adequacy of the pragmatism in Africa's recent leap in development, having spent years in building a workable partnership to sustain meaningful cultural development around the performing arts. To those who criticise China, mainly among the rich countries of the North, this is what the UK Observer has to say: *"China stands accused by some of conducting a new colonial war, ripping the mineral heart out of Africa. But many Africans don't see it that way and are grateful for the huge amount of money that will help lead their own economic recovery - roads, bridges, schools, hospitals. China's investment is changing the face of Africa..."* (Editorial. The Observer, 20.02.11). Can we detect regret or is it jealousy in these dramatic terms? Is that really a war or an act of interested friendship between consenting economic partners? Is that 'ripping out the mineral heart of Africa' or is it clearing finally the arteries so the choking continent may breathe through? As far as we are concerned, friends can only give what they are willing to give, so long as the giving responds to need. Infrastructure is what China is able to provide and it is doing so at such an accelerated pace, namely with one million Chinese workers currently toiling across Africa. What China cannot provide is the deeper motives and the meaningful displays that

Daniel Labonne

must underpin the stories out of Africa. These will come from Africans themselves and the pace imposed by 'friendly' China demands that we get our act together. Africans like Fred Swaniker from African Leadership Academy in South Africa, has understood that *"We need to create our own entrepreneurs and our own talent. "* Note the expression 'create our own talent.' There is a balance to be found between skills, organisation and innovation within a given time frame. Then Swaniker adds that Africans have hardly any reason to be wary about China, if only because it feels and looks like solidarity more than exploitation. *"I believe Africa is where China was 30 years ago."* Africa knows about both exploitation and patience. It should be given credit for discerning the benefit between old friends and new friends.

Imagine what it would be like 30 years from now, with China as an economic superpower and Africans growing in confidence and respect. The missing link to a successful future is 'self-expression.' Not the political meaning given to free-speech, nor the sort of palaver attributed to village squabbles in traditional African settings; but the healthy and creative vigour that anybody picks out from observing closely an African dancer. There again, the pace imposed by 'friendly China' must be matched with an equivalent pace coming from deep within the cultures of Africa. The road, bridges, schools and hospitals could be expected to be matched with high standards displayed in the theatre, dance, opera and film. The early efforts of Nollywood, in Nigeria, are indicating that Africans have not been waiting for aid in this sector. Where 'development funding' failed the ACTPA Project, entrepreneurship has paid off with film production in Nigeria and Ghana. *"In terms of entertainment... we may not have the equipment which developed countries have but we are doing well, "* says Adoga Ibrahim, political Adviser in Nigeria, satisfied that a cinema enterprise is growing fast and African creativity is taking on real meaning as people watch Nollywood films in many parts of the world. In a very conscious effort, Africa must build on the early successes of this budding industry. What is required is adequate training, production skills, management techniques, stage artistry, convincing originality and definite styles 'Made in Africa.' Such cultural development does not happen overnight and without the right place to host the new products. Above all, the right means will determine the ends. Whereby the need to get the funding structure right and ascertain that the resources underground are made to glitter when they surface under the African sunshine.

Africa needs to take a long inward look at what feeds up from the roots, the many deep roots of millennia. Then, it must translate in modern urbanised forms the numerous preserved performing arts. It involves an inventory, a display with the involvement of the traditional performer, a study of each form in a dialogue with the modern performer and finally the devising of the most appropriate treatment of valuables within the tradition and practices. The process of exchange would ensure any one form of performing arts is not treated in isolation. It is not about modernising for its own sake. Cross-fertilisation from a comparative study with high standards expected as an outcome, would ensure that each experiment becomes an education that flatters the culture at source and feeds into the community at large. It is about growing up into mature nations with something to give. Giving is very much a fundamental quality of the hospitable peoples of the continent.

There again, the process of converting the traditional into modern stage productions may benefit from the past 50 years of similar experience in the vast territories and varied arts forms of China. But African performing artists must take the initiatives, trust themselves and believe in their own rich heritage. Then, they must apply the most effective methodologies that would allow the most powerful narrative expected out of Africa. Some of these methodologies had been identified and demonstrated in Mauritius during one experiment in 1988. Neither the treatment, nor the process should come from China, although in circus arts, for instance, there would be much to learn from Chinese performers. However, in due course, there could always be an input for the construction with the right architecture for *'drummas'* at the heart of

Daniel Labonne

the African City. That is precisely why a structure such as FACE is needed, initially, to raise awareness and raise the seed money. In order to make sure that form, content and delivery may become a source of pride and gratifying development for African cities.

But possibly, a closer cultural link exists already with other partner countries like Brazil which might find an obvious interest in FACE and its enterprise in the cultural development of Sub-Saharan Africa. Should, for example, a country like Mozambique or Angola take over from where Zimbabwe left the experiment, no doubt Brazil would even feel more comfortable.

A ROLE FOR BRAZIL

Brazil is making a clear commitment towards playing an active role in the development of Africa. While China strictly looks after its self-interest in economic exchanges that still leaves African countries endowed with much needed infrastructures, Brazil sees a deeper and historic connection with Africa and Africans. For Brazil, it is not economic interests exclusively and it is less a matter of cold calculation, more cultural affinities to future exchanges with Africa. Africans cannot yet believe their good fortune than to have an able and willing 'cousin' making offers and extending a friendly hand. We heard the message from President Lula, echoed by the new Brazilian head of state. In my view, Brazil would be the best partner in the cultural development that advocates the empowering of the performer in sub-Saharan Africa.

Yet, Africa must focus upon relying upon itself. It could achieve that by remaining totally committed to generating its own vision and charting out its own progress; by refraining from asking, opting instead for workable structures that may accommodate the goodwill of new and old friends; by opting for entrepreneurship, no longer relying on governmental initiatives or donor dictates; finally, by refusing to ape other cultures and other successes out of Africa... That is exactly a role that FACE, the Foundation for Arts, Creativity & Exchange, offers to play.

A new vision for a new mission requires a new provision of money. Again, the key role of the African Development Bank in the economic sector must be recognised. But it remains first a bank, then an intergovernmental body with the political and clumsiness that mega structures involve. Yet, a bridge needs to be built between economy and culture. FACE would need to educate the decision makers within Africa. Easier said than done. With economically strong Brazil claiming a cultural link not with one country, but the continent of Africa, it is therefore right that Brazil is invited to take its place around the table so it may play a role in the funding of a strategic plan for the cultural development of Africa. The earlier the better.

That strategic plan integrates the cultural within the economic, the social and the environmental. It views culture as a source of growth, not an impediment for Africans. Sure, a man needs food, shelter and health to survive. But man does not live from bread alone and, to a large extent the human spirit carries the body. A new balance ought to be found between the basic needs of the mortal and the full potential of the social being. The plan places an unusual player at the heart of the vision of the future of the African continent. It gives a powerful voice to the voiceless stuck in the role of victim for the past 250 years. It mobilizes and channels fresh energies in the most positive thrust. It augurs yet unsuspected adventures of the mind and of real peoples. It advocates a creative approach to enhance cohabitation and sharing. Brazil would bring into the equation three other dimensions:

1. the notion of an African Diaspora that includes fractions of populations from other continents and island states;
2. the notion of history that has over two and a half centuries disseminated African populations and cultures;
3. the geographical dimension, whereby Africa has long been much more than the contour of one continent.

Brazil is a friend indeed because it recognizes the historical role of Africa in its own economic development. Brazil is extending a helping hand, not

Daniel Labonne

in assistance, in a partnership rooted in the past but necessarily projected deep into the future. By accepting the extended hand, African partners would find themselves in a rare comfort zone conducive to innovative work and unsuspected progress. In contrast to dealing with earlier partners of Africa, a healthy Brazil-Africa connection would rely upon the performing arts. Samba has helped in the development of the Brazilian personality; Brazilian football has displayed the playfulness and creativity that have developed the game itself. Is it really a coincidence that the national team of France look so multicultural? Brazil's is a success story of cross-breeding. The former president of France, General De Gaulle, once proclaimed 'L'avenir est au métissage' (the future rests on mixed-race offspring). In that respect and for so many reasons, FACE would welcome a strong partnership with Brazil.

In the words and deeds of ex. President Lula, there is no doubt whatsoever of the good faith and the clear commitment of Brazil towards Africa. There is a lot to rejoice and be hopeful for. And one way to rejoice and express the hope of what President Lula calls the 're-encounter' would be to give pragmatic relevance to this different model of cooperation. *"Today we are united for the future. Brazil - not just me - took a political decision to make a re-encounter with the African continent... Brazil would not be what it is today without the participation of millions of Africans who helped build our country... Whoever comes after me has the moral, political and ethical obligation to do much more..."* (President Lula da Silva of Brazil) It is right to grab the extended hand of friendship and begin to translate the rapport in cultural and artistic language. The re-connection is not nostalgic or loaded with some recrimination based upon anger and settling of scores against others. It is an unprecedented offer to look together in the same direction, deep into the future. This new distant ally has grown in economic power and status without denying its roots and without denying the weaker members of the extended cultural family. At least 50% of the population of Brazil claim African roots. FACE would benefit greatly from the support of

Brazilian NGOs and private corporations, whether they operate in Africa or not.

FACE PROMOTES CULTURAL DEVELOPMENT AND THE PERFORMING ARTS

It responds to the most acute need in terms of ensuring lasting benefits in cultural development for Sub-Saharan Africa. First, to raise appropriate funds that African arts and culture deserve in the 21st century; to raise such money from private and corporate sources to ensure lasting benefits, from the guardian of tradition to the average urban citizen; to provide an alternative to the precariousness of event-funding, like sporadic festivals, that tend to export the best and depress the rest; to establish an independent form of funding that assists government initiatives and motivates individual creativity; to keep clear of central government dictates and encourage self-expression; to avoid aid and aim for trade; to educate the young and form the taste of a growing number of spectators; to familiarise the communities with the arts forms from neighbouring countries; to aim for quality and lasting impact of each artistic production. Above all, to ensure the most appropriate training that empowers the performer. Quality, regularity and originality would point towards a growing number of spectators, local, regional and international. There lies the future of a narrative out of Africa, thanks to performing artists. It matters that, from the outset, a roof is placed over the head of the 'empowered performer.' His task will not be easy, but it will be at least as useful as the glorified economist. It is also about giving value, generating economic activities, supplying quality leisure and attracting visitors while educating them the African way. In 1990, ATEX had been treated with suspicion when we advocated the need to organise 'Diaspora Courses' in which the rich visitor would visit Castle Arts in Bulawayo to learn from different African performing coaches. It was a deliberate measure to create revenue and to end dependency... But the African performer was simply expected to be content with grants that came with all the strings that kept him dancing to very strange tunes, indeed...

The morality from another piece of wisdom applies: you can't expect your friends to guess your needs, unless you identify them and begin addressing them first. In French, 'Aide-toi et le ciel t'aidera.' But cultural development must have an economic impact. While quality leisure and complementary education would be delivered to the urban local crowd in the *drumma* at the heart of the African city, tourists should be able to visit in increasing numbers. Incidentally, a tourist is not necessarily somebody travelling from the Northern hemisphere or the Far East. One may first expect regular artistic exchanges between neighbouring countries. For that reason, neighbours would learn to discover and appreciate each other. That is a pre-condition to peaceful relations. Before the ATEX experiments at the Castle Arts in Bulawayo, how many Zimbabweans had seen an Ethiopian dancer or a Mauritian actor on stage?

Is he still dreaming, might the reader ask? The reply comes from the Observer again: "*By the end of this decade, there are expected to be at least 7 cities, among them Dakar in Senegal, Rabat in Morocco and Kano in Nigeria, with consumer markets worth more than $10bn each.... the continent's economy will grow in average annual rate of 7% over the next two decades - faster even than China's.* " Faster than China, you may ask sceptically? Whereby, if one chooses carefully one's friends, they should not mind if occasionally one overtakes them in some sectors. One such sector in which Africa has been well equipped to excel would be the performing arts. What the earlier experiment has demonstrated is clear: there is no need to duplicate what others have been doing; there is no need to look for models outside the shores of the African continent; there is no point trying to compete with rich university departments or prestigious national institutions that depend upon central government funding. It would take decades for Africans to simply familiarise with what they could learn from each other's dances, songs, dramatic games, masks, gymnastics and oral traditions. Cross-fertilisation is the process to be trusted in both training and production, using 'exchange' as an aesthetics at the *drumma*.

Should anybody still have any doubt, just look at China and the excellence of Chinese staged art forms, after 30 years or more of internal cultural experimentation.

TREAT THE PERFORMING ARTS AS RAW MATERIAL

In 2008, Africa has exported $393bn of gas, oil and minerals. Natural resources accounted for one quarter of Africa's growth. These are reassuring figures and certainly a bill of health that demonstrates to what extent the whole continent has been recovering in twenty years. There are two points to be made to enlighten the decision makers who still harbour some doubts about a major scheme with the arts at its core. First, the TIMING is right to invest in people, to glorify their resilience and to liberate the creativity of the peoples of Africa. Secondly, African peoples are unique in this respect that they have treasured their forms of performing arts scrupulously - some would say religiously. To that extent, the dances, the open rituals and participatory forms of performance should be considered another form of raw material, to be valued as highly as the mineral deposits in African soil. That is where the DIAMOND THEORY takes its relevance. The performing arts are deeply rooted within the fabric of the living all across Africa. Actually, the arts form the surest bridge between the worlds of the living and the dead. To live is to be able to sing and dance. Together. Because society has its own traditional way of constant massaging, using what glues people together: the performing arts often symbolised by the drum in grass-root Africa.

In my evaluation of the experiment at the University of London, within the context of theatre studies, I was invited to coin a word to describe the novelty of what I am advocating with respect to ancient practice. I was very tempted to make the case of the *Griot*, as the traditional storyteller and crowd entertainer. I chose to educate without scaring off

Daniel Labonne

the people of goodwill ready to understand the complexity of an unusual continent which happens to have a different concept of time itself. I proposed the word *Drumma* to make the point that the drum lies at the core of Ancient Greek drama, therefore of the perception of modern theatre. First, African performing arts precede Ancient Greece, through Egyptian civilisation and its earlier migration from the South, from the Kush civilisation (modern Sudan). Secondly, time is of the essence. There is a key element within all forms of theatre anywhere that takes us back to the elementary sound of the drum, echoing the human heart and calling upon our common humanity. Time is suspended when the play begins. There has never been but one single character in all plays ever performed. That character is Man, but man conceived in symbiotic representation with the drum, in a celebration of all senses. Various names, roles and circumstances are incidental and they only serve to confirm the uniqueness of mankind. To that extent, the theatre is a vital exercise of collective recognition of the *oneness* of society. The spiritual dimension has never been driven out of the art of theatre, either. In Shakespeare, Racine or Arthur Miller, death remains the preferred game of the theatre artist. Death unifies all human beings and, in all religions, it restores a bridge to a creator. In Africa, the drum restores the link vertically between the world of the living above ground and the world of the ancestors, below ground. *Drumma* is therefore the game that ignites intelligence and consciousness, this unique premise of humans, compared to other creatures. But even then, with the skin of an animal and the hollowed trunk of a trunk, the drum restores the ecological foundation of life that unifies nature, animal, plant, living, dead and the Bigger Spiritual Unknown.

Time has come, in the long awaited awakening of the sleeping continent, to celebrate in the most appropriate forms, the eternal values of *drumma*. To reject the image of poverty once and for all and replace it with the life affirming vigour that permeates African performing arts. It is right to explain and express the depth and richness of African peoples in live representations through dance, drama, masks, costumes and social games. Finally, who remembers the names of rulers of Classical Athens in the years 480-406 BC? No doubt, a lot more people would immediately react to the name of Euripides. Remember what he did for a living? His task during the 74 years of his life: dramatist. In other words, he wrote for the stage, to educate his contemporaries with actors and singers and grant lasting meaning to the vibrant experiments of his city. When all will be gone, the arts will remain. First give the arts its proper place.

A CENTRE, A SCHOOL OR A THEATRE?

FACE will have to get architects and economists involved to find the right answer to the needs and cultural traits of each individual city. Those like me who had been involved in the earlier experiment may keep a modest role if and when required in the future. What really matters is, on one hand, the agent of change and progress - the performer; on the other hand, is the intended beneficiary - the young whose education must be impacted by an empowered performer in Africa. Will the transmission of knowledge and know-how occur in a training centre, in the school or in a new concept of theatre building? That will depend upon the economic means made available and very obviously upon the political will.

The Union of African performing Artists (UAPA), formed in 1984, instructed me to study a school project that could admit and train Africans from all parts and all language groupings. The founding members came mainly from the theatre. I had to devise ways means to remain faithful to a challenging and difficult brief. The results subsequently took the form of training programmes devised for practitioners. The project could not have been an institute, or another university. The rather colourless term 'centre' was given some substance and gathered consensus. But it had relevance as it brought to one central place very dispersed individuals constrained for too long within their own 'islands.' What surprised everyone was the spectacular apparition of the Castle Arts, in Bulawayo, Zimbabwe. The African Theatre Exchange (ATEX) then delivered as promised a host country and a venue for the centre to take root. The funding agencies suddenly became worried. Why? Was it because they are not used to serious work undertaken by artists or Africans delivering concrete results? Was it because the usual condescension towards dependent poor people in constant need, suddenly seemed hollow? When from Sierra Leone, one of the resource persons selected by ATEX, arrived at Castle Arts in 1990 for the first pilot course, he was moved and felt rather overwhelmed. He turned to me and said: '*I do not know what you said to the government of Zimbabwe, Brother, but this place feels like something of a mirage!* ' What he meant was that, far from being a wasteful dreamer myself, I had actually delivered an impossible dream shared by many other fellow performing artists, like him.

But he was right: it was almost too good to be true. For that, the government of Zimbabwe deserves exceptional credit for having listened to the plea of performers and to have responded by handing out the keys so that real artists from all over Africa may meet, exchange and create. They were not disappointed and there are many records of the satisfaction expressed by the host country and all other observers. However, records demonstrate that the sponsors were panicking. I was informally told that they would have preferred a floating event like The African Symposium Workshop in Mauritius, in 1988. But a solid complex, well maintained, a self-contained venue as I had described in the earlier Guidelines, ready to go in Africa? A castle in the then beleaguered Southern Africa? Development was taking too concrete a meaning for the sellers of the unreachable dreams of development from the richer parts of the world... We were only doing our job and we had simply delivered what we had promised: a venue suitable for a unique undertaking. The performing arts of Africa had suddenly found a home after centuries in the wilderness.

All of this in less than a year? With minimal funding carefully timed so that 'short term objectives are met on a project-basis only?' Without any direct supervision from 'foreign experts?' Too much! That could only be either a covert cultural plot or unacceptable arrogance... Thus, the Castle Arts became a victim of its own success. But the world is a complex place and no doubt artists will always be astonished to find out how vicious the real world can be...

FACE is therefore the refusal to give in to negative forces and a determination to remain creative and faithful to the exceptional spirit that prompted the Union African Performing Artists, way back in 1984. That same spirit brought about the mobilisation of decades of limited but effective resources; it resulted in the 'miracle' of Castle Arts emerging in the middle of Southern Africa. The performing arts of Africa deserved nothing less than a home worth of Castle Arts. Since the Castle Arts has been withdrawn unfairly from the passionate and hopeful artists who arrived from West, East, North and South Africa, it would be right to establish a FACE Theatre in each part of Africa. Ultimately, as Africa grows economically, we would advocate that each city in Africa conceives and builds its own FACE Theatre.

In the future, the 'drumma' would be a landmark building at the heart of the African city. It must inspire pride, confidence and belonging. It would fulfil multiple purposes: training centre, performance venue, processing plant and production site for the stage (television and recording studio?). Also available on site, post-production services. Provision must be made to study, research, collect and display live forms of performance. Activities should include craft and fashion workshops, as well as exhibitions. Selected products and services would be for sale in the commercial section. Eventually, the venue should welcome visitors to a museum on the most appropriate theme. It should be able to host and accommodate a visiting troupe with a stage performance from a neighbouring country. It should attract the tourist visitor who wishes to be entertained or learn a maximum, within a pleasant environment... First, it should hold enough knowledge and entertainment for schools and students to become regular customers. It matters that the 'drumma' remains professionally managed with an independent status. Above all,

Daniel Labonne

the *'drumma'* must be seen as the home of the performer in an ongoing process of empowerment.

Given the means, FACE would implement the promises of the earlier experiments at the Castle Arts. It would apply the process of exchange in many ways: in its training methodology, in its touring programmes, in its North-South partnerships, in its original productions. Above all, it would process the variety of raw materials available from across the continent, with a view to giving value, developing an aesthetic and boosting the cultural industry of Africa. Who knows? There might even be one day a unique type of performance Made-in-Africa known as 'Exchange Theatre'...

THE AMERICAN EXAMPLE

Again, should anybody still doubt the feasibility of such an enterprise, claiming that you can't treat 'tribal culture' or valorise what even the urban African would consider 'bad taste,' let's not turn this time to the Greek example... Let's remind people of the extraordinary function given to the cinema, as an art form, by the American people in their soul-searching experiments during the first half of the 20th century. Let us remind their wonderful ability to glamorise the unwashed, uncivilised, lawless behaviour of the lonely homeless ranger of the Wild West. Culture is not only the main export of the US today, the perception of America is largely tributary to the narrative developed thanks to the harnessing of cinema technique, production and distribution. My contention has been crystal clear: what America did with cinema, Africa can do the same with live performing arts.

Another important factor in the major cultural development Americans were able to translate into reality lies in the enterprise culture. Creativity works best when there is no direct link with political power. The funding of the arts must therefore remain clear of interference and preferably private. In so doing, it increases the responsibility of the performer and it provides a balance view to the trusting spectator. Should yet another example prove necessary from America and the world of the performing arts, FACE would need to find inspiration from the exceptional cultural enterprise called 'Motown' which attracted, groomed, produced raw talents who often migrated from the conservative South to the fast developing auto-city of Detroit in the 1950's and 1960's. The world owes to this enterprise the genius of such performers like Aretha Franklin who otherwise might have remained confined to her old parish church. Michael Jackson would not have graced the floors of global stages with his particular style of singing, dancing and mixing (exchanging?) genres. He did so for an ever-growing audience worldwide until his death, aged 50. With hindsight, it only took the abilities of one entrepreneur, Barry Gordy, so the North and the South of this vast and rich country may put resources to good use - human, training, opportunity, production, money. The other crucial factor again: timing was right. Modern popular music worldwide has never been the same after Gordy and Motown.

ARTS AND CREATIVITY IN THE AFRICAN SCHOOL

But the history of black America is very different from the history of black Africa. Furthermore, the star system developed by America could not be transposed to the African situation without damage and frustration. The cultural development that, so far, has failed to take root in Africa will need to somehow fit into the education programme of the young African. Could the performer yet again become the trusted agent to facilitate?

From my understanding, there are basically four types of education:

1. break them down before building them up: *the military drill*;
2. erase every past knowledge and load them with our own stuff: *the blank slate*;
3. just mimic everything I do and you will be all right: *the monkey game*;
4. the doing is what matters, therefore become an apprentice: *practice makes perfect.*

Daniel Labonne

What I am proposing is not a mere rejection of existing methods, nor is it revolutionary for its own sake. The question of need remains central to any applied lesson from the experiment. The young African should not leave a rich and varied heritage at the gate of the school. Allow an exchange of forms, practices and experiences existing across Africa to broaden the horizon and motivate the young mind. Not only would there be an accumulation of cultural capital, but mutual respect would later be a bonus. Then, allow creativity to build a new vocabulary and tap into the imagination. The process may lead to the formulation of a shared view of the world that does not deny anything: neither the order of the modern world, nor the weight of traditional values and practices. Techniques and skills ought to be taught so they may grow on the right foundation. In the process, make sure the individual develops a critical sense and grows in self confidence. Allow the young to indulge into both the practice and understanding of the performing arts while they open their eyes to the outside world. Initially, let the performing arts become the medium of understanding of both self and the world, before the child negotiates imported knowledge. For such a PROCESS OF EXCHANGE to become effective, the performing artist needs specific training so he may eventually be given a place in the formal education of the young.

BACK TO THE FUTURE

Finally, to the urban African who tends to look down on village life and practices, it may be too late to convince him or her that the future does not lie in the latest technology or the next imported gadget. Let us instead focus upon his son or daughter, by facilitating a new African form of education through the arts that reconciles modernity with tradition. For that 'school' to become effective, the investment ought to be placed in the performing artist of Africa who dances as he thinks. And vice-versa.

In Africa, the performing artist must be seen today as being potentially a key player in the next phase of development. He has never cut the ties with tradition; he still has direct access to the common heritage while he holds a mobile phone in his hand. He has inherited the oral tradition while he looks at the real global world in the eye. He is able to dance with a new purpose and teach the lessons of nature and ancient history, without having to ignore the appeals of modernity. No doubt he would be a reliable guide for the young. As he contemplates the present, in his body, in the collective memory and with his own voice, he remembers the whole way from the early beginnings. The rest comes with training, reliable funding, an improved status and a new role in modern African society.

Who knows what the cumulative effect of horizontal exchanges might have? Who can predict where human creativity may lead? Who should doubt about the abilities of a balanced young mind in an expressive body? The young African may not compete by inventing a new gadget, but he may well teach the world how to claim back the 'memory' from invasive technology.

Empower the Performer.

Daniel Labonne

PART 6

People, Facts and Figures

Daniel Labonne

LIST OF PARTICIPANTS IN THE ACTPA PROJECT
Field Study and Pilot Year 1

CONSULTANTS

Mr. Michel Julian	E.T.C.	UK
Mr. Debebe Eshetu	UAPA Director	Ethiopia
Mr. Norman Goldfoot	Business & Management Consultant	England
Ms. Sophia Lokko	University of Ghana Lecturer & Head of Drama	Ghana
Mr. Tim McGee	Central School of Art Registrar	England
Ms. Martha Vestin	Dramatisk Institute Drama teacher	Sweden
Mr. Devi Chaudhuri	Simon & Waterman Partners Accountant	England
Mr. Robert Rakison	Solicitor	England
Prof. John Pick	City University Law Lecturer	England
Prof. Hemmet	City University Law Lecturer	England
Prof. Moody	City University	England
Mr. Jacob Sou	Artistic Director	Burkina Faso
Mr. Prosper Kompaore	Black People Institute Director	Burkina Faso
Mr. Amadu Maddy Lecturer	Gbakenda Theatre	Sierra Leone
Mr. I. Vencatachellum	UNESCO	France
Mr. John Elsom	IATC	England

	Chairman	
Mr John Ytteborg	IATA Secretary General	Denmark
Prof. Adedeji	Drama Specialist	Nigeria
Mr. Jeff Cresswell	Artistic Director	England
Mr. Bo Karre	SIDA Former Head of Ed.Div.	Sweden
Prof. Alphonse Blague	Former Head of African Institute Republic	Central African
Mr. Iver Mackay	Translator	England/France
Mr. Cliff Moustache	Leader of theatre groups	Seychelles
Mr. Louis Akin	National Ballet Director	Cote D'Ivoire
Mr. Ogah Abah	H.B.University Lecturer	Nigeria
Mr. Tafatoana Mahoso	N.A.C.Z.	Zimbabwe
Mrs. Alberta Arthurs	Rockfeller Foundation Head of Arts,Humanities	U.S.A.
Mrs. Suzanna Laffont	Technician	New Zealand/UK
Mr. Gerard Telot	Violonist/Music Teacher	Mauritius
Mr. Stephen Chifunyise	Dramatist/Writer	Zimbabwe
Mr. Makhili Gassama	Minister of Culture	Senegal
Ms. Susan Sato	Rockfeller Foundation Asst.Arts & Humanities	U.S.A.
Mr. Ebbe Carlsson	SIDA Consultant	Sweden
Mr. Kodjo Hadzi	ACCT	Paris/Ghana
Mr. El Caba Toure	ACCT	Paris/Senegal

Daniel Labonne

Ms. Anna Pentila	Actress	Finland
Ms. Eva Maria Haukinen	Actress	Finland
Ms. Manuela Suero	Artistic-Director	Mozambique
Ms. Blondell Cummings	Dancer Choreographer	U.S.A.
Ms. Cecil Ekoue	Dancer	Cote D'Ivoire
Mr. F. Nii-Yartey	Ghana Dance Ensemble Head	Ghana
Ms. Penina Mlama	Dar-Es-Salaam Head of Drama Dept.	Tanzania
Mr. Dele Charley	Tabule Theatre	Sierra Leone
Mr. Pierre Tressia	Radio Presenter	Cote d'Ivoire
Mr. Joe Legwabe	Teacher, Drummer, Dancer	England/South Africa
Mr. Etienne Goyemide	Writer	Central African Republic
Mr. Saddick Balewa	Technician, Cameraman	Nigeria
Mr. Jacques Masson	Technician, Cameraman	France
Ms. Jennifer Williams	B.A.A. Director	England/U.S.A.
Mr. Hugh Lovegrove	I.T.I. President	England
Ms. Jane H.Young	B.T.A. Former Director	England
N.C.V.O.		England
Mr. Alain Knubley	Company Secretary	England
Mr.Teegate Medghin	Scriptwriter	Ethiopia
Cde. Girma Yilma	Minister of Culture	Ethiopia
Mr. E. Chambulikazi	Lecturer	Tanzania

Ndugu Massimbi	Bagamayo Arts Centre Director	Tanzania
Mr..C.R.Musiwa	Ministry of Ed.& Culture Deputy Secretary	Zimbabwe
Mr..F.Mutokonyi	Ministry of Ed.& Culture Assistant Secretary	Zimbabwe
Mr..I.Sibanda	Ministry of Ed.& Culture Secretary	Zimbabwe
Hon. Mrs Fay Chung	Minister of Ed. & Culture	Zimbabwe
Mr. E.Iriebi	CAFAC Director	Cote d'Ivoire
Mr. A.Ouedraogo	Presenter/Animator	Togo
Mrs. A. Amegatcher	Ministry of Ed. & Culture Principal Administration Secretary	Ghana
Ms. Dzifa Glikpoe	Theatre company Artistic Director	Ghana
Mr. Asiedu Yirenkyi	School of Performing Arts Lecturer	Ghana
Mr. Yeboah Nyamekye	Arts Council of Ghana Executive Director	Ghana
Mr. Woode	Ghana News Agency Editor	Ghana
Dr. Martin Owusu	Ghana Drama Studio	Ghana
Mr. Nanabanin Dabson		Ghana
Dr. M. Ben-Abdalla	Ministry of Ed. & Culture PNDC Secretary	Ghana
Mrs. Violette Decker	Sierra Leone Broadcasting	Sierra Leone
Dr. Johnson	Fourah Bay College Head of English Department	Sierra Leone

Daniel Labonne

Mr. Ron McJohnson	Ministry of Information and Broadcasting	Sierra Leone
Mr. Coker	Daily Mail	Sierra Leone
Mr. De Souza George	Institute of African Studies Cultural Studies	Sierra Leone
Dr. Cecil Fyle	Institute of African Studies Director	Sierra Leone
Mr. Brest Kakou	National Institute of the Arts Director	Cote d'Ivoire
Mr. S. Omari	African Development Bank Deputy Director Training Department	Cote d'Ivoire
Mr. Morr Fall	African Training Centre for Management, Director	Cote d'Ivoire
Mr. Kragbe	Ministry of Culture Director of External Affairs	Cote d'Ivoire
Mr. Couzy	Ministry of Culture Technical Adviser	Cote d'Ivoire
Mr. P.R. Anouma	National Commission for UNESCO, Secretary General	Cote d'Ivoire
Mr. Jerome Carlos	National Newspaper 'Ivoire-Dimanche,' National Radio T.V. Editor	Cote d'Ivoire
Mr. Grekou Zadi	University of Abidjan Lecturer (Letters)	Cote d'Ivoire
Mr. Makanga	Regional Centre for Cult.Action Director	Togo
Mr. Marcel Diouf	Organisation of Africa Unity Cultural Counsellor	Ethiopia
Mr. Guingane	Regional Centre for Cult Action Ex-Director	Burkina Faso

Students	CRAC	Togo
Mr. Djibrill Fall	Social & Cultural Affairs Director, Permanent Sec, SeneGambia	Gambia
Mr. Marcel L.Thomassi	Ministry of Information & Tourism	Gambia
Mr. Mustapha Joof	Gambia National Drama Association President	Gambia
Mr. Sering Seck	Gambia National Drama Association Trainer/Producer	Gambia
Mr. Babou M.S. Sowe	Executive Committee of The Gambia National Drama Association. Representative	Gambia
Mr. Momodou G.Joof	Dept.of Youth Sports & Culture Asst. Cultural Officer	Gambia
The Secretary General	National Commission for UNESCO	Gambia
Daniel Sorano	Actors & Actresses	Senegal
Mr. Abdoulaye Badiane	Ministry of Culture Director of Cabinet	Senegal
Mr. Nomar L.N'Diaye	Altervision-Media Afrique Director of Projects	Senegal
Mr. Louma Sarr	National Commission for UNESCO. Secretary General	Senegal
Mr. Pathe Gueye	National theatre Daniel Sorano, Director	Senegal
Mr. Pathe Diagne	Panafrican Black Arts Festival, commission FESPAC	Senegal
Mr. Diop	National Conservatory of the Arts. Director	Senegal

Daniel Labonne

ACTPA COURSE I (1990)
PARTICIPANTS

NAME	AGE	OCCUPATION	COUNTRY
Actpa Course 1:		Directing a Dance Drama in Contemporary Africa	

Trenees

Trainees

NAME	AGE	OCCUPATION	COUNTRY
Ms.Justine Sawadogo	27	Actress/choreographer	Burkina Faso
Ms.Bibiane Matoko	46	Dancer	Congo
Mr. Melaku Tsegaye	29	Dancer/Actor/Teacher	Ethiopia
Ms.Faustina Dugbenu	37	Singer/Actress/Dancer	Ghana
Mr.Gaston Valayden	41	Teacher/Actor	Mauritius
Mr.Vivian Pin	26	Dancer	Mauritius
Mr. Robert Isaacks	23	Actor/Culture Producer	Namibia
Mr.J'Baptiste N'kuliyinka	42	Director of National Ballet	Rwanda
Mr. Salisu Abubkar	30	Senior Cultural Asst.Dancer	Nigeria
Mr. Felix Kpokpa	38	Drummer, actor	Côte d'Ivoire
Ms. Kiswigu Bernard	32	Artist, Drama Teacher	Tanzania
Ms.Sithembile Mpofug		Dancer	Zimbabwe
Ms.Maidei Mupozo	15	Dancer	Zimbabwe
Ms.Lizzie Muchaka		Performer	Zimbabwe
Ms.Eldorah Mathe		Dancer	Zimbabwe
Mr.Ignatius Chiyaka		Dancer, Drama Teacher	Zimbabwe
Mr.Lerato Ndlovu	24	Dancer, Poet, Musician	Zimbabwe

Academic and Artistic Specialists

NAME	AGE	OCCUPATION	COUNTRY
Mr. F.Nii-Yartey	45	Choreographer/Researcher	Ghana
Mr. Louis Akin	56	Choreographer/Director	Cote d'Ivoire
Mr. Stephen Chifunyise		WriterDrummer/Dancer	Zimbabwe

Course Co-ordinators

NAME	AGE	OCCUPATION	COUNTRY
Mr. Debebe Eshutu	48	Actor/Director	Ethiopia
Mr.Amadu Maddy	53	Writer/Teacher/Actor Director	Sierra Leone

Artistic Direction

Daniel Labonne 40 Theatre Director/ Researcher Mauritius

ACTPA COURSE II

1991

Theme: Anthropology and Performing Arts - LUCY & ME

TRAINEES:

Name	Country
1. Mr. A. Dakisaga	Burkina Faso
2. Ms A. Zewdu	Ethiopia
3. Ms. Kiros	Ethiopia
4. Ms. Z.C. Dogdo	Côte d'Ivoire
5. Mr. N.A. Sowah	Ghana
6. Miss. S.Torgbede	Ghana
7. Ms. S. Mwangola	Kenya
8. Ms. M. Virahsawmy	Mauritius
9. Mr. S. Abubakar	Nigeria
10. Mr. D. Lumumba	Nigeria
11. Ms. K. Bernard	Tanzania
12. Mr. P. Lwanga	Uganda
13. Mr. I. Chiyaka	Zimbabwe
14. Mr. L. Ndlovu	Zimbabwe
15. Ms. N. Mayinda	Zaire
16. Mr. E. Ngaboyicondo	Rwanda

SPECIALISTS

1. Mr. D. Eshetu	Ethiopia
2. Mr. F. Nii-Yartey	Ghana
3. Mr. K. Mwambayi	Zaire
4. Mrs. D. Harper Wills	Guyana

VISITING INSTRUCTORS

1. C. Merry	UK
2. S. Reynolds	UK

RESEARCH/ART DIRECTION
(in Ethiopia/France)

1. D.Labonne	Mauritius

ADMINISTRATION

1. H.Babajee	UK/Mauritius
2. S. Telot	UK/ Mauritius

Daniel Labonne

CHRONOLOGICAL REPORT
ACTIVITIES ONLY

FROM 1985 TO 1991 (6 YEARS)

MEMORANDUM ON TRAINING SCHOOL (SWEDEN)	APRIL	1985
INFORMATION TOUR (Paris/London)	MAY/JUNE	1985
LABONNE MOVES FROM I.COAST TO LONDON	AUGUST	1985
CONSULTATIONS IN ZIMBABWE	OCTOBER	1985
VISIT TO CANADA	DECEMBER	1985
CONSULTATIONS IN SWEDEN	JANUARY	1986
CONSULTATIONS IN MAURITIUS	MARCH	1986
RESEARCH IN ETHIOPIA	APRIL	1986
RESEARCH IN TANZANIA	APRIL	1986
WORK SESSIONS IN DENMARK	MAY	1986
PUBLICATION OF BROCHURE (UAPA)	MAY	1986
CONSULTATIONS IN HOLLAND	JUNE	1986
OPENING OF ATEX OFFICE IN UK	FEBRUARY	1987
CONSULTATIONS IN PARIS AND BRUSSELS	MAY	1987
RESEARCH IN COTE D'IVOIRE	JULY	1987
RESEARCH IN GHANA	JULY	1987
RESEARCH IN TOGO	JULY	1987
RESEARCH IN SIERRA LEONE	JULY	1987
RESEARCH IN SENEGAL	JULY	1987
PUBLICATION OF GUIDELINES	SEPT	1987
PUBLICATION OF PROPOSAL DOCUMENT	OCTOBER	1987
INT'L SCIENTIFIC COUNCIL MEETING (LONDON)	OCTOBER	1987
ROUND TABLE MEETING IN PARIS	MARCH	1988
ATEX SUB-OFFICE MOVES TO MAURITIUS	JUNE	1988
AFSYMWORK IN MAURITIUS	OCTOBER	1988
CONSULTATIONS IN PARIS	DECEMBER	1988
CONSULTATIONS IN MONACO	AUGUST	1989
CONSULTATIONS WITH UNESCO/ZIMBABWE	NOVEMBER	1989
TECHNICAL MISSION TO ZIMBABWE	FEBRUARY	1990
CONSULTATIONS WITH HOLLAND	JUNE	1990
CASTLE ARTS IS OBTAINED FOR ACTPA	JULY	1990

CONSULTATIOONS WITH ZIMBABWE GOVT.	JULY	1990
OPENING OF ACTPA COURSE 1	SEPT	1990
CONSULTATIONS IN FINLAND	OCTOBER	1990
PREMIERE OF "FOOTPRINTS"/OPENING CEREMONY	NOVEMBER	1990
EVALUATION MEETING WITH MR.MUSIWA (LDN)	FEBRUARY	1991
RESEARCH ON LUCY & ME IN ETHIOPIA	MARCH	1991
TAKE-OFF OF ACTPA COURSE 2 IN ZIMBABWE	APRIL	1991
CASTLE ARTS ROUND-TABLE (ZIMBABWE)	JULY	1991
PREMIERE OF PRODUCTION 2 "LUCY & ME"	JULY	1991
CONSULTATIONS IN CÔTE D'IVOIRE	AUGUST	1991
OFFICIAL STATEMENT OF ZIMBABWE GOVT.	SEPT	1991
EVALUATION MEETINGS WITH MR.MUSIWA IN LDN.	NOV/DEC.	1991
ACADEMIC EVALUATION LONG STUDY (UNI.LON)	1995 - 2001	

NOTES:

1. DURING ALL THAT PERIOD, REPORTS ARE PRODUCED, PROMOTION AND MARKETING ARE UNDERTAKEN THE ACTUAL RESEARCH IS PERMANENT. ACTPA TRAINING PROGRAMME IS DEVISED, RESEARCHED, BUDGETED, IMPLEMENTED.

2. FROM 1987 TO 1991, ATEX UNDERTAKES PLANNING, CO-ORDINATION AND FUND-RAISING. MEETINGS AND CONSULTATIONS ARE HELD IN LONDON.

3. CITY UNIVERSITY (ARTS POLICY AND MANAGEMENT) ASSISTS IN THE RESEARCH AND STUDY BY PRIVATE STUDENT DANIEL LABONNE.

4. GOLDSMITHS COLLEGE (UNIVERSITY OF LONDON) CREDITS POST STUDY AND EVALUATION BY PRIVATE STUDENT DANIEL LABONNE.

FACTS AND FIGURES

NUMBER OF YEARS FOR PRE-PILOT RESEARCH AND PREPARATION	5 YEARS
NUMBER OF COUNTRIES VISITED FOR RESEARCH AND PREPARATION	19
NO. OF CONSULTANTS INVOLVED DURING RESEARCH	34 (Professionals) 66 (other)
NUMBER OF ACTIVITIES INSERTED IN PREPARATION	56
NUMBER OF COUNTRIES WHICH HOSTED EVENTS DURING PREPARATION	6
NUMBER OF NATIONAL ORGANISATIONS WHICH HAVE ASSISTED DIRECTLY INTO RESEARCH AND PREPARATION	10
NUMBER OF INTERNATIONAL ORGANISATIONS THAT GAVE ASSISTANCE	5
NUMBER OF VISITS ABROAD	30
NUMBER OF VISITS TO ZIMBABWE BEFORE THE OPENING	6
NUMBER OF VISITS TO SCANDINAVIA THAT LED TO THE JOINT FUNDING	6
NUMBER OF MONTHS OF FIELDWORK, RESEARCH, DOCUMENTATION, PLANNING, COORDINATION AND FUNDRAISING	60
TOTAL FUNDS RAISED FOR RESEARCH AND PREPARATION (1987 - 1990)	£ 80 606.25
FUNDS SPENT PER MONTH (1987- 1991)	£ 1,343 (AVERAGE)
ACTUAL COST PER MONTH INCLUSIVE OF UNPAID MANAGEMENT	£ 4,966

ACTPA AT CASTLE ARTS

PILOT PROJECT YEAR 1

STATISTICAL REPORT

NO. OF STUDENTS WHO HAVE ATTENDED COURSES IN CASTLE ARTS	40
NO. OF COUNTRIES WHICH HAVE BEEN REPRESENTED IN ACTPA COURSES	16

NO.OF DAYS OF ACTIVITIES FOR YEAR 1	156
NO. OF ORIGINAL STAGE PRODUCTIONS "MADE IN CASTLE ARTS"	2
NO.OF INTERNATIONAL TRAINERS-INSTRUCTORS ENGAGED FOR COURSES IN CASTLE ARTS	12
NO. OF ZIMBABWE TRAINEES WHO FOLLOWED THE TWO MAIN COURSES AT CASTLE ARTS	14
NO. OF ZIMBABWE CITIZENS ENGAGED BY ACTPA AT CASTLE ARTS DURING YEAR 1	25
NO. OF VISITING INSTRUCTORS WHO HAVE TAUGHT AT CASTLE ARTS	3
NO. OF ORGANISATIONS THAT HAVE CONTRIBUTED TO THE FUNDING OF YEAR 1	8
NO. OF ARTISTIC GROUPS FROM MATABELELAND WHO PERFORMED AT CASTLE ARTS	8
NO. OF OUTREACH WORKSHOPS THAT HAVE BEEN GIVEN BY CASTLE ARTS RESOURCE PERSONS TO ZIMBABWEANS	4
NO. OF WOMEN-TRAINEES ENGAGED FOR THE ACTPA COURSES	18
NO. OF MEN-TRAINEES ENGAGED IN ACTPA COURSES	22
NO. OF ENGLISH SPEAKING TRAINEES ENGAGED IN ACTPA COURSES	36
NO. OF FRENCH SPEAKING TRAINEES ENGAGED IN ACTPA COURSES	8
NO. OF PERSONS WHO HAVE TRAVELLED TO ZIMBABWE FOR THE VARIOUS ACTPA ACTIVITIES	55
NO. OF TRAINEES WHO HAVE BENEFITTED DIRECTLY FROM ACTPA INCLUDING AFSYMWORK-MAURITIUS	165
NO. OF RESOURCE PERSONS WHO HAVE BEEN ENGAGED FOR ACTPA WORKSHOPS INCLUDING AFSYMWORK	25
NO. OF AFRICAN COUNTRIES WHICH HAVE PROVIDED DIRECT ASSISTANCE TO ACTPA	2
NO. OF REPORTS PRODUCED FOR THE ACTPA PROJECT	17
NO. OF PROFESSIONAL CONSULTANTS WHO HAVE DIRECTLY BEEN ENGAGED TO DEVELOP THE ACTPA CONCEPT	10
NO. OF TRAINEES WHO HAD TO LEAVE THE PROGRAMME BEFORE THE COURSE ENDED	2
PERCENTAGE OF ATTENDANCE UNTIL COMPLETION OF COURSES AT CASTLE ARTS	95%

Daniel Labonne

ACTPA PROJECT COMPREHENSIVE FINANCIAL STATEMENT

1987 – 2012

20th March 2012

(In Pound (£) Sterling)

Period	Total Cost ACTPA	Fund Agencies Grants (financial)	Host Country Contribution (In kind)	Personal Investment (Capital/Kind)	Unpaid fees to to ATEX (research/mngmt)
Pre-pilot					
1985 – 1987	53, 826 00	22 869 00		9 400 00	21 557 00
Pilot Project					
1987 – 1990	379 731 00	169 960 00	(23 353 00)	36 318 00	150 100 00
1991 – 1992	146 622 00	71, 262.00	(30 360 00)		45 000 00
Post-Pilot					
1996 – 2002	29 380 00			12 380 00	17 000 00
2011 – 2012	11 110 00			6 110 00	5 000 00
27 years	620 069 00	264 091 00	53 713 00	64 208 00	238 657 00

(*see notes below*)

Notes on the comprehensive financial statement.

a. The budget prepared on 18 December 1988 and circulated to the funding agencies projected both income and expenditure. The expenditure for year one amounted to £748, 200. Pressure from underfunding limited the programme and its impact. Only £264, 091.00 were made available by the financial partners. During year 1 at Castle Arts, only two short courses were approved for funding.

b. The latest expenses incurred personally include the production of a documentary film that explains how the ACTPA Project leads to the foundation FACE and the revival of the project. A fact-finding mission was organised in 2011 to Tunisia, Ethiopia and Mozambique, funded from my pocket. Several promotion documents including a website, a documentary video and a brochure are being produced, representing current additional investment.

c. To this date, consultants are having an input into legal, strategy, PR, publishing and fund-raising. Not to mention the ongoing technical research on African performing arts and cultural development.

d. A 3-year budget had been agreed upon with the main sponsors and the host country. Like in any project, the early investment and unpaid management costs were in anticipation that funding would increase and revenue would be created within the 3 years. The initial objective to break even.

e. The achievements of the project have largely depended upon ATEX operating from London. Moving from Ivory Coast to London with the family in 1985 has been one early decision that involved capital on behalf of the project co-ordinator. Setting up ATEX as a UK company and opening an office in Covent Garden also involved investment and risk. The office had 1 full-time employee and 1 part-time employee from day 1. The drama teacher and theatre director had to give up contracts and career in the arts to

Daniel Labonne

engage increasingly into the research and management of the project. Not to mention, attending to the needs of a young family without depending upon the system.

f. No funds were provided between two activities. Months and years of research, planning, fund-raising and promotion had to rely upon personal input from the co-ordinator and his family.

g. No funds were provided for the cost of original productions, the approved activity being a training programme in strict terms. The managers had to demonstrate the viability of their method and have something to show to the world. We saved on the money raised and injected capital whenever necessary to deliver.

h. Show business and the entertainment industries involve big money and generate jobs and serious revenue. The funding reduced the possibilities and pushed the experiment towards underperformance and condemned our efforts to poor standards. Yet, the feedback from spectators and observers demonstrated that we just about managed to avoid underrated cultural products, unfit for the larger market being targeted.

i. The host country's contribution had to be accounted for. Managing the asset provided by the host country implied maintenance, furnishing, equipment, staffing and reliable logistics like any school. Above all, the Castle Arts demanded management skills that had to satisfy the government and secure the international residents. The sponsors refused to consider the 'school', insisting upon isolated 'floating' projects covered by one budget at a time.

j. A second course involved a change of strategy at fundraising level and convincing new financial partners, namely The Ministry of Development of the Netherlands and the Ministry of Foreign Affairs of Finland – FINNIDA to whom we are particularly grateful.

k. The reader will appreciate that no casualty had been reported that affected any of the international individuals who attended our programmes, either in Mauritius and in Castle Arts, Zimbabwe. No scandal either could be recorded, in spite of the variety of people from dozens of countries. No complaint about training, accommodation, food, standard of teaching or production had matched the underfunding of the project. There was no accident to report. Nor has there been any court case for bad debts, although the project lost the promised funding after course 1.

l. During 27 years, from 1985 to 2012, the same person has consistently invested into a project that concerns dozens of countries and potentially millions of people in Sub-Saharan Africa. From the statement above, the combined value of that investment, by adding personal input and unpaid management, amounts to £302 865 00 without interest.

m. The host country has taken back the Castle Arts after the project was stopped prematurely. The funding agencies had paid for activities only and they had exactly what they had paid for. The investment over years has yet to deliver. Since the experiment still responds to objective needs and cultural development is yet to have an impact on real people, all might not be lost.

n. The latest investment has taken the form of this book you now hold in your hands, thus taking the bulk of the information and the contradictions of development towards a better future.

o. To conclude, the experiment points towards private enterprise, so the investment may prove viable, create jobs and, generate lasting benefits for both its clientele and its future investors.

p. For the project to finally meet all its objectives, after 27 years of commitment, the exhausted researcher may have to place the project in the hands of business professionals.

Daniel Labonne

PART 7

Photo Album

Faces and Places on the Way to Castle Arts

Daniel Labonne

THE ACTPA PROJECT

In Pictures

This album originally had been put together in 1993 under the title 'The Other Side of the Dream.'

This pictorial report is made out mostly of photographs taken by Daniel Labonne along the formative years of the ACTPA Project. They are not of high quality and were never meant to be published. The reader will notice the lack of glamour that reflects poor funding to undertake a rather ambitious task. But the pictures do provide evidence that real people were involved, that the project was far from being either elitist or political, that many countries had been consulted. ACTPA was far from being an ego trip; on the contrary, it often became a heavy burden to carry. More significantly, the empowerment of the performing arts in Africa has remained the constant focus along decades of work to this day. From UAPA to ATEX, from ATEX to ACTPA, from ACTPA to FACE, the question of needs underpins each initiative taken to clear a neglected area of development: culture and the arts. Original artwork by Keith Jurianz.

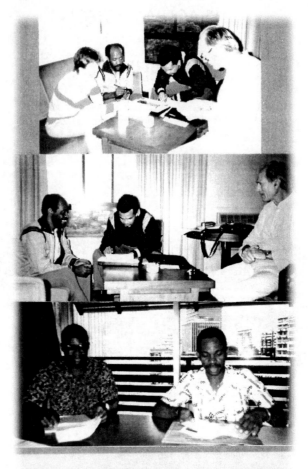

Daniel Labonne

As one outcome of the Stockholm Colloquium on African Theatre, a delegation from Africa and from Sweden pays a visit to Zimbabwe.

TOP: left to right
1985

Martha Vestin	(Sweden. Theatre Director)
Debebe Eshetu	(Ethiopia. Actor. UAPA President)
Daniel Labonne	(Mauritius. Theatre director. UAPA V.President and Treasurer. Researcher)
Bo Karre	(Sweden. Education Officer. SIDA)

SECOND: photo down

In good spirit, begins a long and difficult task in a hotel room, Harare. (left to right) Debebe Eshetu, Daniel Labonne and Bo Karre.

THIRD: photo down
1987

First things first: field study of theatre and arts training across Africa. Here, a visit to Côte d'Ivoire, in West Africa by Daniel Labonne.

Left: Grekou Zadi of the University of Abidjan
Right: Pierre Ignace Tressia, Performer and presenter at Radio Cote D'Ivoire

BOTTOM:
1987

More negotiations towards finding a host country for the ACTPA centre. Daniel Labonne pays another visit to Zimbabwe. An empty stage under an open sky... Progress is slow at first in pushing the project through.

Daniel Labonne

TOP:
1986

A delegation of 4 consultants travels to assess the situation of the performing arts in East Africa. Funds are raised to study Ethiopia and Tanzania. Here, Dar-Es-Salaam, in Tanzania.

MIDDLE:
1985

A campaign in the North also proves necessary, to inform and raise funds. Here, Daniel Labonne visits Toronto, Canada. Consultations with Universities and Funding Agencies in Toronto, Ottawa and Montreal.

BOTTOM:
1985

Addis Ababa, Ethiopia. Here, the National Theatre of Addis. The field work had begun with Ethiopia in 1985. Later, in 1991, the research within the framework of Course 2 at Castle Arts takes the researchers to the National Museum of Addis, where Lucy, the human ancestor, 'resides.'

Daniel Labonne

TOP PHOTO:

1986

Back to Sweden, fresh discussions prove necessary namely with the Swedish International Development Authority - SIDA. This trip is undertaken by the project coordinator, Daniel Labonne. A stop-over in Denmark to develop relations with another partner-organisation - IATA (the International Amateur Theatre Association).

SECOND PHOTO:

1987

In London, the International Scientific Council (ISC) Meets to broaden the support for the ACTPA Project. ATEX (African Theatre Exchange) organises the meeting. The meeting is financed personally by Daniel Labonne.

From left to right:

The members of the ISC
Indrassen Vencatachellum (UNESCO)
John Ytterborg (IATA)
Martha Vestin (Swedish Dramatic Institute)
Prof. Joel Adedeji (Nigeria)

THIRD PHOTO:

1988

In Paris, consensus is reached.
At the Francophone Headquarters (ACCT)
ATEX organises a Round Table, to devise the best
Form of partnership that suits the ACTPA Project.
Funding is the main item on the agenda.

From left to right:

Prof. Amadu Maddy (Sierra Leone)
Dr. T Mahoso (Zimbabwe)
Martha Vestin (Sweden)
Susan Sato (Rockefeller Foundation. USA)
Monsieur Hadzi (France -Togo)
Alberta Arthurs. Rockefeller Foundation - USA)

Daniel Labonne

1988

Mauritius. ATEX Organises the African Symposium Workshop - AFSYMWORK.
AFSYMWORK tests out in the filed the various practices and methods used in the training of performing artists, worldwide.

AFSYMWORK is a clear success. The format pays off: A combination of practical research, seminars, workshops, performance and exchange.
Left, Cliff Moustache, a training expert from Seychelles and Norway poses after a reception offered by a sugar factory to the international participants.

MIDDLE:

1988

Family picture. The participants to AFSYMWORK relax at the end of two weeks of intense work.
Left (next to the djembe) the elder Louis Akin from Côte d'Ivoire.
Standing, back row, showing the V sign, the musician and dance teacher Joe Legwabe from South Africa.

BOTTOM:

1990

Back to the negotiation table, in Harare, after London, Paris and Mauritius.
Zimbabwe confirms once again its willingness to host the centre. ATEX clarifies the remaining issues.
Centre, Mr. Francis Mutokonyi, nominated as the key officer for the Ministry of Education and Culture to deal with ATEX about the ACTPA centre in Zimbabwe. Present at this session, a consultant from Unesco.
The Technical Mission conducted jointly by ATEX and Unesco is welcomed by the Ministry of Education and Culture. Centre, Mr. Isaac Sibanda, chairman of a work session in Harare. To his right, Daniel Labonne (ATEX). To his left, Indrassen Vencatachellum (UNESCO).

Daniel Labonne

TOP:
1990

Efforts are finally rewarded with a metamorphosis. A self-contained building, with many facilities, including accommodation, restaurant, rehearsal rooms and performance venue is chosen among other proposed buildings in the country. What had been so far known as Castle Arms in Bulawayo is made available to ATEX to establish the ACTPA Project.

Castle Arms is renamed Castle Arts by ATEX.

MIDDLE:
1990

Here, the keys of the Castle Arms are handed over to Daniel Labonne (second to the right) by representatives of several ministries of Zimbabwe.

BOTTOM:
1990

September 1990, Bulawayo, Zimbabwe. Unveiling a symbolic figure cast in iron, Mrs Fay Chung, Minister of Education and Culture officially opens ACTPA at Castle Arts Next to her, wearing the national dress of Ethiopia in white, Debebe Eshetu. Standing behind the statue, the founder of ACTPA at Castle Arts, Daniel Labonne.

Daniel Labonne

TOP:

London 1987

The International Scientific Council gives its blessing to the ACTPA Project. From left to right, Indrassen Vencatachellum (Unesco), John Ytterborg (IATA), Daniel Labonne (ATEX), Martha Vestin (Sweden), Prof. Joel Adedeji (Nigeria)

MIDDLE:

France 1988

The policy meeting in Paris is given a name: The ATEX Round Table. The meeting achieves an unusual international resolve to grant support from competing interest groupings. ATEX had a difficult task: to secure the funding for the ACTPA Project, without antagonising anybody.
The participants to the ATEX Round Table, Paris:
The Agency for Technical and Cultural Cooperation - ACCT. Paris
The Rockefeller Foundation - USA
The Swedish International development Authority - Sweden
The African Theatre Exchange (ATEX) - London
The Institute for Black Peoples - Burkina Faso
The Arts Council of Zimbabwe - Zimbabwe
The Union of African Performing Artists - Ethiopia
Theatre Practitioners represented by Amadu Maddy - Sierre Leone

BOTTOM:

Mauritius 1988

AFSYMWORK - the African Symposium Workshop turns out to be an event that demonstrates the feasibility of the ACTPA Project and the ability of ATEX. The enthusiasm is widespread and unanimous among local and foreign participants alike, after two long weeks of work.

Daniel Labonne

TOP:

1990

Zimbabwe:

The performing group BLACK MFOLOSI welcomes the ACTPA Project to Bulawayo, on behalf of an enthusiastic artistic community.
Here, the group at its early beginnings. Later, they became well-known and travelled widely, out of Africa.

MIDDLE:

1990

The ACTPA Production Workshop and the original stage-show FOOTPRINTS translate into reality the concept researched and promoted for years.
Here, the trainee-artists together with their specialist resource persons pose for a family picture at the Castle Arts, Bulawayo. They came to Zimbabwe from 15 different countries.

BOTTOM:

1991

LUCY & ME is the title of the second training programme. The course pushes further both training process and production work. The 'exchange process' advocated by ATEX is confirmed and it establishes the method of training proposed at the ACTPA.
Participants have a smile on their face, proud of their common endeavour in spite of openly discussed difficulties.

Daniel Labonne

TOP:
1984

Building bridges between the vast cultural gaps. The dream emerged in the South, as a vision of grass-root Africa. Many years of listening along a patient research were initially required.

MIDDLE LEFT:
1991

... Geographical Divides
The dream evolves in the North. ACTPA is first studied, formatted, promoted. In this picture, Professor Kalingayi Mwambayi in front of the ATEX offices in London.
Kalingayi Mwambayi from Zaire/Congo is a founding member of the UAPA.

MIDDLE RIGHT:
1988

... North and South Divides
Here, from left to right: Alberta Arthurs (USA), Martha Vestin (Sweden), Ebbe Carlson (Sweden), Prosper Kompaore (Burkina), Debebe Eshetu (Ethiopia)

BOTTOM:
1988

... Racial Divides
Here, Eva Maria Haukinen of Finland and Blondell Cummings of USA. Two performing artists who came to make a contribution to AFSYMWORK in Mauritius.

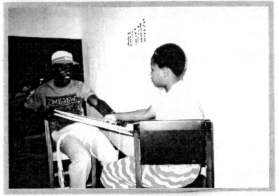

Daniel Labonne

TOP:

1988

... Linguistic Divides

From left to right in Paris: Monsieur Hadzi of ACCT (Togo), Amadu Maddy (Sierra Leone), Susan Sato (USA), Dr. T Mahoso (Zimbabwe)

MIDDLE:

1990

... Gender Divides
... Regional Divides

Here, trainees during course 1 OF ACTPA at Castle Arts: Felix Kpokpa (Cote D'Ivoire), Madei Mpozo (Zimbabwe)

BOTTOM:

1990

Bridging Tradition and Modernity

Here, Francis Nii Yartey of Ghana, recruited by ATEX to teach at Castle Arts, is filming, using a video camera at Great Zimbabwe ruins.

Daniel Labonne

TOP:

1990

A bridge across generations of African performers
Here, the specialist choreographer, elder Louis Akin of Côte d'Ivoire,
recruited by ATEX to teach and direct at Castle Arts, in a fraternal
embrace with young Ignatius Chiyaka, a trainee dancer from Zimbabwe.

MIDDLE:

1990

Bridging Culture and Development

A troupe of young performers in a public demonstration at the
Commercial Centre of Harare, Zimbabwe.

BOTTOM:

1990

Because the Child is the Father of Man

Professor Amadu Maddy extends a hand to a child. For, at the end of the
road, it will be the African child who is expected to benefit from the
training process and the education delivered by ACTPA.

LE CAFAS/ACTPA DEVIENT UNE REALITE

LA MISSION TECHNIQUE CONDUITE CONJOINTEMENT PAR L'UNESCO ET L'ATEX EN JANVIER 1990.

Optimisme et satisfaction exprimés par Madame le Ministre de l'Education et de la Culture du Zimbabwe (ici au centre) qui accueille le Centre Africain de Formation des Artistes de Spectacle sur le sol Zimbabwéen.

Autour du Ministre Faye Cheung (de gauche à droite):
M. D. Labonne (ATEX), M. C. Musona, assistant chef du cabinet; M. Isaac Stranda, chef de cabinet, M. L'envoi attaché/cum de l'Unesco et M. F. Mandkawa, directeur de la culture.

LES ARTISTES DE SPECTACLE DU ZIMBABWE EXPRIMENT LEUR JOIE ET LEUR GRATITUDE POUR LA FORMATION ET LES PERSPECTIVES OUVERTES PAR LE CAFAS CHEZ EUX

Ici, une représentation impromptue de la troupe Black Mhlosi à Bulawayo.

32

Daniel Labonne

The ACTPA Dream Becomes a Reality

A technical mission to Zimbabwe jointly conducted by UNESCO and ATEX in January 1990 leads to a venue, chosen for ACTPA in Africa.

Optimism and satisfaction expressed by the Minister of Education and Culture of Zimbabwe (centre) who welcomes the African Centre for The Training of Performing Artists on Zimbabwean soil

Around the Minister Fay Chung (from left to right),Mr. D. Labonne (ATEX) M. C. Musiwa (assistant Head of Cabinet), Mr. Isaac Sibanda (Head of Cabinet), Mr. Indrassen Vencatachellum (Unesco) and Mr. F. Mutokonyi, Head of Culture.

Performing artists of Zimbabwe express their joy and their gratitude for the new opportunities created as ACTPA is physically grounded in Zimbabwe.

Here, an impromptu performance of the group Black Mfolosi, in Bulawayo.

Daniel Labonne

Hat's off!

Excitement and Pride as the African performer arrives at the Castle Arts, a home for performing arts in Southern Africa.

Daniel Labonne

The Castle Arts is offered to ATEX to Accommodate ACTPA

1990

The right compound and the right standard had been described in the ACTPA Guidelines in 1987. 3 years later, the Zimbabwe government delivers Castle Arms in Bulawayo.

The axis between the Castle Arts (Zimbabwe) and ATEX in Croydon (UK) becomes increasingly important. Perhaps more crucial than the earlier network built by ATEX across the African continent.

Here, Sheila Telot of ATEX, at the reception desk of Castle Arts, Bulawayo, Zimbabwe.

1991

Mr. Henri Babajee (left) and Mr. Cuthbert Musiwa (right). They both deserve credit for the successful monitoring of the two training programmes of ACTPA at Castle Arts in 1990-1991. Both are photographed here at the ATEX office in Croydon. Centre, Daniel Labonne.

Daniel Labonne

ATEX Takes on the Difficult Task of Defending the Interest of Many Stakeholders, by Managing Both ACTPA and the Castle Arts.

The Castle Arts

TOP:

Here, offices and rehearsal rooms:

In 1990, yes, ACTPA has finally found a home. However, the Castle Arts presents new challenges. Zimbabwe becomes the new powerful player; Managing the Castle involves enterprise skills; Furnishing and equipping a castle cost more money; The Security of trainees requires special provisions; the quality of the training remains paramount.

MIDDLE:

Main hall at castle Arts:

Several visits to Zimbabwe had proved necessary to produce a document that spells out the terms of reference which allows ATEX to accept the offer of the Castle Arts from the host country, Zimbabwe.

BOTTOM:

Here, the recording studio and the stores:

The ground also needs maintenance, therefore staff, tools, management. In the course of year 1, the host country merely observes. Mr. Musiwa is then delegated to London to evaluate the performance of the project manager, ATEX. Progress, problems and future planning are outlined. Inversely, Mr. Babajee of ATEX is posted at Castle Arts, Bulawayo to attend to the many logistics issues on the ground. In London, fundraising continues.

Daniel Labonne

The Castle Arts

TOP:

Here, the bar and refectory:

The training programme takes off only 3 months after the Castle Arts had been made available for a trial period. ATEX had to deliver to reassure the partners. Neither the time nor the money was right. But the pressure to deliver was real, while the funds were allocated 'for projects only.'

MIDDLE:

Here, the swimming pool and part of the wall around the garden:

The performer is given a different status with ACTPA at Castle Arts. Discipline and respectability are other issues that determine the efficiency of an international training programme at Castle Arts. The day-to-day management of adult-trainees pose many issues to keep everyone satisfied and creative.

BOTTOM:

Part of the dormitories where trainees and trainers had their own rooms:

No major incident had been recorded during the pilot year. This fact must be weighed up against the backdrop of the real implications of recruiting, transporting, accommodating, feeding and training foreign students, with different cultures, mostly speaking different languages.

Daniel Labonne

Castle Arts Welcomes Tradition and Modernity

TOP:

1990

Performing artists from local communities are regularly invited to perform at the castle. They do so with pleasure; the trainees learn from popular art forms.

MIDDLE:

1990

The National Troupe of Mozambique pays a visit of several days to the Castle Arts, Bulawayo.

They are accompanied by Swedish consultant, Ebbe Carlson.

BOTTOM:

1990

Other visitors travel from Namibia and elsewhere to observe the work in progress in ACTPA at Castle Arts.

Daniel Labonne

The Official Opening Ceremony of ACTPA at Castle Arts.

On 18th September 1990, at the end of the training programme 1, special guests converge to Castle Arts, coming from Harare, Scandinavia, London, Holland and Australia...

TOP:

Personalities from the business community of Bulawayo regularly attend open cultural evenings organised at Castle Arts.

MIDDLE:

Performances devised and rehearsed over weeks are presented by trainees at Castle Arts. The discussion and feed-back become part of the training process.

BOTTOM LEFT:

The president of the UAPA, Debebe Eshetu, acts as master of ceremony, on behalf of performing artists of all Africa.

BOTTOM CENTRE:

The governor of Matabeleland expresses the deeper meaning of hosting an international centre like ACTPA, as felt by the community.

BOTTOM RIGHT:

The ministry of Education and Culture, Mrs. Fay Chung, underlines the link between unity, culture and training as components of a viable development for Africa.

Daniel Labonne

Building a Network of Friends and Supporters

TOP:

Specialists participants to the workshop seminar in Mauritius. They came from Tanzania, Seychelles, Côte d'Ivoire, South Africa and Burkina.

MIDDLE LEFT:

Family picture around (centre wearing a suit) the director of the African Cultural Institute, Mr. Alphonse Blague (Central African Republic). In front of him, the delegate from Madagascar.

MIDDLE RIGHT:

Happy participants to AFSYMWORK in Mauritius. They come from Denmark, Norway, Tanzania, Seychelles, USA.

BOTTOM:

Mr. Bo Karre, an early friend from Sweden, pays a private visit to Castle Arts, Bulawayo.

Daniel Labonne

Winning the Support of the North

TOP:

Here, in Holland, circus artists Zouzou Yaya Haha and his colleague Rosalie, as well as researcher Kees Epskamp of CESO (absent from the picture) gave their full moral and intellectual support by opening the doors of some Dutch organisations for Daniel Labonne (left) during his visit.

MIDDLE LEFT:

Thanks to these friends, the government of Holland provided a financial support to ACTPA:

The Utrecht School of Performing Arts took a genuine and direct interest in the progress of ACTPA and the work undertaken by ATEX. Up to the last minute. Here (left in middle photo left) Rien Sprenger, head of theatre department and Thera Jonker, head of international relations.

MIDDLE RIGHT:

Danish friends have been active and helpful in Unlocking the support from the Scandinavian authorities to the work of ATEX and the success of the ACTPA Project. Here, photographed in Copenhagen with Daniel Labonne, the general secretary of the IATA, John Ytterborg and the director of Danish Amateur Theatre Association (DATS), Mr. Erwin.

BOTTOM:

Swedish friends have been particularly committed. In early days, photographed with Daniel Labonne in Stockholm, Bo Karre (left) and Martha Vestin (middle).

Daniel Labonne

Diplomatic Work Each Step of the Way

To obtain and keep essential support for ACTPA and cultural development in Africa.

1985-1991

TOP:

A view of the port, Stockholm:

Many visits to Stockholm, the Swedish capital, were organised between 1984 and 1991, in order to explain the needs for training and the awkward situation of performers in Africa.

Without SIDA (the Swedish International Development Authority) ACTPA would have never taken off and found the means to materialise. The project was promoted to Swedish organisations and artists as a self-help scheme and a fresh approach to North-South direct partnership.

MIDDLE:

The Minister of Education and Culture of Mauritius, M. A. Parsuramen, expresses the support of his ministry and the government to the ACTPA project. Left, the Minister. Extreme right, Daniel Labonne.
Fourth left, Minister M.F. Roussety, reiterated the support later at AFSYMWORK in Mauritius, 1988.

BOTTOM:

Mr. C. Musiwa, the Zimbabwe official on his official visit to ATEX in London. Here with Mrs Sharon Robinson, project director at the Commonwealth Foundation.

Daniel Labonne

The Economic Impact of the ACTPA Project

Here, during a site visit in Harare, a representative of the Zimbabwe Ministry of Foreign Affairs (left) and a consultant from UNESCO (right) speaking to an engineer (middle).

Where to locate the pan-African school for maximum impact?

Daniel Labonne

TOP:

1990

Cultural workers must indeed travel far and work hard.
Whereby the need for adequate training. Here, consultant Daniel
Labonne visits yet another potential venue proposed by the host
country, Zimbabwe, to host the ACTPA training centre.

MIDDLE:

1990

The Castle Arts has been chosen and approved. The castle must provide
accommodation, food, leisure and protection besides the technical
training. Trainees, international specialists and other staff benefit.

BOTTOM:

1991

Video equipment is purchased, transported and installed at Castle Arts,
for the needs in technical training in production skills and documentary
work.

Here, the instructor and video technician, Steve Reynolds hired in
London to run a training workshop as part of the training programme 2,
LUCY & ME.

Daniel Labonne

1989

In London, the ATEX personnel toil for 12 hours in the day to push the ACTPA Project through. At least 3 international sessions with Castle Arts each day to monitor progress. Here, administrator and translator Floryse Dubarry.

1990

Hello, this is Castle Arts...

ATEX had received the Castle Arts empty and without personnel. The venue had to be furnished, equipped then staffed before the course could take off.

Besides, accountants and other external consultants were instructed regularly throughout all the phases of a complex project. The ACTPA Project is also about sound project management.

MIDDLE LEFT:

The popular cook at Castle Arts.

MIDDLE TOP:

The receptionist receiving calls sometimes from Congo or Rwanda.

MIDDLE BOTTOM:

ATEX administrator, Sheila Telot, in consultation.

BOTTOM:

It does cost money to provide minimum comfort, health and safety to African Performing Artists. It is often a matter of cleanliness while the personnel keep a smile on their face... These are the basic conditions to keep the international trainees motivated and productive.

Daniel Labonne

1990-1991

Trainees need to be transported while food supplies must be purchased each day... Personnel must cover 24 hours at Castle Arts.

TOP LEFT:

Car rental was one item on the agenda for the pilot project.

TOP RIGHT:

Daily visits to the market for the requirements at the castle.

MIDDLE:

The course leads to a production and included are design and costume making. First the machines and the material are purchased. Then, local expertise is put to good use, under artistic direction.

BOTTOM:

September 1999. Course 1 comes to a close, a first production is ready for stage, and the opening ceremony is being planned.

A stage is built within the walls of Castle Arts, blending existing structures with appropriate performance areas.

Essential to the production, building material, local personnel, transportation etc.

Daniel Labonne

1990-1991

A recording session at the studio at Castle Arts:

TOP LEFT:

The playwriting coach Doris Harper-Wills from Guyana, and selected by ATEX.

TOP RIGHT:

The personnel recruited to do the house work at Castle Arts. Some reside at the Castle.

MIDDLE:

Bulawayo airport:

Many trips are needed for coordination between the authorities in Harare and Castle Arts in Bulawayo.
55 tickets in total have been purchased for international flights within the framework of the ACTPA Project.

BOTTOM:

Musicians and instrument makers have been hired to participate in the productions at Castle Arts.

Daniel Labonne

1990-1991

TOP:

In business terms, ATEX has demonstrated the feasibility of the ACTPA Project and the potential of the chosen venue, Castle Arts, in Bulawayo, Southern Africa.

Castle Arts was actually converted from a deserted complex into an international centre that delivers high quality training and a venue for quality performances.

MIDDLE:
1988

Such an applied research at such a high standard of involvement and delivery requires a thorough field study and prior assessment of existing institutions that deliver training programmes. Here, a theatre workshop inside the Theatre of Port Louis in Mauritius.

BOTTOM:
1985

Inter African training centres had been operational for decades in other areas than the performing arts. Here, the centre for management and advanced training of civil servants (CAMPC) in Abidjan, Cote D'Ivoire.

Daniel Labonne

The Art of Dance

TOP:

The ABC of dance is taught by a specialist from Ghana, Francis Nii Yartey, recruited by ATEX.

MIDDLE:

The trainee from Namibia who had never danced on stage before coming to Castle Arts:

For hours, days and weeks on end, the trainee-performer practices and rehearses, with a little help from fellow performer from Nigeria, Salisu Abubakar, himself a dancer.

BOTTOM:

Comes the date of the premiere, FOOTPRINTS is greeted by officials and all as a triumph, it is a personal victory for the Namibian performer.

Daniel Labonne

The Art of Costume-Making

Costume is an art in its own right.

TOP:

Performing artists from Mauritius, Côte d'Ivoire and Congo are at work in the costume workshop of ACTPA at Castle Arts.

MIDDLE:

Assisted by a fellow trainee from Ghana, the actor from Ethiopia, Melaku, tries on an original costume, under the surveillance of an instructor from Sierra Leone.

BOTTOM:

Metamorphosis of characters, on stage for the performance of FOOTPRINTS. Out of nowhere, appears a demi-god...

Daniel Labonne

Movement with a Meaning

LEFT:

A course on movement conducted by the elder Louis Akin. Movement and function are not dissociated in African dance. The prop needs to be part of the movement.

MIDDLE:

Posture, make-up, togetherness, props, music, light...
And do not forget to smile! So many techniques taught and mastered within weeks at Castle Arts.

BOTTOM:

Movement with a meaning. Development, remember, is ultimately the result of a shared effort together, which implies both responsibilities and rights.

The individual often reaps what he has sown. Figuratively and literally. Here, Trainee Felix directs fellow students. Movements from the plantation to the stage.

Daniel Labonne

Theatre Arts

TOP:

A situation in the Dance Drama FOOTPRINTS. Standing, the actor from Mauritius, Gaston Valayden.

MIDDLE:

The craft of the performing artist combines aptitude to the right attitude. Centre, the performer from Ethiopia, Melaku Segai shows his mastery.

BOTTOM:

Projecting oneself using theatre arts, beyond one's own constraints. Beyond personal identity, beyond national boundaries, towards other cultures. Here, the Ghanaian performer communicates with body, spirit and a smile...

BELOW - 1990

Footprints

An original stage production
Conceived and created at Castle Arts

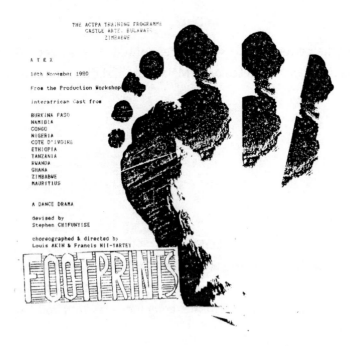

THE ACTPA TRAINING PROGRAMME
CASTLE ARTS, BULAWAYO
ZIMBABWE

A T E X

16th November 1990

From the Production Workshop

Interafrican Cast from

BURKINA FASO
NAMIBIA
CONGO
NIGERIA
COTE D'IVOIRE
ETHIOPIA
TANZANIA
RWANDA
GHANA
ZIMBABWE
MAURITIUS

A DANCE DRAMA

devised by
Stephen CHIFUNYISE

choreographed & directed by
Louis AKIN & Francis NII-YARTEY

FOOTPRINTS

Daniel Labonne

The Concept of Exchange

Exchange applied to the arts delivers some results:

Sharing and exchanging using performing arts rest upon the right method of training. Such a method could be put to good use, in order to benefit the young. Therefore, ACTPA had a concern for the training of performers that would equip them with the skills to train others.

Music playing fosters togetherness.

Kalingayi and Sally

Daniel Labonne

TOP:

He is a French-speaking performer...

He has learnt something about Kenya. He travelled to Castle Arts from Zaire, hired by ATEX as a resource person in the training programme 'LUCY & ME' in 1991.

Here, touching the reality of a dream symbolised by the statue of the performing artist at Castle Arts.
The statue created by a Bulawayo sculptor was commissioned by ATEX in 1990.

BOTTOM:

She is an English-speaking performer...
She has learnt something about Zaire... She travelled to Bulawayo from Kenya, as a trainee, to study the techniques that would allow her to practice the performing arts with some impact back home.

Her name is Salome Mwangola, trainee-performer selected for the course 2 'LUCY & ME' in 1991. Here, she reflects over the achievement of ACTPA as a symbol of hope and optimism.

Some thirty performing artists, including Kalingayi and Salome, were actually taught...
Contemporary Africa
Performing Arts
About themselves
The role of the artist in African Society
The responsibility of the performer
Techniques of expression in performing arts
Variety of forms of expressions
Video techniques
Techniques of training
Production techniques and problems

Daniel Labonne

Exchange as a Training Method for Performing Artists in Africa.

TOP:
1990

First, the method was tested in Mauritius, during the African Symposium Workshop (AFSYMWORK). Here, a workshop in open air, under the direction of a specialist from Madagascar.

MIDDLE:
1990

Later, at Castle Arts in Zimbabwe, the concept is put in practice in a real training situation, involving some 30 trainees, coming from a dozen countries.

BOTTOM: LUCY & ME:
1991

This is the second training programme. The course confirms the viability of the method. The method is consolidated further so that it benefits the performing artist of Africa.

Here, proudly wearing a costume for the stage show at Castle Arts, Ngaboy Icondo, the selected performer from Rwanda.

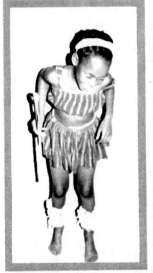

Daniel Labonne

TOP:

Opportunities are offered to the trainee-performer to develop his self-confidence, a personal style and the techniques of a presenter.

MDDLE:

This young Zimbabwean dancer is happy to demonstrate her dance routine to international trainees, residing at Castle Arts.

BOTTOM:

Every Thursday, a theatre show at Castle Arts where local performers are invited to perform.

Daniel Labonne

TOP:

Training Course 2 is researched at the National Museum of Addis Ababa where Daniel Labonne meets with the real Lucy, the human ancestor.

MIDDLE:

1991

This young trainee performer from Zimbabwe smiles with satisfaction, following three solid months of hard work at Castle Arts. The arts of the rest of Africa came to her doorstep.

BOTTOM:

1991

Judy Mitoma of Rockefeller Foundation (USA) pays a visit to Castle Arts and shows her appreciation of the planning and the seriousness of the training programme at the level of management.

Here, posing between administrator Mr Henri Babajee (right) and to her left, Mr. Debebe Eshetu (resource person/UAPA), both having been hired to run course 2 LUCY & ME at Castle Arts.

LUCY ET MOI
A UNE DIMENSION
UNIVERSELLE

La recherche comprend une
visite en Ethiopie; une autre
en France et une
documentation sur les
trouvailles archéologiques.
(le livre ci-joint est édité par
Penguin Books)

1991

Daniel Labonne

Addressing the Concept of Time in African Culture

Exchange Between Africa And The Diaspora

Research covers a visit to Ethiopia, then a visit to France, not to mention the documentation about archaeological findings, including this book by Donald Johanson edited by Penguin Books.

1991

In academic terms, LUCY & ME, the theme of the course was Anthropology and Performing Arts. The course points towards the field of exploration initiated by ACTPA at Castle Arts.

The process followed was as follows:
1. Field study in Ethiopia
2. Preparation of the course at ATEX in UK
3. Fund-raising and selection of participants
4. Exchange techniques taught at Castle Arts, Zimbabwe
5. New playwriting at Castle Arts
6. Rehearsals and production of an original play
7. Production of a video film
8. Mini tour of the production

Here Doris Harper-Wills, from Guyana, who ran a workshop on new playwriting. She brought other contributions as a woman resource person and a representative of the African Diaspora.

Daniel Labonne

ACTPA proved to be a journey into the unknown...

Between 1991 and 2011, the world has changed profoundly. The cold war has come to an end, technology has established the Internet as an unavoidable virtual dimension, new superpowers are emerging while vital resources are declining... Africa is growing in self-confidence, signalled by the remarkable success of Football World Cup 2009 in South Africa.

Was ACTPA an experiment that came too early? In 2011, the findings might establish that the cultural dimension of development does matter. The Arts might still be the alpha and omega of development for Africa...

Young Africans form nearly 50% of the continent's population. They have a right to be taken into a brighter place with a different story of life and energy from Africa. Performing arts have a key role to play in this process. The world also expects better and more from Africa. Let the performing artists step forward in a free flow of creativity...

From the experiments of the ACTPA Project, a healthier vision is now required and a comprehensive plan must emerge to enable the implementation, across Africa, of Development Through Creativity.

Daniel Labonne

Different Perspectives to Target a Vast Audience

The audience across the African continent is vast and aware of the rules of live performance.

The African public can also be demanding, because performing arts is practised by most individuals and communities.

Allow the African performer to face the African public first, across borders, across language barriers and across styles.

Sub-Saharan Africa offers limitless possibilities in terms of live art forms. Training the performer begins by enriching the vocabulary by learning from each other.

An adequate programme of training should keep the performer close to the young.

TOP:
From the roof of Castle Arts, contemplating possibilities and challenges.

MIDDLE & BOTTOM:
In the streets of urban Africa, a young performer walks on tight rope for spectators.

Hope Mixed With Anxiety Among Resource Personscin 1990: What If Castle Arts Is Taken Away From Performers of Africa?

Daniel Labonne

In 2012, Face is the Answer to Their Prayers

With time, the candle sends a different message. It used to be a celebration at the end of a promising first year of ACTPA at Castle Arts. It may be seen today as a candle in remembrance of Louis Akin, the African dance specialist who died a couple of years after his assignment at Castle Arts.

The candle may also stand as a prayer for a handful of committed mature performers who had been totally convinced by a most promising experiment.

Is it a case of anxiety about the risk of losing both the momentum and the credit for such innovative work? Is the world ready for the full expression of the vital force within African performing arts? Will decision-makers accept that the economist does not hold all the answers? That in Africa, the performer may have a special to play? Is Africa ultimately ready to celebrate with FACE in the 21st century?

The simple historical fact is that ACTPA at Castle Arts has been a reality shared and tested by responsible performers who witnessed the achievement.

Photo taken at Castle Arts. (Clockwise from bottom right) Louis Akin (Côte d'Ivoire), Amadu Pat Maddy (Sierra Leone), Stephen Chifunyise (Zimbabwe), Francis Nii Yartey (Ghana), Debebe Eshetu (Ethiopia).

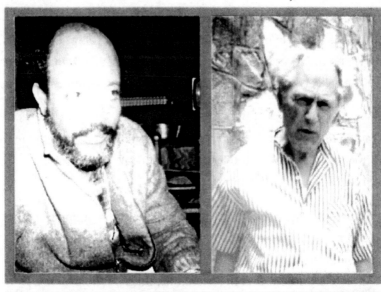

Daniel Labonne

Thank You to Some Key Individuals Behind The ACTPA Adventure

TOP: left

He had the maturity in terms of age, professionalism, diplomatic abilities as president of the UAPA. DEBEBE ESHETU (Ethiopia)

TOP: Right

He had the wisdom of an experienced development worker endowed with deep human qualities. BO KARRE (Sweden)

BOTTOM:

She has been a pillar supporting the early efforts of a unique project. She became a bridge between cultures in a proactive approach to North-South collaboration.

Daniel Labonne

TOP:

He had the listening ear on behalf of the host country. CUTHBERT MUSIWA (Zimbabwe)

MIDDLE LEFT:

They both had the talent and the smile...

Left, PROSPER COMPAORE (Burkina Faso) and Professor ALPHONSE BLAGUE (Central African Republic)

MIDDLE RIGHT:

He has always been the right man at the right time... INDRASSEN VENCATACHELLUM (UNESCO)

BOTTOM LEFT:

He had the essential diplomatic qualities and real friendship for African Performing Arts. JOHN YTTERBORG (International Amateur Theatre Association) Norway

BOTTOM RIGHT:

She had the patience and the administrative skills... SHEILA TELOT (ATEX)

Friends of today and tomorrow

Three of the close friends of ATEX in the UK were Michel Julian of European Theatre Coordinate, Tim McGee of Central School of Speech and Drama in London and Hugh Lovegrove, ex. chairman of the International Amateur Theatre Association. I owe a special thank-you to Professor John Pick, head of Department of Arts Policy and Managementat City University. Progress would have been impossible for me without the British Theatre Association (ex BTA). Later, at Goldsmiths College, University of London, Gerald Lidstone supervised my post project evaluation for six long years. Deepest gratitude to my old friend, the knowledgeable and accomplished Ivorian performer Louis Akin, now deceased. Mrs. Madeleine Gobeil (ex UNESCO) deserves a salute for her friendship and support in difficult times. Mrs Jennifer Williams of the British American Arts Association made a significant contribution. Mr John Mapondera of Zimbabwe played a delicate role along the diplomatic process that led to finding a host country for ACTPA. Henri Babajee brought trust and enlightenment in the darker days of a testing project. The employees at Castle Arts were cheerful representatives of the Bulawayo community. In Ethiopia, Professor Brahane of Addis National Museum extended a helping hand, then opened Lucy's safe resting place...

A special mention for the role of the Ministry of Foreign Affairs of the Netherlands and the Utrecht School of Performing Arts. They showed the utmost interest for the work in progress at Castle Arts and, jointly with FINNIDA of Helsinki, they made the second training programme in 1991 possible.

Over a period of 26 years (1985-2011), so many other friends of the project outnumber the weaker doubters of a meaningful enterprise. To all these friends and supporters, we say a humble THANK YOU, on behalf of performing artists of Africa who did benefit from the practical research and the training delivered by ACTPA.

For a long time to come, the government of Zimbabwe will deserve the gratitude of performers of Africa, past, present and future. The minister Dr. Fay Chung always found the right words and sincerely wanted a permanent ACTPA to grow in close proximity to her ministry.

Finally, a word for the spouses and the families who spent months and years, sharing the anxiety and enduring the absences of those who called themselves 'theatre workers' with a difficult cause to defend.

With FACE, a new generation will be invited to join in an exciting adventure and become friends of a permanent centre of training, creativity and exchange.

Daniel Labonne

PART 8

What the World Had to Say

Daniel Labonne

THE EXPERIMENT CONDUCTED BY ATEX

As seen by partners in cultural exchange from 30 countries in the World.

From Zimbabwe

"...My Ministry is presently taking the necessary steps towards the early establishment of the African Centre for the Training of Performing Artists (ACTPA). We would also appreciate all the measures you could take in due course to ensure that technical and material assistance for the Regional Centre be foreseen in the Draft Programme and Budget for the next biennium 1991-1993..."

Hon. Fay Chung, Minister
Ministry of Education and Culture

From United Kingdom

"...Anything that can develop greater understanding between nations especially between developing African countries and the rest of the world can only be for the common good. Art and cultural exchange are undoubtedly ways that can break barriers and achieve that greater understanding quicker and easier than any others just because they are common languages in communication between peoples..."

Ken Harris
Esq., Asst. Director
Croydon Chamber of
Commerce & Industry

From France/Unesco

".J'ai le plaisir de vous faire parvenir le contrat relatif à la préparation par l'African Theatre Exchange(ATEX) d'une étude en vue de la réunion d'experts sur le programme d'action pour la diffusion des spectacles en Afrique."

En me félicitant du concours de l'African Theatre Exchange à la réalisation de cette activité del'Unesco..."

Ms. Madeleine
Gobeil, Responsable
de la section de la Promotion des Arts
Unesco

From the Netherlands

"...A pan-African Theatre School to have animators, facilitators, performing artists, educators working out an African didactics and curriculum in the performing arts. According to me this is the only ways to sustain the African identity in the performing arts and to develop a more structural basis for exchanging experiences within the African continent..."

Mr. Kees P. Epskamp, staff member
Centre for the study of education in
developing countries, CESO.

From Sweden

"...Yesterday I had a meeting at SIDA with Carlsson. I heard the latest news from your meeting and he gave me copies of all the papers... I only want to send my spontaneous congratulations..."

Ms. Martha Vestin, Theatre Director

Daniel Labonne

From Nigeria

"...I have today received my copy of your open letter of 30th April 1989, and I wish to congratulate you on all the efforts made so far and to assure you of continued solidarity and support.

I was recently elected Dean of the Faculty of Arts of our University (with effect from August 1st 1989). As Dean, I should be able to put the resources of our faculty at the disposal of ACTPA, whenever I am called upon to do so..."

Prof. Dapo Adelugba, Secretary general
Nigeria Centre of the I.T.I.

From Canada

"...The protection and development of the performing arts in Africa is a matter of concern for all those who wish to see truly endogenous development, compatible with the cultural environment.

The centre could be a resource for Canadian institutions implementing projects in Africa which wish to use popular theatre forms in their community development work..."

Mr. Charles Morrow, Chief
Dev, Communications Sector
CIDA

From Mauritius

"...I am going to, here, promise in my own name and I am sure in the name of the Minister of Education, Arts and Culture, that on Government's side, all the support will be given..."

Hon. M.F. Roussety, Minister
Ministry of Civil Service of Mauritius

From Oslo

"...We are glad to learn that the project at long last will be on the move... At a forthcoming Nordic meeting in Oslo in May this year among the cultural affairs units the project will be discussed..."

R.Anderssen-Rysst
Head of Cultural Affairs Unit
N O R A D

From Denmark

"..We wish you all success with the symposium which we have been happy to support by ensuring participation of Danish experts as well as two representatives from Tanzania and Ghana..."

Soren Dyssegaard
Director of Information,
Ministry of Foreign Affairs

From UNESCO

"...Comme mes collègues de la Division du développement culturel et de la création artistique ont eu l'occasion de le dire, lors des récents entretiens qu'ils ont eus avec M. D. Labonne, Coordonnateur du projet, l'Unesco est sensible aux perspectives nouvelles qu'offrira le CAFAS pour la promotion de la créativité artistique et le renforcement des échanges artistiques en Afrique..."

Henri Lopes, Sous-Directeur Général
Section Culture et Communication

From Gabon

"...Le Centre International des Civilisations Bantu (CICIBA) est heureux de vous écrire pour vous proposer de créer une collaboration entre votre AFRICAN THEATRE EXCHANGE et lui..."

I.Obenga M. Directeur Général
Centre International des Civilisations
Bantu

From Holland

"...The African Center for Training Performing Artists which is to be established in Zimbabwe and which you have a coordinating role was one of our main topics... It was felt that the center might be an excellent location for the training in circus arts..."

M. Zouzou
International Circus Arts Exchange

From Angola

"...Con esta razon soy mucho interasado de entrar en contacto con tu escuela caso que me necesite par dar aulas de danza africana estoy en plena disposicion perio tiene que mandar una carta o un convite en mi nombre se este fuera estare la con ustedes..."

Muicha Gracia
UNAC

From Bonn, Germany

"... We feel that cultural aspects become more and more important. Perhaps we could find ways and means to assist you in establishing an inter African training centre for performing artists..."

Dr. Josef Muller, Head
German Foundation for Int'l Development

From Senegal

"...Je saisis cette opportunité pour vous renouveler l'engagement de l'ICA à initier une coopération fructueuse entre le CRAC de Lomé et le CAFAS, au sein d'une coopération agissante entre l'ICA et l'ATEX.

Alphonse Blagué, Directeur Général
Institut Culturel Africain

From Commonwealth Foundation, London

"...Thank you very much for your letter of 5th February with the good news that Zimbabwe will actually be hosting ACTPA and you will be launching your first training programme in September 1990. With my best wishes for success in your enterprise..."

J.F.H.Tsang Mang Kin Deputy Director
The Commonwealth Foundation

From Zaire

"...Je vous remercie pour votre lettre du 30 octobre qui vient de m'arriver. C'est avec plaisir que nous aimerions, dès le depart, établir des liens de collaboration entre l'ATEX et le CALDAS..."

Prof. Monyem M.K.Mikanza
Sec. Excutif, CALDAS

From Paris IFPC

"...One more step has been passed in your effort to coordinate experience and policies in the field of theatre training in Africa. The international fund for the promotion of culture showed its interest in your activities in African theatre by contributing to the publication of the brochure of the Union of African Performing Artists in 1985..."

Jean-Baptiste de Weck, Director
International Fund for the Promotion of Culture Unesco

From Burkina Faso

"...Salue le projet de création d'un centre de formation des interprètes du spectacle à Harare (Zimbabwe) à l'initiative de l'African Theatre Exchange (ATEX)

Résolutions 1-19
Conférence des Ministres Africains
de la Culture 21-29 Mars 1988

Daniel Labonne

From Miami, U.S.A.

"...ACTPA is also of great interest to us, and we are hoping that we can establish vibrant exchange programmes between all three institutions. ATEX could be instrumental in realising this goal, and I trust that I can count on your support with this venture..."

G. Cresswell, *Artistic Director*
Cayman National Theatre Company

From Ethiopia

".. RECOGNISING the enormous task accomplished by ATEX, in promoting the interests of African Performing Artists, both inside and outside the Union;

FULLY AWARE that there will not be progress without the ability to organise, to strategise, to fundraise and to promote, all these having been successfully achieved by ATEX..."

Debebe Eshetu, *Chairman*
Union of African Performing Artists

From UN

"...Je vous félicite pour les nombreuses initiatives que vous continuez de prendre pour développer le théâtre en Afrique, en l'occurrence pour contribuer à la Décennie mondiale du développement culturel..."

Basile Koussou, *Secrétaire*
Décennie Mondiale du
Développement Culturel

From Côte d'Ivoire

"...Je fais confiance au dynamisme et à la rectitude de l'ATEX en affaire pour accepter de lui confier également la représentation exclusive des intérêts du Ballet..."

Louis Akin, *Directeur*
Ballet National de Côte d'Ivoire

From Tchekoslovakia

"...It is why we send you this letter. Dear Sheila, Please, help us! Can you find some sponsors or some patrons of arts which will be willing to give the money to some Czechoslovak young artists for some crazy but nice project..."

Jan Papez, student of directing
Academy of Art - Prague

From Paris

"...L'ACCT suit toujours avec grand intérêt les activités de l'ATEX et vous serait obligée de lui communiquer les résultats des travaux du Symposium en vue d'éventuelles actions conjointes dans le futur..."

Abou El Caba Toure, Directeur Général
Culture et Communication - ACCT

From Burkina Faso

"... Après avoir pris connaissance du projet initié par ATEX en vue de la création d'un centre africain de formation en art du spectacle, j'ai le plaisir de vous confirmer tout l'intérêt que mon département attache à telle initiative.   Nous souhaiterions également que ATEX puisse appuyer nos efforts en vue de la mise en oeuvre de structures nationales de formation..."

Alimata Salembere Le Secrétaire d'Etat
Ministère de l'Information et de la Culture

From Bruxelles, E.E.C.

"...Your initiative appears to us to be a worthwhile experience in the field of training of performing artists.

The Commission and the Performing artists of Africa may come closer some day..."

B.Amat A.
Head of Division
E.E.C.

Daniel Labonne

From OAU

"...En conséquence, le Secrétaire Général de l'OUA réaffirme tout son soutien à votre initiative et se félicite vivement de l'aboutissement prochain des efforts que vous n'avez cessé de déployer depuis longtemps. C'est également l'occasion de remercier le Gouvernement du Zimbabwe qui a si généreusement accepté d'abriter le CAFAS.

Dr. M.T.Mapuranga, Sec.General adjoint,
Organisation de l'Unité Africaine

From Dakar, Senegal

"... Je suis heureux de vous assurer du soutien total du Sénégal et de ma disponibilité, ainsi que celle de mon département, pour vous recevoir à l'occasion de votre visite en Afrique de l'Ouest..."

B.B.Dieng Conseiller Technique
Ministère de la Culture du Sénégal

From I.T.I. UNESCO

"...The committee has a firm interest in encouraging methods of training which are not European-based and has taken steps to ensure than its membership is truly multicultural and international. We are therefore delighted that the Government of Zimbabwe has felt able to devote money and resources to a project which will, we feel sure, enable African artists to develop a clear voice in the international arena. The committee wishes to give maximum support to this initiative..."

J.N.Benedetti, President
International Theatre Institute

From New York, U.S.A.

"... We are confident that your efforts on behalf of African theatre are very important, and we are hopeful that you will be able to advance those efforts significantly.
Good luck in this exciting adventure..."

Alberta Arthurs
Director for Arts & Humanities
The Rockefeller Foundation

From Tanzania

"... We are pleased to inform you that your association has been brought to our attention with great recommendation as being one whose aims and activities could be very beneficial to the development of theatre in Tanzania.
We are interested in establishing artistic links with African Theatre Exchange..."

C.R.Maliwanga for Principal Secretary
Ministry of Community Development,
Culture, Youth and Sports of Tanzania

From England

"... Your scheme sounds most interesting and it is greatly to your organisation's credit that you have achieved so much. At some stage, I would like to meet you and see if there is scope for useful collaboration..."

Mark Featherstone-Witty, Founder
British School of Performing Arts (BRIT School)

Portrait of the African Performer
Myriam Makeba

Miriam Makeba (1932-2008), singer performer, was rightly nicknamed Mama Afrika. She is credited as being the first African artist who managed to take African music worldwide. Her country, South Africa, removed her citizenship because she actively campaigned against the Apartheid system. She returned home after the Apartheid system collapsed and kept on performing and campaigning for other freedom and causes. Makeba must be saluted for choosing to sing in African languages, for turning her exile into a plea for better understanding of Africans through music. As a woman of substance, being a performing artist was never a curse, but a source of empowerment to educate the world about the broader picture and the human appeal. She never gave in to the star system and resisted the temptation to be reduced to a mere political activist.

Epilogue

Changing the Perceptions of Africa

There are two views about Africa and Africans. Samuel P. Huntington only accepts that 'possibly' an African civilization existed, accepting Ethiopia only as a civilization in its own right. Historian Sam Walker insists that the most sophisticated civilizations did exist in Africa, namely in the kingdoms of Mali, in Kush (ancient Sudan) and of course in Ancient Egypt. Cheikh Anta Diop goes further than Walker by qualifying African civilization as the mother of all civilizations, historically preceding and inspiring Ancient Greece and Mesopotamia. Both perceptions are valid as we contemplate the future. Huntington excludes Africa from any role to play in the 'clash of civilizations', implying that it would either be reduced to a mere spectator or once again suffer the consequences of future conflicts. However, he does accept that in the future, a new civilization may emerge with South Africa leading. Spectator? Or is it a different role all together that Africa needs to define for herself? And since 'clash of civilisations' implies tensions conducive to war, why not imagine a function resolutely turned towards peace for African peoples?

Walker and Diop seem more committed to restoring the truth and undertaking some fundamental repair to the damaged integrity of a civilization which only tends to be identified in the modern arena either as victim or backward. Their task has already begun and, for decades, it has been about educating the world and correcting perceptions about black Africa. But it remains an uphill struggle as mainstream education and the media remain negative towards Africa. In that sense, Lilian Thuram confirms the need to assemble every now and again all the pieces of the 'African puzzle'. In our own research, we also respond to

Daniel Labonne

the same need to attend to this gaping wound on the side of the human comprehensive history. Not so much for the world's sake, but for the sake of populations concerned by the continent's cultural development. This said, it does matter to educate the young everywhere about the full dimension of what it means to live globally. In the process, one may restore an inclusive perception and some repair to the memory may operate. Hopefully, one can expect some healing to the damaged body of human experience. Fleshing up the old bones of Lucy, 'the mother of mankind'...

But the context of our study is more focused: it is about the cultural development of Sub-Saharan peoples. It takes into account the failure of development over a long period and the inefficiency of aid. There is an urgent need to build bridges within the African continent, across borders, in order to repair fragmented cultures, fragmented histories, fragmented personalities... In such a delicate task, the old tired African Griot most certainly must be called upon. Oral tradition must be tapped into while it is still alive. In south-Saharan Africa, the performing artist ought to be trained to play a key role of mediator between tradition and modernity, between the spiritual and the temporal, between the virtues of integrated living and the stress of frenetic competition. That empowering role combines healing, educating and developing a creative attitude faced with conflicting forces that have kept the African story locked up for too long. Time is pressing and there is unprecedented pressure felt by all cultures to dig deep and come up with fresh ideas for survival and peace. For everyone on earth, the future is becoming increasingly a very narrow gate to pass through... At the same time, it is a challenge that this experiment does not ignore.

Africa remains the memory of the world. The term 'Africa' goes widely beyond a geographical concept. There is a mystical sense to the word, better understood whenever scientific fact establishes with unanimity that human life emerged on the African continent. Was it the Romans who invented the name as they venerated the goddess Africa when they colonised the north of the continent? Up to the 15th century, the development of Africa was more or less in pace with the other parts of the world, especially Asia, the Middle East and Europe. Once, there had been trade on the east coast and on the west coast of the continent and universities had been established namely in the kingdom of Mali. Nowadays, the voice of Africa has been suppressed and stifled only to be restored by the media whenever a new war opposes weakened leaders in a purposeless struggle, unless calamity strikes. But while the developed world may continue to perceive development in terms of the smallest percentage of their respective national budgets, Africans have no choice. From South, East or West, they have had to bravely tackle their development by trial and error. It is in this broader context that this ongoing research must be assessed. For development to be meaningful to the average citizen of Sub-Saharan Africa and for it to deliver a balanced individual within a more peaceful environment, a vision from within the culture must be allowed to emerge. To facilitate this phase of development, a contribution from the performing artist in Africa cannot be discarded. That is a modest claim to make.

There are tasks to be attended to that cannot be left to the politician, to the economist or to the teacher. Unless, across Africa, the school could make room to accommodate the performing artist as a co-educator. First, the latter must be adequately trained... Sure, the supply of water, attending to disease and combating hunger will continue to matter. Attending to these basic needs is fully recognised, fully understood. Mobilization against these have long begun and, as we have seen, new partnerships are being tested. But there are equally vital needs, whereby the performer could be equipped to deliver a healing process, following the damaging partitioning of a continent, the ongoing legacy of the cruelest form of slavery and the most unfair exploitation of raw materials. Somebody needs to repair the fractured picture. Anger and terror should not be the only options to the frustrated thinking young person. Restoring the memory through dance, storytelling and creative arts could be as useful a job as a sports officer's within the modern

Daniel Labonne

school. Allowing the African to tell that story to fellow Africans across the continent matters more than celebrity culture and impressing the outside world.

Our research has delivered a strategic plan that gives meaning to EMPOWERING THE PERFORMER.

From practice to theory, this experiment has grown to the next phase, from theory to practice, by providing a pragmatic response to the challenges of cultural development by focussing upon specialised training and the active involvement of the performing artist of Africa. The role of performing arts permeates all areas of life in sub-Saharan Africa and this situation is quite unique in the 21st century, considering the large populations concerned. Training should lead to improved education for the young, a network of distribution for productions Made-in-Africa, ultimately justifying the need for the most appropriate distribution outlets. The performer would become an agent for the development of African peoples by motivating them to play a more creative role in their own vision of development, by giving them self-worth and by impacting upon urban development across sub-Saharan Africa. Live shows, staged drama, television and feature films would eventually multiply the benefits. A coherent picture would also need to exist on-line.

'*DRUMMA*' AS A BUILDING THAT RESPONDS TO NEED.

It would be wrong to limit the meaning of the new word '*drumma*' to some political claim about the real origins of modern theatre or a vain attempt to re-write history. It would be equally wrong to think prestige where priorities drag all initiatives to the level of basic living conditions. In our applied research, it is neither about ambition, nor romanticism. It is certainly not about race. The future matters and we shall survive together or we won't. But in Africa, the young are desperate for new answers to endemic problems. How do you remedy to the desperation that places a weapon in the hands of a 15 year old? Besides, human talent is limitless and nobody has the monopoly of intelligence. We are all intelligent differently. Therefore, the word *'drumma'* should be read within the perspective of possible progress in cultural development for real peoples, numbering nearly one billion. At this stage of our research, the best reading of the word would be to suggest that the 'empowered performer' would eventually require a new home in the future. *'Drumma'* could conceptualize such a 'home' as a new building that both inspires and characterizes the urban development of African cities.

From initially describing the fundamental need for humans to dramatize self perception and the uniqueness of a conscious being as well as drama preceding formalized ancient Greek theatre, the term *'drumma'* has grown into responding to the need to conceptualize a new building that would collect, process, display what Africa and Africans have best to offer. Both to the urban dweller and the frequent visitor. The *'drumma'* would in its own right become a 'diamond' that attracts and gives standard where there had been none before.

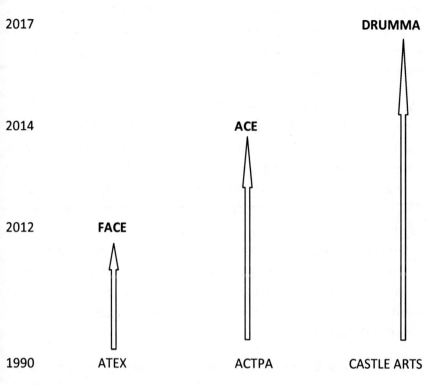

2017   **DRUMMA**

2014   **ACE**

2012   **FACE**

1990   ATEX   ACTPA   CASTLE ARTS

FACE has a huge mountain to climb. The experiment has demonstrated how unstable the continent can be, how unreliable the partners could become along a development process. The most promising independent country can be torn by internal conflict and banned by world opinion within a decade. Old friends of yesterday may remain motivated by sheer self-interest with their own political agenda and economic survival. Money is both the solution and the problem. Most damaging is the lack of interaction between neighbouring countries, with traditionally similar cultures. Development ought to remain an organic process whereby growth delivers both health and happiness. If the performing arts have remained alive across the continent, punctuating each stage of the social life within micro communities, they deserve to be trusted to accompany national and regional development. But governments have other priorities. Culture is underfunded, based upon the development history from elsewhere. How many African embassies have a cultural attaché? When was the last time a troupe from Mali invited to perform in Zambia? Out of Africa, how many of the 54 countries of Africa could the average person list down outright from memory? Who professionally attends to the need to improve the image of Africa and Africans?

Africans can only rely upon themselves. That is one tough lesson to learn from our experiment. FACE is one translation of this reckoning. Aid will not do the job required to ensure lasting progress and sustainable growth. Therefore, we need to make new friends, like Brazil, and deserve their active involvement, provided we know what we want. Provided we spell out what we need and try hard enough to address our predicament. Tourists will never gladly visit an African city, unless there is quality entertainment, attractive cultural landmarks and a unique emotional experience through the arts. Singing, dancing, storytelling and music remain uniquely vibrant across Africa. They should be trusted to give meaning and relevance to 'cultural development' applied to this sub-region of the world.

In my introduction, I quote Lilian Thuram as an unexpected contributor to an experiment in the performing arts. One may say: Lilian Thuram is mostly known as a football player who defended the selection of France in winning the World Cup and he is not an artist... To counter these objections, there is one basic rule confirmed by Thuram's book (*Mes Etoiles Noires*): there is an urgent need to do something about the world we live in and initiatives are welcome from all those able and of good faith. But there may be a couple of serious points in quoting Thuram. Africa and Africans have fully embraced football as a global sport. Many capital cities in Sub-Saharan Africa have found the means to build remarkable stadia. The question is: to what extent does a stadium in Abidjan express the deeper personality of the Ivorian citizen? Where is the evidence that football in Africa fosters social cohesion and tolerance? No doubt, the global appeal of football has influenced positively sports as entertainment. Sure, exceptionally talented African players, like Didier

Drogba of Chelsea Football Club, have become world stars. However, how many Londoners each year would travel to Ivory Coast to discover Drogba's country, watch a football match or partake in the local cultures? There is a need for an inside-out cultural development, comparable to the outside-in effect of football, which delivers an exclusive expression of the personality and the cultures of a country. Why not a building as culturally relevant to Africa, as football is a cultural expression of the British people and personality? One final point: the footballer may not be an artist, but he is undoubtedly a performer. In fact, the footballer has somehow stolen the show from the performing artist. The phenomenon is relatively new for Africa, largely due to the extended appeal of live television. It would not be wrong for Africans to assess creatively the impact of football on the young and on society as a whole. Why not imagine a link between sports and the arts? That link might take different forms: shared funding, integrated urban development, the education of the young with an equal emphasis on sports and the performing arts... FACE proposes to open a healthy debate, explore new avenues for progress and build a new viable partnership for effective cultural development in Africa. Only independent funding and cultural enterprise could deliver. That is why FACE has been set up to receive and handle substantial amounts of money to service a gaping need that is not being attended to by anybody else.

How realistic is FACE? the reader may ask. It is as realistic as we have been all along this applied research over decades. Sure, we remain in the realm of ideas and we have to navigate in choppy waters with political undercurrents. But progress has a price and the political classes of Africa need to be educated to think outside the box. Besides, we have grown to understand that cultural development is a ferociously guarded backyard for the rich and powerful. The best ideas tend to end up on the stock market or in a Hollywood production. That is why economists in Africa have been trained to literally ignore the cultural dimension of development. Does that make a better economist or a weaker leader?

The political class keeps the creative artists begging for favours, rather than grant them rights and make room for creativity. The challenges of Africa are often so overwhelming and the history of poor leadership in sub-Saharan Africa is universally parroted. Is it unrealistic to suggest that the quality of education is to be blamed, from infant school to university, for such poor leadership? But, again, we must leave the blame game to others. Recently, we have been realistic when we visited informally potential host countries for a permanent African Centre of Exchange – ACE. Mozambique is one of these deserving countries in Southern Africa. Mauritius has engaged into a policy of setting up a knowledge hub that would attract a clientele from the neighbouring countries. But the choice of the next host country for ACE remains open. FACE is already talking to regional financial organisations in Africa and targeting corporations with long term interests in a prosperous African continent.

More publications may follow this book, based upon the various reports and essays on the experiment. To be absolutely realistic, a dramatic treatment of what exactly happened at Castle Arts on a day-to-day basis would provide material for a novel or a soap opera. The author of this book would be content with writing to limit direct involvement in the management of the performing arts school. The reader will welcome the decision that a proportion of the sales on the book EMPOWERING THE PERFORMER will go towards FACE, the foundation. It is realistic to believe that cultural development through the performing arts would require goodwill from North and South, the most reliable partnership and considerable amounts of money. But, as one may see, we are not relying upon charity but we are setting the example. Charity begins at home. In our case, enterprise is even healthier than charity and home is as big as a continent...

Sotigui Kouyate and Myriam Makeba have earned themselves the place of royalty in the gallery of performers for the youth of Africa to visit. Setting up such a gallery is one of the tasks that FACE needs to undertake. Perhaps the best way to start would be to do it online. The youth worldwide would access it more gladly. But there rests another challenge for ageless Africa: assert its values and translate its teachings live, before technology renders the naked human voice obsolete, manipulated beyond recognition. I shall try to treat this issue in another book. Suffice it to claim that performing artists may have a brand new to role to play, besides mediating between the culturally meaningful life of the village and the risky fast lanes of city life in an increasingly global environment.

He came from north-west Africa and the French-speaking part of the continent: Sotigui Kouyate had this unique voice that moved audiences from deepest Africa to the brightest summit of Hollywood cinema; from the distant era of Dogon culture to the latest theatre experiments of Peter Brook in Paris. She came from southern Africa and the English-speaking part of the continent: Myriam Makeba combined this image of the woman, the eternal African and the patriot. She sang in African languages and caught the ears of the world with a motherly voice surging from very far indeed. Yes, it took twenty seven years of the life of Nelson Mandela to defeat the Apartheid regime in South Africa. But one must not underestimate the ongoing campaign of the lonely female performer, as Myriam Makeba wandered across the globe in exile from her own (then) racist country. She became the sobbing voice and the beating heart of a beloved yet divided country. Both Mandela and Myriam Makeba revealed unexpected values of the African personality: arms and violence do not always triumph; resistance with dignity may in the end deliver the most precious of human treasures, beginning with freedom and equal human rights; singing, smiling and dancing win the hearts.

Both Kouyate and Makeba stand as exemplary performers with a life well spent, against all odds, a fair distance away from the trappings of celebrity culture, constantly aware of a very deep plural heritage. Both performers tried and succeeded, through their arts, to bring people together. Between the two of them, they gave a concrete meaning to the plural forms of performing arts. In my view, they do in their own way provide flesh to the dry bones of Lucy... Empowering the performer of Africa could not remain a vague concept with wishful thinking. I must thank these wonderful performers for their assistance in offering valid testimony and concrete meaning to what this book is all about.

I am inviting them to accompany the efforts of the Foundation for Arts, Creativity & Exchange, as FACE revives a 'unique and timely' project, within permanent structures.

APPENDIX

For the record, we reproduce two original documents and we quote two visitors to Castle Arts and 2 selected trainees who all demonstrate the capital of hope, support and enthusiasm from North and South, invested into our experiment.

RESOLUTION OF THE OAU/AFRICAN UNION
Conference of Ministers of Culture
(Cameroon 1990)
*

LETTER FROM SWEDEN
After a private visit to Castle Arts in 1990
*

UNSOLICITED FEED BACK AFTER A PERFORMANCE OF THE DANCE
DRAMA 'FOOTPRINTS'
Letter of a spectator from the US
(Harare 1990)
*

EVALUATION IN 1997
2 Performers selected and trained in ACTPA at Castle Arts
reflect upon their experience
*

RESOLUTION ON THE CENTRE FOR THE TRAINING OF AFRICAN PERFORMING ARTISTS

The Conference of African Ministers of Culture, meeting in its Third Ordinary Session in Yaounde, Cameroon, on 17 and 18 May 1990,

Recalling the provisions of the Cultural Charter for Africa,

Considering that the formulation and implementation of national cultural policies as well as the execution of the Plan of Action and Stretegy for the World Cultural Development Decade require competent and well-trained staff

Desirous to ensuring the success of the African Cultural common market and the medium-term Cultural Development Plan.

Recalling Resolution CMAC/RES. 2 (II) adopted by its Second Ordinary Session (OUAGADOUGOU , march 1988) on the training of cultural development personnel,

Having heard the statement by the Zimbabwean delegation:

1. TAKES NOTE, with satisfaction of the progress made in the proposed establishment of the Centre for the Training of African Performing Artists in Harare, at the initiative of the African Theatre Exchange (ATEX);

2. NOTES, that the project will commence with nine-week sessions of pilot workshops for 15 to 20 participants from Member States,over a period of 3 years;

3. URGES Member States to participate in the training projects and to support the future establishment of a permanent centre after the trial period;

4. REQUESTS UNESCO to assist in the implementation of the project within the framework of the World Cultural Development Decade.

Letter from Sweden
following a private visit during ACTPA Course 1 at Castle
Arts, in the absence of Daniel Labonne.

3/12/90

Dear Daniel,

...

We felt they (all the participants in the first course) formed a wonderful inter-African group together, in spite of languages difficulties which were obvious, eager to learn from each other and eager to teach each other. We congratulate you on the selection of teachers, they were exquisite personalities, all three of them. On the whole, our impression is that the 1st of April 1985-idea of an ACTPA somewhere in Africa has materialized in a way that exceeds all expectations. The Castle Arts is a dream place for the training of any artists and those who were the first to be given the opportunity of using it did profit from it. It is easy to imagine the Castle Arts as the focal point of inter-African exchange in the performing arts within a very short time.

Please accept our congratulations for what has been achieved so far. We are aware that without you and your efforts there would be no ACTPA, nor would it be without the participation of all those that you mobilized for this idea.

The lovely group of African artists we met in Bulawayo are scattered now, so we cannot reach them collectively. Please tell those of them with whom you are in touch how happy we were to meet them and thank them for their hospitality and their attention.

With warm wishes for ACTPA's continued success at beautiful Castle Arts.

Bo & Marianne KARRE

United States Information Service - USIS

Century House East
Mezzanine Floor. Baker Avenue
P.O. Box 4010 . Harare, Zimbabwe
Telephone: 72895017/8/9

November 15, 1990

Mr. Daniel Labonne, Director
ACTPA Training Programme,
The Castle Arts
P.O.Box NE 49
Bulawayo

Dear Mr. Labonne,

I had hoped to talk with you after the performance at Girls' High School the other night, but unfortunately I was not able to do so.

I just want to let you and the cast, the director-choreographers, the musicians, the costumers and everyone else associated with FOOTPRINTS—know that I thought it was a splendid production. It was very professionally mounted and performed and certainly bodes well for the future of ACTPA!

The accomplishment of FOOTPRINTS is even more remarkable when one considers that performers from no less than twelve countries — often speaking different languages and coming from widely differing artistic traditions - were involved, and that there was less than two months of preparation time. This is truly a Phase I to be proud of, and one can only hope that there are many, many phases still to come.

Please allow me to take this opportunity to congratulate you, and everyone involved with ACTPA, on the occasion of the official ceremony to open the training program on November 18, and to

Daniel Labonne

wish ACTPA a long and successful future in Zimbabwe. The contribution which ACTPA can make to the culture of the continent as a whole, promises to be very great indeed. And of course I hope to pay you and the Castle a visit when I am next in Bulawayo.

Sincerely,

(signed)
Dr. RAY ORLEY
Cultural Attaché

FEEDBACK from 2 trainees
during an evaluation conducted 6 years after they attended the inter-African Training Programmes.

"There is no doubt that ACTPA II was a wonderful experience and had immense potential. I grew as an artist beyond my previous expectations... As an artist, my training had been very western in orientation and Eurocentric in perspective. It was refreshing to have the focus and centre shifted. The trainers were competent and so willing to give of themselves, which immensely increased our motivation... As a direct result of ACTPA, I decided to go into theatre and drama education. Before ACTPA II, I was teaching in a general education college. Upon my return, I went into various types of theatre – drama – education work and am presently a resource person and a member of the Nairobi Theatre Academy Executive Committee and IDEA (International Drama + Theatre + Education Association)... With each new experience Africa goes through, it seems the need grows to define and find a new way of educating the young to find and understand themselves in the light of their past and future. Performing arts could hold the key to a challenging path to achieving this, if more courses as LUCY and FOORPRINTS were held."

SALOME MWANGOLA (Kenya)

Salome Mwangola was a female performer selected for course II in ACTPA at Castle Arts, in 1991.

*

"This was a very well organised project which should be recorded in the History of the Performing Arts in Africa and has to be emulated and imitated by all progressive elements of our society... It will take death to erase the memories of such a superb experience in the life of a mediocre artist such as myself as I was before the occasion."

LERATO NLOVU (Zimbabwe)

Lerato Ndlovu was a male performer who attended course I in ACTPA at Castle Arts, in 1990.

"The new Africa must use the traditions of Africa
as well as the culture of the world
to produce a unique and healthy vision of the future."

FAY CHUNG
Minister of Education and Culture, Zimbabwe
At the opening ceremony of ACTPA at Castle Arts,
November 1990. Bulawayo.

Daniel Labonne

BIBLIOGRAPHY

Donald Johanson (with Maitland Edey). *Lucy. A Young Woman of 3.5 Million Years*. William Morrow and co. Inc. New York. 1983

Jean Marc Henry - Basile Kossou. *La Dimension Culturelle du Developpement*. Nouvelles Editions Africaines. Unesco. 1985

Robin Walker. *Before the Slave Trade. African World History in Pictures*. Black History Studies Publications. 2008.

Samuel P. Huntington. *The Clash of Civilizations*. Simon and Schuster UK Ltd. 1997

MIcheal Young and Geoff Whitty. *Society, State and Schooling*. The Falmer Press. 1977.

Bill Williamson. *Education, Social Structure & Development*. Macmillan Press Ltd. 1979.

David Williams, Peter Brook. *A Theatrical Casebook*. Methuen. 1989

Bakari Traore. *The Black African Theatre and Its Social Functions*. Ibadan University Press 1972.

Robert C. Toll. *The Entertainment Machine. American Show Business in the 20th Century*. Oxford University Press. 1982

Wole Soyinka edited by Richard Drain. *Drama and the African View world*. Routledge. 1995.

Richard Schechner. *By Means of Performance. Intercultural studies of theatre and rituals*. Cambridge University Press. 1990.

Phil Murray. *Empowerment. A practical guide to personal success*.PeFECT WORDS and MUSIC Limited. 1995.

John Pick. *The Theatre Industry*. Comedia. 1985.

Patrice Pavis. *Theatre At The Crossroads of Culture*. Routledge. 1992

Kwesi Owusu . *From Notting Hill Carnival: De Road is the Stage and the Stage is De Road*. Richard Drain. Routledge. 1995.

Anthony O'Connor. *The African City*. Hutchinson University. Unoversity for Africa. 1983.

V.Y.Mundimbe. *The Invention of Africa. Gnosis, philosophy and order of knowledge*. Blomington. Indiana University Press. 1988.

Maria Ley. Erwin Piscator. *The Piscator Experiment*. The South Illinois University Press. 1970.

Baz Kershaw. *The Politics of Performance*. Routledge. London. 1992.
Micheal Jackson & Ivan Karp. Personhood and Agency. *The experience of self and other African cultures*. 1990.

Hunter & F. Steward. *African strategy for self-help Africa. Popular Islam south of the Sahara*. Edited by J.O.Y. Peel & C.C. Stewart. Manchester University Press. 1985.

Jacques Hallack. *Setting education priorities in the developing world*. UNDP-UNESCO. International Institute for Educational Planning, Pigmalion Press. 1990.
Kwame Gyekye. *An essay on African philosophical thought. The Akan conceptual scheme*. Cambridge University Press. 1987.

John Gabriel. *Racism, Culture, Markets*. Routledge, 1994.

Erich Fromm. *To have or to be?* Abacus. 1979.

Claude Fabrizio. *The cultural* dimension *of development*. UNESCO Publishing. 1995.
Hansel Ndumbe Eyoh. *From Hammocks to Bridges*. Yaounde University Press. 1986.

Xavier Dupuis. *Culture et Developpement. De la reconnaissance a l'evaluation*. Unesco/ICA. 1991.

Cheikh Anta Diop. Translated by Yaa-Lengi Meema. *Civilisation ou Barbarie*. Lawrence Hill. Chicago. 1991.

Yaya Diallo and Micehell Hall. *The Healing drum*. Destiny books. 1989.
Aidan Foster Carter. *The sociology of development*. Causeway Press Ltd. 1985.
William J. Baumol. *Performing Arts. The Economic Dilemma. A study of problems*. M.I.T. Press. London 1968.

Rustom Barucha. *Theatre of the world: Performance and the Policy of Culture*. Routledge. London & NY. 1993(1990).

Karin Barber. *African Popular Culture. The International African Institute*. UK. 1995.
Samir Amin. *Delinking. Towards a Polycentric World*. Zed rboks Ltd. 1985.

Lilian Thuram, *Mes Etoiles Noires. De Lucy a Obama*. Editons Points. 2011

Daniel A. Bell & Avner de-Shalit. *The Spirit of Cities.* Princeton University Press.

Dozens of Reports from ATEX Archives.

Various Magazines and Newspapers including the Observer, UK.

Daniel Labonne. *Development Through Creativity.* MPhil thesis. Goldsmiths College. University of London. Drama and Theatre Arts.

Daniel Labonne

DANIEL H. LABONNE (MPhil)

Writer and playwright

Daniel Labonne is a writer, a theatre artist and researcher. Actor, playwright, stage director and poet, he has worked internationally, especially in Africa. Born in Mauritius and a British Citizen, he shares his time between his native island and London. He holds a postgraduate degree (Mphil) from Goldsmiths College, University of London and studied Arts Management earlier at City University. He has been an adviser to the Minister of Culture of Mauritius and the artistic director of the London based African Theatre Exchange (ATEX) and the Samuel Coleridge-Taylor Society in Croydon, UK. Daniel Labonne is mainly known as the project manager of the ACTPA Project - African Centre for the Training of Performing Artists, a unique cultural development project for the African continent, implemented in 1990's at Castle Arts, Zimbabwe. He is the founder of FACE. Having earned his living mainly as a social entrepreneur, he may finally devote maximum time to writing books, plays and lyrics. He writes in French, English and Kreol. Married with two grown up sons. Latest book published: CAP SUR L'ILE MAURICE (Papa Laval), a Creole opera.

dhlabonne@aol.com
www.dhlabonne.com
www:face-performing-arts.com

Lightning Source UK Ltd.
Milton Keynes UK
UKOW05f2335110214

226312UK00016B/861/P